GHOSTS OF ARZAWA

BEYOND THE TROJAN WAR MYTH

R JAY DRISKILL

RED PIRATE MEDIA

Where the Aegean meets Anatolia, empires clashed and heroes were born—this is the story of Arzawa's place in the Trojan legacy.

Eric Cline

ALSO BY R JAY DRISKILL

SUNSET IN BRONZE SERIES:

KINGS OF STONE: THE HITTITE ENIGMA

RAIDERS OF THE BRONZE AGE COLLAPSE: THE SEA PEOPLES IN LEGEND, HISTORY, AND ARCHAEOLOGY

GHOSTS OF ARZAWA: BEYOND THE TROJAN WAR MYTH

SONG OF A LOST CITY: TROY IN MYTH, FICTION, AND FACT

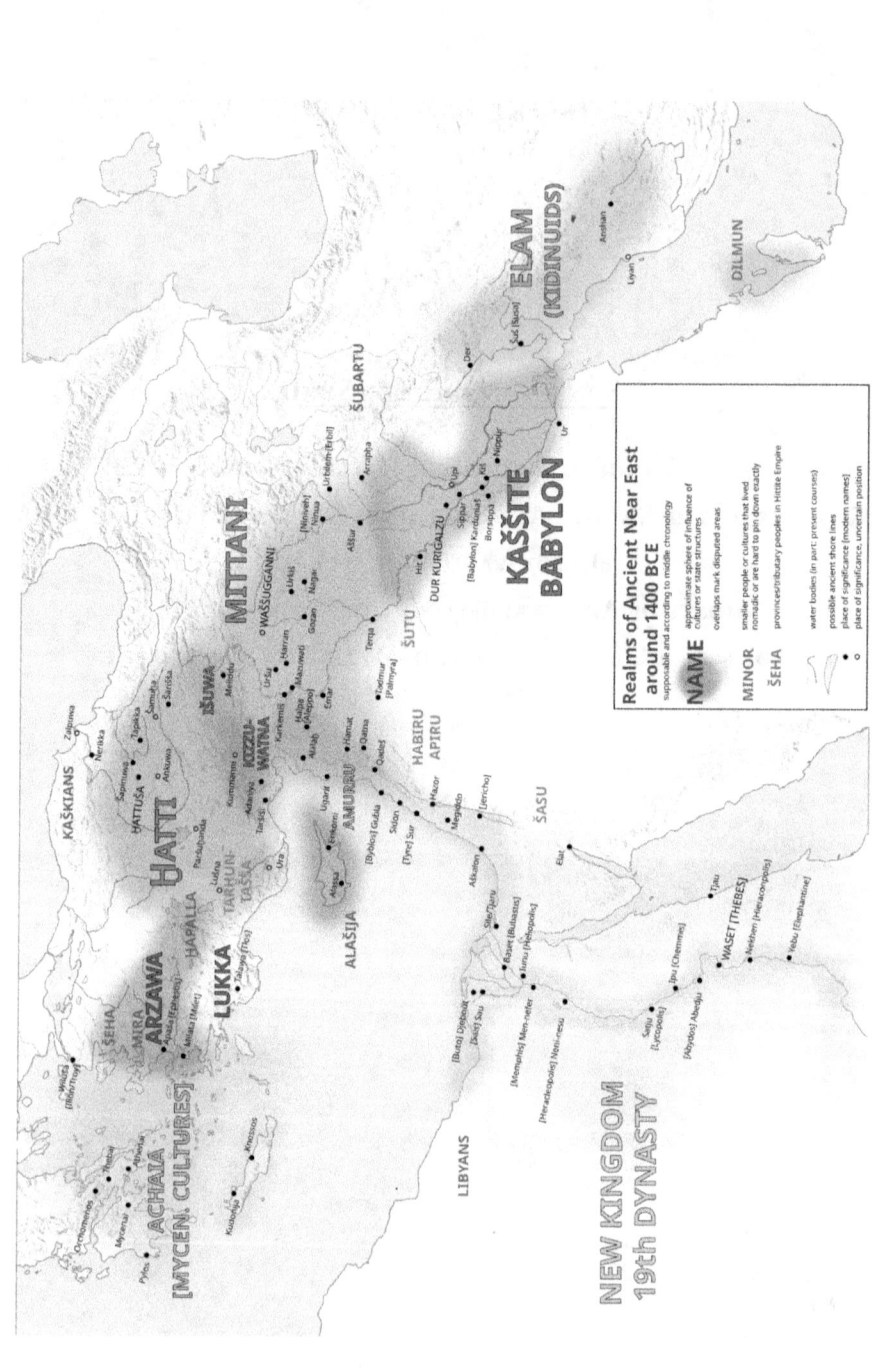

Realms of Ancient Near East
around 1400 BCE
supposable and according to middle chronology

NAME approximate sphere of influence of
cultures or state structures

overlaps mark disputed areas

MINOR smaller people or cultures that lived
nomadic or are hard to pin down exactly

ŠEHA province/tributary peoples in Hittite Empire

water bodies (in part: present courses)

possible ancient shore lines

● place of significance [modern names]

○ place of significance, uncertain position

KAŠKIANS

ACHAIA
[MYCEN. CULTURES]

SEHA
MIRA
ARZAWA
LUKKA
HAPALLA
HATTI
HATTUŠA
TARHUN
TAŠŠA
KIZZU
WATNA
IŠUWA
MITTANI
WAŠŠUGGANNI
ŠUBARTU

ALAŠIJA

AMURRU
HABIRU
APIRU
ŠUTU
DUR KURIGALZU
KAŠŠITE
BABYLON
ŠASU

ELAM
(KIDINUIDS)

DILMUN

LIBYANS

WASET [THEBES]

NEW KINGDOM
19th DYNASTY

CONTENTS

PREFACE

The Kingdom That History Almost Forgot

Pretend you're an archaeologist working in the sweltering heat of central Turkey, carefully brushing dirt from what appears to be just another clay tablet fragment from the ancient Hittite capital of Hattusa. The cuneiform signs are partially broken, frustratingly incomplete, but as you begin to decipher them, a phrase jumps out at you that makes you sit up straight. Someone—a Hittite scribe writing over three thousand years ago—has described a western Anatolian warlord as being "slippery as an eel."

Now, I don't know about you, but when I read something like that in an ancient text, I immediately want to know more. Who was this person who so thoroughly frustrated the Hittites that their scribes resorted to fishy metaphors? What had he done to earn such colorful—and clearly exasperated—description from one of the ancient world's superpowers?

The answer, as it turns out, leads us into one of the most fascinating and underappreciated stories of the Late Bronze Age: the rise and fall of the kingdom of Arzawa, and the remarkable individuals who emerged from its ashes to continue defying imperial power long after the kingdom itself had fallen.

The Problem with Ancient Celebrity

The warlord in question was named Piyamaradu, and if you've never heard of him, you're not alone. Despite successfully resisting and outmaneuvering the Hittite Empire for decades—no small feat, considering the Hittites were essentially the Romans of their day—Piyamaradu remains virtually unknown outside the small circle of scholars who study Late Bronze Age Anatolia. This anonymity isn't unusual; it's actually the norm for most ancient historical figures who didn't happen to live in Egypt, Mesopotamia, Greece, or Rome.

But here's the thing that really gets to me as someone who has spent years studying the Bronze Age collapse and its aftermath: the figures and kingdoms we don't know about were often just as important—sometimes more important—than the ones that made it into our history textbooks. They shaped events, influenced the course of civilizations, and left traces that we're still uncovering today. Yet they remain obscure, overshadowed by their better-documented neighbors and adversaries.

Piyamaradu operated in the political landscape created by the defeat and fragmentation of Arzawa, a powerful kingdom that had dominated western Anatolia for centuries before the Hittites finally brought it to heel. And if Piyamaradu is unknown to most people today, Arzawa is even more so, despite the fact that it controlled some of the most strategically important territory in the ancient world—the crucial link between the Aegean and the Near East.

Why We Remember Some and Forget Others

This brings us to one of the most fundamental questions in historical study: why do some civilizations, kingdoms, and individuals get remembered while others fade into obscurity? The answer usually comes down to a combination of factors: who won the wars, who wrote the most records, and—perhaps most importantly—whose records survived to be discovered by modern archaeologists.

The Hittites, who eventually conquered Arzawa, left us thousands of cuneiform tablets detailing their history, their diplomatic correspondence, their

2

religious practices, their legal codes—you name it. Their capital at Hattusa has been excavated extensively, and we can reconstruct their political and cultural development in remarkable detail. The Mycenaean Greeks, who interacted with Arzawa through trade and diplomacy, may not have left us extensive written records, but they inspired legends that eventually became Homer's epic poems, ensuring their place in Western cultural memory.

But Arzawa? The Arzawans apparently didn't believe in extensive record-keeping, at least not in ways that have survived for us to find. We have to piece together their story largely from external sources—primarily Hittite and Egyptian records—and from archaeological remains. It's like trying to understand a conversation by hearing only one side of it, or reconstructing a movie from the reviews written by critics who didn't particularly like it.

This documentary disparity has profound implications for how we understand the ancient world. History, as they say, is written by the victors, but it's also preserved by the prolific record-keepers and discovered by archaeologists lucky enough to dig in the right places. The result is a deeply skewed picture of the past, one that privileges certain voices and perspectives while marginalizing others.

The Underdog Appeal

As someone who has spent considerable time studying the Bronze Age collapse—that mysterious period around 1200 BCE when multiple civilizations across the eastern Mediterranean seemed to fall apart simultaneously—I've always been drawn to these forgotten kingdoms and overlooked historical actors. There's something compelling about the underdogs, the peoples and places that mainstream history passed by but that played crucial roles in shaping the ancient world.

Perhaps it's because their stories feel more relatable somehow. The great empires of antiquity—Egypt, Assyria, the Hittite Empire—can seem almost abstract in their power and grandeur. But kingdoms like Arzawa, struggling to maintain their independence against expanding imperial powers, facing the challenge of preserving their cultural identity while adapting to changing political realities—these dynamics feel surprisingly familiar.

Or maybe it's simply that there's more detective work involved in studying these forgotten civilizations. When you're working with abundant textual sources, as we have for Egypt or Mesopotamia, much of the basic historical framework is already established. But when you're trying to reconstruct the story of Arzawa, every new discovery—whether it's a diplomatic letter mentioning trade relations or an archaeological finding that reveals previously unknown cultural connections—can fundamentally change your understanding of how things worked.

Imperial Systems and Their Discontents

The story of Arzawa and its aftermath—including the emergence of figures like Piyamaradu—illuminates something crucial about how ancient imperial systems actually functioned. We often think of empires as monolithic entities that either controlled territory completely or didn't control it at all. But the reality was far more complex and interesting.

Take the Hittite Empire, for instance. Despite their reputation as master warriors and administrators, the Hittites often found it more practical to work with local power structures than to replace them entirely. They preferred vassal relationships to direct control, puppet rulers to provincial governors. This system had obvious advantages—it was cheaper to maintain and often more politically stable—but it also created opportunities for savvy local actors to exploit.

This is where someone like Piyamaradu becomes so fascinating. He wasn't simply a rebel fighting against empire; he was a sophisticated political operator who understood how imperial systems worked and how to game them. The Hittite texts describe him with a mixture of frustration and grudging respect, referring to his ability to slip away just when they thought they had him cornered, his talent for manipulating boundaries and exploiting competing jurisdictions.

What's particularly striking is how the Hittite kings repeatedly tried to bring Piyamaradu into the fold through negotiation rather than conquest. They offered him official positions, territorial control, recognition of his authority—classic imperial strategies for co-opting troublesome local leaders. The fact that these negotiations went on for decades suggests that Piyamaradu was too powerful and too useful to simply crush, but too independent and too disruptive to ignore.

The Art of Political Balancing

Reading through the diplomatic correspondence that mentions Piyamaradu, you get the sense of someone who understood the political landscape of his time with remarkable sophistication. He operated in a world where multiple powers—the Hittites, various Mycenaean Greek kingdoms, local Anatolian city-states, and others—were constantly jockeying for position and influence. Rather than choosing sides definitively, he seems to have mastered the art of playing these powers against each other.

This kind of political balancing act requires extraordinary skill and nerve. You have to understand not just the immediate interests of each power, but how those interests might shift over time. You need reliable intelligence about what's happening in distant capitals. You have to maintain relationships with multiple parties while avoiding commitments that might limit your future options. And you have to be prepared to switch sides or disappear entirely when the political winds change.

In many ways, Piyamaradu's approach reminds me of the strategies employed by successful small states throughout history—think of Renaissance Venice navigating between the Ottoman Empire and various European powers, or modern Switzerland maintaining neutrality while engaging with all sides. It's a high-risk, high-reward strategy that can provide remarkable freedom of action for those skilled enough to pull it off.

Archaeological Insights into Forgotten Worlds

One of the things I find most exciting about studying kingdoms like Arzawa is how archaeological evidence can illuminate aspects of ancient life that textual sources barely mention or ignore entirely. The material remains of Arzawan cities reveal sophisticated urban planning and architectural techniques that combined elements from multiple cultural traditions—Anatolian, Mycenaean Greek, and others.

For instance, excavations at sites associated with Arzawan culture have uncovered evidence of advanced metallurgical techniques, suggesting that the kingdom was not just politically important but also economically sophisticated. The bronze-working traditions developed in western Anatolia during this period influenced metalworking practices across the eastern Mediterranean. Yet you won't find much about Arzawan metallurgy in ancient texts, because ancient scribes generally weren't interested in technical details of production.

Similarly, burial practices and religious artifacts from Arzawan sites provide glimpses of how ordinary people maintained cultural traditions even as political structures changed around them. The persistence of certain ritual practices and artistic motifs across periods of political upheaval suggests that cultural identity could be remarkably resilient, surviving even when kingdoms fell and new powers took control.

Trade connections revealed through archaeological analysis show how the kingdom of Arzawa participated in vast networks of exchange that transcended political boundaries. Pottery styles, jewelry designs, and even architectural elements moved along these trade routes, creating a kind of cultural diffusion that operated independently of political control. This reminds us that ancient peoples weren't as isolated or parochial as we sometimes imagine—they were connected to broader worlds of cultural and economic exchange.

The Challenge of Popular History

One of the ongoing challenges in studying periods like the Late Bronze Age is how to make these complex historical dynamics accessible to general readers without oversimplifying them. The technical details of archaeological evidence and textual analysis are crucial for understanding how ancient societies actually worked, but they can be intimidating to non-specialists.

I've always believed that the key is to focus on the human stories within these larger historical patterns. People are naturally drawn to narratives about individuals facing challenges, making difficult choices, succeeding or failing in their endeavors. When you can connect technical analysis of pottery types or architectural remains to broader questions about how ancient people lived, worked, and understood their world, the details become not just tolerable but fascinating.

The story of Piyamaradu, for instance, gives us a lens through which to examine the complex dynamics of imperial expansion and local resistance. His decades-long cat-and-mouse game with the Hittite Empire illuminates how ancient political systems actually functioned, how power was negotiated and contested, how individuals could carve out space for autonomous action even within seemingly hegemonic systems.

Similarly, the rise and fall of Arzawa provides a framework for understanding broader patterns of political and cultural change in the Late Bronze Age. Rather than seeing it simply as a victim of Hittite expansion, we can recognize it as a significant power that helped shape the political and cultural landscape of western Anatolia. Its story offers insights into how ancient kingdoms maintained their identity and independence in an increasingly interconnected world.

Modern Resonances

Perhaps one reason I find these ancient dynamics so compelling is how relevant they feel to our contemporary world. Today's global system, like that of Bronze Age Anatolia, features complex interactions between centralized powers and local actors who maintain influence through careful manipulation of boundaries and relationships.

We see echoes of Piyamaradu's strategies in modern geopolitics—small states or non-state actors who successfully exploit the competition between great powers to maintain their independence and pursue their interests. The techniques may have changed, but the underlying dynamics of how to preserve autonomy and agency within larger power structures remain remarkably consistent.

The challenges faced by kingdoms like Arzawa—how to maintain cultural identity while adapting to changing political realities, how to benefit from international connections while preserving local traditions, how to resist imperial pressure without triggering overwhelming retaliation—these are issues that resonate across historical periods.

This doesn't mean we should view ancient history as simply a mirror of contemporary concerns. The specific contexts and cultural frameworks of Bronze Age Anatolia were unique to their time and place. But studying how ancient peoples dealt with challenges that have structural similarities to modern problems can provide valuable perspective on our own experiences and choices.

The Importance of Scholarly Rigor

Throughout my career, I've tried to balance academic rigor with public accessibility, and working on topics like Arzawa makes this balance particularly important. Because we have limited sources for these forgotten kingdoms, it's tempting to fill in gaps with speculation or to make dramatic claims that go beyond what the evidence actually supports.

But I believe we do a disservice to both scholarship and public understanding when we sacrifice accuracy for excitement. The real stories of ancient civilizations are fascinating enough without embellishment. The challenge is to present them in ways that convey their significance and human relevance while remaining true to what we can actually demonstrate from archaeological and textual evidence.

This means being honest about the limitations of our knowledge. When we're reconstructing the story of Arzawa primarily from external sources, we need to acknowledge that we're seeing it through the eyes of its enemies and rivals. When we're interpreting archaeological remains, we need to be clear about what we can confidently conclude and what remains speculative.

At the same time, we shouldn't let these limitations paralyze us or prevent us from drawing broader insights from the evidence we do have. The goal is to strike a balance between healthy skepticism and interpretive boldness, to push the boundaries of our understanding while remaining grounded in solid scholarship.

Restoring the Forgotten

My hope in writing about kingdoms like Arzawa and figures like Piyamaradu is to restore them to their rightful place in our understanding of ancient history. This isn't just about giving credit where credit is due, though that's certainly part of it. It's about developing a more complete and nuanced picture of how ancient civilizations actually developed and interacted.

When we focus exclusively on the great empires and well-documented civilizations, we risk creating a distorted view of the ancient world—one that overemphasizes centralized power and underestimates the importance of local agency and regional dynamics. By paying attention to forgotten kingdoms and overlooked historical actors, we can better understand the full complexity of ancient political and cultural systems.

This has implications beyond academic history. The stories we tell about the past shape how we understand the present and envision the future. If our historical narratives focus primarily on great empires and powerful rulers, we may be less attentive to the ways that local communities and individual actors can influence larger historical processes.

But if we include stories like that of Arzawa and Piyamaradu—stories of sophisticated resistance to imperial power, of cultural persistence through political change, of small actors successfully navigating between competing great powers—we develop a richer understanding of how historical change actually works.

Looking Forward

As archaeological techniques continue to improve and new discoveries are made, I'm optimistic that we'll learn more about kingdoms like Arzawa and figures like Piyamaradu. Each new finding has the potential to shift our understanding of Bronze Age Anatolia and the broader ancient world.

But even with our current limited knowledge, these stories offer valuable insights into enduring patterns of human political and cultural interaction. The tension between imperial expansion and local autonomy, the challenge of maintaining distinctive identities in an interconnected world, the strategies available to those who must navigate between competing powers—these dynamics have shaped human society for millennia and continue to do so today.

In studying the experiences of ancient peoples who faced similar challenges, we gain not only historical knowledge but perspectives that remain relevant to understanding our own world. The kingdom of Arzawa may have fallen over three thousand years ago, and Piyamaradu may have slipped away into historical obscurity, but their stories continue to illuminate fundamental questions about power, resistance, and the preservation of human agency in complex political systems.

That, ultimately, is why forgotten kingdoms matter. They remind us that history is not just the story of the powerful and well-documented, but of all the peoples and communities who struggled to shape their own destinies within the constraints and opportunities of their times. In recovering their stories, we enrich our understanding not only of the past, but of the enduring human capacity for creativity, resilience, and hope in the face of overwhelming challenges.

R Jay Driskill
March 2025

INTRODUCTION

The Lost Kingdom: Rediscovering Arzawa

I magine trying to piece together the history of the United States using only documents written by its enemies. Picture reconstructing American society from British colonial records, Confederate propaganda, and Soviet intelligence reports, with maybe a few archaeological sites thrown in for good measure. Welcome to the world of studying ancient Arzawa.

Hidden away in the mountains and valleys of western Turkey, between the glittering Aegean Sea and the snow-capped peaks of the Taurus range, lay one of the Bronze Age world's best-kept secrets. For generations, scholars fixated on the obvious superpowers of the ancient Near East: Egypt with its towering pyramids and golden pharaohs, Mesopotamia with its vast libraries of cuneiform tablets, the mighty Hittite Empire ruling from its mountain fortress at Hattusa. Meanwhile, tucked away in what seemed like a backwater corner of Anatolia, was a kingdom that came tantalizingly close to vanishing from history altogether.

This is the story of Arzawa—a name that means nothing to most people today but once commanded respect from the pharaohs of Egypt and struck fear into the hearts of Hittite kings. It's a tale of archaeological detective work at its finest, where every pottery sherd and broken tablet adds another piece to one of history's most challenging puzzles.

The Great Rediscovery

The recovery of Arzawa's history reads like an academic adventure story. For decades, the kingdom existed only as a footnote in Hittite texts—usually as some troublesome neighbor causing problems on the empire's western frontier. Scholars knew it was there, somewhere in western Anatolia, but that was about it. Then something remarkable happened.

As Anatolian specialist Trevor Bryce puts it, "The recovery of Arzawa's history from fragmentary evidence offers a masterclass in archaeological detective work. Each excavation season, linguistic analysis, or theoretical reframing adds new pieces to a puzzle that grows more fascinating as it becomes more complete" (Bryce, 2016: 345).

What changed everything was a combination of new archaeological discoveries, fresh interpretations of old texts, and a growing recognition that the ancient world was far more interconnected than we'd previously imagined. Suddenly, Arzawa wasn't just some peripheral kingdom getting beaten up by the Hittites. It was a sophisticated political entity with its own distinctive culture, international connections that reached all the way to Egypt, and a remarkable ability to survive and adapt in one of history's most turbulent periods.

The transformation has been nothing short of revolutionary. Arzawa has emerged from the shadows to take its rightful place as a major player in Late Bronze Age geopolitics—a kingdom whose rise and fall helps us understand how the ancient world really worked.

A Kingdom Worth Knowing

Why should we care about a kingdom that disappeared three thousand years ago? The answer goes far beyond simple antiquarian curiosity. Arzawa matters for several compelling reasons, each of which illuminates broader patterns in human history.

First, Arzawa provides a masterclass in political survival under impossible conditions. Try to imagine building and maintaining a unified kingdom across some of the most challenging terrain in the ancient world—rugged mountains, deep valleys, and scattered settlements connected only by treacherous mountain passes. The strategies Arzawan rulers developed to hold their realm together offer fascinating insights into the relationship between geography and political power.

Then there's Arzawa's position at one of history's great crossroads. This wasn't some isolated mountain kingdom cut off from the wider world. Arzawa sat squarely at the intersection of the Aegean and Near Eastern cultural spheres, creating a unique synthesis that borrowed from both traditions while developing something distinctly its own. The kingdom's material culture, religious practices, and political institutions reveal just how permeable cultural boundaries were in the ancient world—a lesson that resonates strongly in our own globalized age.

The complex relationship between Arzawa and the Hittite Empire also illuminates timeless patterns of imperial ambition and local resistance. The Hittites' strategy of conquest, division, and administration—and the persistent challenges they faced in keeping control—reveals the practical limitations of imperial power that would-be conquerors throughout history have had to confront.

Finally, and perhaps most intriguingly, Arzawa's connections to the world described in Homer's epics make it relevant to one of archaeology's most enduring debates: was there really a Trojan War? While Troy itself (known to the Hittites as Wilusa) maintained a complicated relationship with Arzawa, understanding the kingdom's role in western Anatolian politics provides crucial context for the conflicts that may have inspired the *Iliad*.

The Challenge of Reconstruction

Studying Arzawa is like trying to solve a jigsaw puzzle with half the pieces missing and no picture on the box. The Arzawans, unlike their more famous neighbors, left behind no great libraries of texts, no detailed royal inscriptions, no comprehensive legal codes. What we know about them comes primarily from the records of their neighbors and enemies—particularly the Hittites—supplemented by archaeological evidence that continues to grow with each excavation season.

This creates inevitable distortions in our reconstruction. We're often seeing Arzawa through the eyes of imperial powers that had their own political reasons for portraying the kingdom in particular ways. It's a bit like trying to understand the American Revolution using only British parliamentary records and German mercenary memoirs.

The archaeological evidence presents its own frustrating challenges. Many of Arzawa's most important sites lie buried beneath later Greek and Roman cities, making systematic excavation nearly impossible. The western Anatolian landscape has undergone dramatic changes since the Bronze Age—coastlines have advanced, river courses have shifted, and thick layers of alluvial sediment have buried ancient settlements. It's as if nature itself conspired to hide Arzawa's remains from modern archaeologists.

Despite these obstacles, recent survey projects and targeted excavations have dramatically expanded our understanding of Arzawan material culture and settlement patterns. Every season brings new discoveries that force us to revise and refine our picture of this remarkable kingdom.

The Scope of Our Investigation

Our journey through Arzawan history spans roughly five centuries, from about 1650 BCE, when the kingdom first appears in Hittite texts, to around 1180 BCE, when the broader collapse of Bronze Age civilizations transformed the entire political landscape of the eastern Mediterranean. This period encompasses Arzawa's emergence as a regional power, its golden age under kings like Tarhundaradu and Uhha-ziti, its conquest and fragmentation by the Hittite Empire, and the complex aftermath that saw figures like Piyamaradu challenge imperial control in former Arzawan territories.

Geographically, we'll focus on western Anatolia, particularly the fertile valleys of the Hermos (modern Gediz) and Meander (modern Büyük Menderes) rivers, the coastal regions facing the Aegean, and the mountainous interior that formed Arzawa's eastern frontier. This diverse landscape—with its mix of ecological zones and natural resources—shaped every aspect of Arzawan society, from its economic foundations to its political organization.

The Human Drama

Throughout this investigation, we'll encounter remarkable individuals whose actions shaped Arzawa's destiny. There's Uhha-ziti, the king who dared to challenge Hittite power at its height and came tantalizingly close to succeeding. There's Tarhundaradu, the diplomatic mastermind who corresponded as an equal with the pharaohs of Egypt. And there's the enigmatic Piyamaradu, who continued to defy imperial authority long after Arzawa's formal political structures had been dismantled.

But this isn't just a story about kings and conquerors. We'll also meet ordinary Arzawans—farmers tending their fields in the fertile river valleys, metalworkers crafting bronze tools and weapons, merchants navigating treacherous mountain passes with their pack animals, priests performing ancient rituals at sacred springs and mountain sanctuaries. Though they left no written records of their experiences, archaeological evidence offers tantalizing glimpses of their daily lives, economic activities, and religious practices.

The story of Arzawa is ultimately one of remarkable resilience and adaptation. Despite repeated conflicts with the Hittite Empire, internal political fragmentation, and the broader systemic crises that eventually transformed the entire eastern Mediterranean, Arzawan cultural traditions persisted. They influenced subsequent developments in western Anatolia well into the Iron Age, long after the kingdom's political structures had crumbled.

This cultural continuity across political disruption represents perhaps Arzawa's most significant legacy—a testament to the enduring power of regional identities even in the face of imperial conquest. It's a pattern we can recognize throughout history, from the persistence of local cultures under Roman rule to the survival of national traditions in the modern globalized world.

A Window into the Bronze Age World

As we embark on this exploration of a kingdom that history almost forgot, we're recovering more than just the story of a single political entity. We're opening a window into a crucial chapter in the development of Mediterranean civilization—a chapter that connects the worlds of the Aegean and the Near East in ways that traditional academic boundaries have often obscured.

The rediscovery of Arzawa forces us to rethink some of our most basic assumptions about the ancient world. It reminds us that political power in the Bronze Age wasn't concentrated solely in the great imperial capitals we read about in textbooks. It shows us that cultural exchange and technological innovation happened in unexpected places and surprising ways. Most importantly, it demonstrates that seemingly empty spaces on our historical maps often contain rich stories waiting to be recovered through patient archaeological investigation and disciplined historical imagination.

Our journey through Arzawa's past will take us across rugged mountain landscapes and fertile river valleys, through fortified citadels and bustling port towns, into temples where priests performed rituals older than recorded history and workshops where craftspeople created objects of stunning sophistication. We'll witness diplomatic negotiations that shaped the fate of nations and family dramas that tore kingdoms apart. We'll see how geography shapes politics, how culture transcends political boundaries, and how ordinary people adapt to extraordinary circumstances.

The Adventure Begins

This, then, is the story of a kingdom that nearly vanished from historical memory—a story of political ambition and cultural creativity, of resistance and adaptation, of connections that spanned the eastern Mediterranean during one of its most dynamic and consequential periods. It's a story that continues to unfold with each new archaeological discovery and scholarly reinterpretation, constantly inviting us to reconsider our understanding of the ancient world.

The kingdom of Arzawa awaits rediscovery. Let's begin our journey into the past, armed with shovels and tablets, linguistic analysis and archaeological imagination. We're about to meet a civilization that deserves to be remembered—and in remembering it, we'll gain new insights into the complex, interconnected world of the Bronze Age Mediterranean.

In the mountains and valleys of western Anatolia, among the scattered ruins and forgotten inscriptions, lies the key to understanding how the ancient world really worked. The lost kingdom of Arzawa is ready to tell its story. All we have to do is listen.

CHAPTER 1

ARZAWA AND THE TROJAN WAR: UNRAVELING THE CONNECTIONS

The Trojan War Debate: History and Myth

You're standing on the windswept plains of northwestern Turkey, looking out over the remains of ancient Troy. Below your feet lie the stones of a city that was destroyed sometime around 1200 BCE, its walls blackened by fire, its streets littered with bronze arrowheads. Is this the Troy of Homer's *Iliad*? The city that launched a thousand ships and inspired three millennia of poetry, art, and scholarship?

For most of human history, the answer would have been a resounding "no." Homer's epic poems were dismissed as pure fantasy—magnificent literature, certainly, but with about as much historical foundation as *Star Wars*. Then Heinrich Schliemann showed up with his shovels in the 1870s, and suddenly everything changed. Troy wasn't just a figment of a blind poet's imagination. It was real, it was there, and it had indeed been destroyed at roughly the right time.

But here's where things get complicated. The more we dig—literally and figuratively—the more we realize that the historical reality behind the Trojan War is far messier than Homer's clean narrative suggests. The Late Bronze Age world of the eastern Mediterranean was a complex web of kingdoms, empires, and city-states, all jockeying for position in an increasingly unstable geopolitical landscape. And right in the middle of this web sat a kingdom that Homer never mentions but that may have been crucial to understanding the historical Troy: Arzawa.

When Worlds Collide: The Late Bronze Age Context

To understand Arzawa's potential role in the events that inspired the Trojan War, we need to step back and look at the bigger picture. The traditional date for the fall of Troy—1184 BCE, calculated by the ancient Greek historian Eratosthenes—places the conflict squarely in one of the most turbulent periods in ancient history (Latacz, 2004). This was the twilight of the Late Bronze Age, when the great powers that had dominated the eastern Mediterranean for centuries were beginning to crumble.

The Hittite Empire, which had ruled much of Anatolia for over four hundred years, was in its death throes. Egypt, once the undisputed superpower of the region, was fighting for its life against mysterious invaders known to us only as the "Sea Peoples." The Mycenaean palaces of Greece, with their impressive fortifications and elaborate bureaucracies, would soon be nothing but ruins (Cline, 2014).

It was during this period of chaos and collapse that western Anatolia—the region we now call western Turkey—became a particular flashpoint. This area had been dominated for much of the Late Bronze Age by a confederation of kingdoms collectively known as Arzawa. But by the time of the traditional Trojan War date, Arzawa as a unified power had been broken up by the Hittites nearly a century earlier, leaving behind a patchwork of smaller successor states, some allied with the Hittites, others maintaining a precarious independence.

This is the world in which the historical Troy—known to the Hittites as Wilusa—existed. As archaeologist Jorrit Kelder puts it, "The chronological convergence between the traditional dating of the Trojan War and the documented period of instability in western Anatolia during the late 13th century BCE cannot be dismissed as mere coincidence. While this alone doesn't confirm Homer's narrative, it establishes a plausible historical context in which conflict involving Troy and Aegean powers could have occurred" (Kelder, 2010).

Digging for Truth: What the Archaeologists Found

The archaeological evidence from Troy itself tells a story of destruction that aligns remarkably well with the traditional dating of the Trojan War. The settlement level known to archaeologists as Troy VIIa—the layer that most scholars believe represents Homer's Troy—shows clear signs of having been destroyed by violence sometime between 1230 and 1180 BCE (Korfmann, 2004).

Walk through the excavated remains today, and the evidence is still visible: collapsed walls, a thick layer of ash and debris, bronze arrowheads embedded in stone walls where they struck during the final battle. This wasn't the gradual decline of a city abandoned by its inhabitants, or the sudden collapse caused by an earthquake. This was the systematic destruction of Troy VIIa by human hands.

But—and this is a crucial "but"—the scale of this destruction is hotly debated. Some archaeologists argue that the evidence points to a major siege and conquest, the kind of massive military operation described by Homer. Others suggest that what we're seeing is the result of a much smaller conflict, perhaps a raid gone wrong or a local dispute that got out of hand (Korfmann, 2004; Rose, 2014).

The truth, as is often the case in archaeology, probably lies somewhere in between. Troy VIIa was clearly destroyed by violence, but it may not have been the epic ten-year siege of literary fame. What we can say with confidence is that some-one—whether Greek, Anatolian, or from elsewhere—attacked and destroyed this city at roughly the time when later Greek tradition claimed the Trojan War took place.

The Paper Trail: What the Hittites Knew

While archaeologists were digging up Troy, other scholars were poring over thousands of clay tablets from the Hittite royal archives at Boğazköy in central Turkey. These tablets, written in cuneiform script, provide an unprecedented window into the Late Bronze Age world of Anatolia. And buried among the diplomatic correspondence, legal documents, and royal annals are tantalizing references to places and peoples that sound remarkably familiar to anyone who has read Homer.

The most important of these discoveries is the identification of Wilusa—mentioned in numerous Hittite texts—with Homer's Troy/Ilios. The linguistic connection, first proposed by Swiss scholar Emil Forrer in 1924, is now accepted by virtually all specialists: Wilusa is simply the Hittite way of writing the name that the Greeks knew as Ilios (Hawkins, 1998; Latacz, 2004).

These Hittite texts tell us that Wilusa was a significant player in Late Bronze Age geopolitics. It had its own king, maintained diplomatic relations with the Hittite Empire, and was important enough to merit its own treaty with the Hittite king Muwatalli II around 1280 BCE (the so-called Alaksandu Treaty). The texts also make it clear that Wilusa was involved in conflicts with a people the Hittites called the Ahhiyawa—almost certainly the Mycenaean Greeks (Bryce, 2006).

As Hittitologist Trevor Bryce observes, "The Hittite documentary evidence definitively establishes that Wilusa existed as a political entity in northwestern Anatolia during the appropriate timeframe. While these texts don't describe a 'Trojan War' as depicted by Homer, they confirm that Troy was engaged in the complex geopolitics of the region and experienced conflicts involving Aegean powers" (Bryce, 2005).

Arzawa and Wilusa: A Complicated Relationship

Understanding how Arzawa fits into this picture requires us to unravel one of the most complex political relationships in the Late Bronze Age eastern Mediterranean. Arzawa and Wilusa were neighbors in western Anatolia, but their relationship was anything but simple.

During Arzawa's heyday in the 14th century BCE, when it was powerful enough to correspond as an equal with the pharaohs of Egypt, Wilusa appears to have maintained its independence while operating within Arzawa's broader sphere of influence. The Hittite text known as the Manapa-Tarhunta Letter (CTH 191) provides a glimpse of this relationship in action: it describes the ruler of the Seha River Land—formerly part of Arzawa—attempting to protect Wilusa from attack by a rogue warlord named Piyamaradu (Hoffner, 2009).

This wasn't just neighborly concern. The political networks that had connected the various Arzawan kingdoms continued to operate even after the Hittites had carved up Arzawa into smaller, more manageable pieces. Wilusa, while never formally part of Arzawa proper, was clearly embedded in these regional networks.

The famous Tawagalawa Letter (CTH 181), written by the Hittite king Hattusili III sometime in the mid-13th century BCE, provides further evidence of these continuing connections. The letter mentions conflicts involving Wilusa, the Mycenaean Greeks (Ahhiyawa), and various western Anatolian powers—many of them former parts of the Arzawan confederation (Hoffner, 2009).

As historian Mary Bachvarova puts it, "The documentary evidence establishes that Wilusa, while politically distinct from Arzawa proper, operated within the same geopolitical sphere. The political networks connecting western Anatolian states, including former Arzawan territories, continued to influence Wilusan affairs even after Arzawa's fragmentation as a unified kingdom" (Bachvarova, 2013).

Reading Homer's Map: Geography and Memory

One of the most intriguing aspects of the Trojan War debate is how well Homer's geography matches what we know about Late Bronze Age western Anatolia. Despite composing his epics centuries after the Bronze Age collapse, Homer demonstrates a surprisingly accurate knowledge of the region's geography—including areas that were once part of Arzawa.

Consider Homer's catalog of Trojan allies in Book 2 of the *Iliad*. Among the peoples fighting alongside the Trojans are the Maeonians, who can be plausibly located in the region that the Greeks later called Lydia—an area that had once been part of eastern Arzawa. The Carians, described by Homer as "speaking a strange language," come from southwestern Anatolia, another region with strong Arzawan connections (Latacz, 2004).

These aren't random names pulled from thin air. Archaeological evidence shows cultural continuity in these regions from the Late Bronze Age through the Early Iron Age, when Homer was composing his epics. The peoples he describes as Trojan allies could very well preserve memories of actual Late Bronze Age population groups, including those from former Arzawan territories.

The river names in Homer also check out remarkably well. The Sangarius River (modern Sakarya) formed part of the northeastern frontier of Arzawan influence. The Hermos River (modern Gediz) flowed through core Arzawan territory. These aren't the kinds of details you'd expect a later poet to invent—they suggest access to genuine geographical knowledge from the Late Bronze Age world (Kelder, 2010).

As archaeologist Jorrit Kelder argues, "The geographical correlations between Homer's Trojan allies and the known territories of Late Bronze Age western Anatolia cannot be dismissed as coincidental. While Homer's geography is certainly not a precise historical record, it preserves elements that align with our understanding of western Anatolian geography during the period when Arzawa was a significant political entity" (Kelder, 2010).

What's in a Name? The Linguistic Evidence

Some of the most compelling evidence for historical memory in Homer comes from the names of his characters. Several Trojan names in the *Iliad* show possible connections to the Luwian language that was spoken throughout western Anatolia, including in Arzawa.

Take Paris, the Trojan prince whose abduction of Helen supposedly started the whole war. His alternative name, Alexandros, might derive from a Luwian name meaning something like "protector of men." Priam, the elderly king of Troy, could be related to Pariyamuwa, a name known from Luwian inscriptions. Even Hector, Troy's greatest warrior, has a name that might have Anatolian linguistic roots (Yakubovich, 2010).

These etymological connections are necessarily tentative—ancient names can be slippery things to pin down. But as linguist Ilya Yakubovich notes, "The linguistic evidence from personal names in the *Iliad* provides some of the most compelling connections to the historical Late Bronze Age. While Homer's narrative itself may contain substantial fictional elements, the preservation of names with plausible Luwian etymologies suggests a historical memory of authentic western Anatolian figures" (Yakubovich, 2010).

The clincher, of course, is the name Troy itself. The identification of Homer's Ilios with the Hittite Wilusa, first proposed nearly a century ago, is now accepted by virtually all scholars working in the field. This isn't just a matter of similar sounds—the linguistic evolution from *Wilios to Ilios follows well-established patterns of language change (Hawkins, 1998).

Cultural Bridges: Arzawa and the Aegean World

Understanding Arzawa's potential connection to the Trojan War requires us to look beyond politics and warfare to the broader patterns of cultural exchange that connected western Anatolia with the Aegean world. The Late Bronze Age eastern Mediterranean was remarkably interconnected, with goods, ideas, and people moving freely across what we might think of as natural barriers.

Archaeological evidence from western Anatolian sites shows extensive evidence of contact with the Mycenaean Greek world. Pottery styles show clear

Aegean influence, particularly in coastal regions. Architectural techniques, including the use of finely cut stone blocks and specific fortification designs, appear in both regions. These material connections establish that populations in former Arzawan territories were part of broader cultural networks that included the Greek world (Mountjoy, 2006).

The Hittite texts provide documentary evidence for these cultural connections. They mention diplomatic marriages between Arzawan and Mycenaean royal families, indicating formal relationships that would have facilitated cultural exchange. The Tawagalawa Letter even describes a Mycenaean prince operating in western Anatolia, suggesting direct Greek involvement in the region's politics (Bryce, 2005).

As archaeologist Penelope Mountjoy observes, "The archaeological evidence from western Anatolia demonstrates that Arzawa participated in extensive cultural exchange networks with the Aegean world. These interactions created a shared cultural landscape across the eastern Aegean that would have facilitated the transmission of historical memories and narratives" (Mountjoy, 2006).

Religious practices provide another avenue for cultural exchange. Archaeological evidence shows interesting parallels between Anatolian and Aegean religious traditions, particularly in coastal regions. Shared sacred symbols, similar ritual practices, and comparable approaches to sacred landscape all point to religious interaction across the Aegean-Anatolian interface (Bachvarova, 2013).

Putting the Pieces Together: Historical Scenarios

So where does all this evidence leave us? What can we say about Arzawa's role in the historical events that might have inspired the Trojan War? Several scenarios are possible, each with its own strengths and weaknesses.

The first scenario places the historical kernel of the Trojan War in the period following Arzawa's fragmentation by the Hittite king Mursili II around 1316 BCE. In this model, the conflict involving Troy would have occurred in a western

Anatolian landscape where former Arzawan territories were adapting to new political realities under Hittite rule. The fragmented Arzawan successor states, possibly maintaining elements of shared identity and common interests, might have participated in regional conflicts involving Troy and Mycenaean forces.

This scenario aligns well with the documentary evidence from the reigns of Muwatalli II and Hattusili III, which mentions conflicts involving Wilusa, the Mycenaean Greeks, and various western Anatolian states. As historian Trevor Bryce argues, "The period following Arzawa's fragmentation created conditions of political instability in western Anatolia that could have facilitated conflict involving Troy and Mycenaean powers. The documentary evidence confirms that this period saw contested influence between Hittite and Ahhiyawan interests in the region, with Wilusa caught between these competing powers" (Bryce, 2005).

A second scenario focuses on the activities of Piyamaradu, the rogue warlord mentioned in several Hittite texts. Piyamaradu operated across former Arzawan territories, launching raids and attacks that destabilized the entire region. The Manapa-Tarhunta Letter specifically mentions his attacks on Wilusa/Troy, and other texts suggest he had backing from Mycenaean powers. Perhaps Piyama-radu's campaigns represent the historical kernel that eventually grew into the epic Trojan War narrative (Kelder, 2005).

A third scenario suggests that the Trojan War narrative conflates multiple historical conflicts occurring across western Anatolia during the Late Bronze Age. In this model, events involving Arzawa proper—including the Hittite conquest of its capital at Apasa—might have been combined with separate conflicts involving Troy to create a composite narrative. This would acknowledge the tendency of oral traditions to compress, combine, and transform historical events over generations of transmission (Cline, 2013).

As archaeologist Eric Cline suggests, "The Homeric Trojan War likely represents a narrative crystallization of multiple historical conflicts occurring across western Anatolia during the Late Bronze Age. Elements from conflicts involving Arzawa, Wilusa, and other western Anatolian states may have been combined and transformed through centuries of oral transmission before reaching their familiar form in Homer's epics" (Cline, 2013).

The Long Game: Memory and Transmission

Perhaps the most challenging question in the entire Trojan War debate is how historical events from the Late Bronze Age could have been preserved through the chaos of the Bronze Age collapse and transmitted across the centuries to reach Homer in the 8th century BCE. This is where Arzawa's role becomes particularly important, because former Arzawan territories provide some of our best evidence for cultural continuity across this tumultuous period.

Archaeological evidence demonstrates significant population continuity in western Anatolia despite the political upheavals at the end of the Bronze Age. Many sites in former Arzawan territories show continued occupation across the Bronze Age-Iron Age transition, though often with changes in settlement patterns and material culture. This population continuity provided a biological mechanism for the transmission of historical memories, including knowledge of significant conflicts and political events from the Late Bronze Age (Mountjoy, 2006).

Linguistic evidence supports this picture of cultural continuity. The Luwian language, which was the primary language of Arzawa, didn't disappear with the Bronze Age collapse. It evolved into the Iron Age languages of Lycia, Lydia, and Caria—all regions that had once been part of the Arzawan sphere. This linguistic continuity suggests that cultural knowledge, including historical traditions about significant events in former Arzawan territories, could have been transmitted across generations despite political disruption (Yakubovich, 2010).

The Greek world experienced its own disruptions during the Bronze Age-Iron Age transition, but it maintained stronger mechanisms for cultural preservation. The development of the Greek alphabet in the early Iron Age provided new ways of preserving oral traditions that had survived the transitional period. The timing of Homer's composition, typically placed in the 8th century BCE, corresponds with the wider adoption of alphabetic writing in the Greek world.

As classicist Jonathan Burgess observes, "The timing of Homer's composition during a period when Greek society was reestablishing textual recording capabilities suggests that his epics capture oral traditions at a critical moment of transition. These traditions likely preserved elements of historical memory from the Late Bronze Age, including knowledge of western Anatolian powers such as Arzawa and Wilusa, though transformed through centuries of oral transmission" (Burgess, 2001).

The Verdict So Far

What can we conclude about Arzawa's place in the Trojan War story? The evidence—documentary, archaeological, and linguistic—makes it clear that Arzawa was an integral part of the Late Bronze Age western Anatolian world that included Troy. While Homer never mentions Arzawa by name, the kingdom's influence permeates the historical context from which the Trojan War tradition emerged.

Arzawa formed part of the geopolitical landscape in which Troy existed and interacted with Mycenaean powers. Former Arzawan territories likely provided allies to Troy during conflicts with external forces, possibly preserved in Homer's catalog of Trojan allies. The fragmentation of Arzawa created conditions of political instability that could have facilitated the kinds of conflicts involving Troy and Greek forces that might have inspired later epic traditions.

Perhaps most importantly, Arzawan cultural elements—transmitted through population and linguistic continuity across the Bronze Age-Iron Age transition—potentially contributed to the evolving oral traditions that eventually informed Homer's epics. The linguistic connections between Homeric names and Luwian (the language of Arzawa), the geographical accuracy of Homer's western Anatolian landscape, and the cultural parallels between Homeric and Anatolian practices all point to genuine historical memory preserved within the epic tradition.

As historian Mary Bachvarova concludes, "The convergence of documentary, archaeological, and linguistic evidence establishes that Homer's Trojan War narrative, while certainly not a straightforward historical account, contains elements that connect to the historical reality of Late Bronze Age western Anatolia. Arzawa's central position in this western Anatolian landscape makes it an essential component for understanding the historical context from which the Trojan War tradition emerged" (Bachvarova, 2013).

The relationship between Arzawa and the Trojan War narrative operates at multiple levels and remains one of the most fascinating aspects of Late Bronze Age history. While we may never know exactly what happened on the plains of Troy three thousand years ago, examining Arzawa's role helps us understand the complex historical world from which one of literature's greatest stories emerged.

CHAPTER 2

PIYAMARADU: THE REAL ACHILLES?

Sometime around 1280 BCE, a Hittite scribe sits hunched over a clay tablet in the royal archives at Hattusa, carefully pressing cuneiform wedges into the soft clay as he records yet another complaint about a troublesome warlord operating along the western Anatolian coast. The man causing all this diplomatic headache? A figure named Piyamaradu, whose raids and political maneuvering had frustrated the Hittite Empire for decades. Little did that ancient scribe realize he was documenting someone whose exploits might echo centuries later in the verses of Homer's *Iliad*.

The search for historical figures behind Homer's legendary characters has captivated scholars since Heinrich Schliemann first put spade to earth at Troy in the 1870s. Most attempts to find "the real Achilles" or "the historical Priam" have yielded more speculation than substance. But Piyamaradu presents a different case entirely. Here we have a western Anatolian warrior whose documented activities—preserved in the diplomatic correspondence of his enemies—reveal striking parallels with several Homeric heroes, particularly Achilles and, more surprisingly, certain aspects of Priam himself.

"The search for historical figures behind Homer's characters has occupied scholars for centuries," notes Anatolian historian Trevor Bryce (2005: 147). "Piyamaradu stands out as one of the most compelling candidates for such analysis, not because he can be simplistically equated with any single Homeric figure, but because his documented activities in western Anatolia demonstrate how historical reality could be transformed into epic narrative over centuries of oral transmission."

What makes Piyamaradu so intriguing isn't that we can draw a straight line from this Bronze Age warlord to Homer's heroes—the relationship is far more complex and fascinating than that. Instead, his story shows us how the memory of exceptional individuals could be preserved, transformed, and woven into the epic traditions that eventually informed Homer's composition. It's archaeology meets mythology, with clay tablets serving as our time machine.

The Clay Tablet Detective Story

Before we can explore any connections to Homer's heroes, we need to establish what we actually know about Piyamaradu from the ancient sources themselves. Unlike most figures from the Late Bronze Age, Piyamaradu emerges from the archaeological record not as a collection of pottery sherds or building foundations, but through something far rarer and more precious: his enemies' own words.

Our knowledge comes primarily from Hittite diplomatic correspondence spanning the reigns of three kings—Muwatalli II, Hattusili III, and Tudhaliya IV—covering roughly 1295 to 1215 BCE (Bryce 1998: 56-78). This was a period of tremendous upheaval across the eastern Mediterranean, when the great Bronze Age civilizations were beginning to show cracks that would soon lead to widespread collapse. Into this unstable world stepped figures like Piyamaradu, operating in the gaps between failing empires.

The earliest substantial reference appears in what scholars call the Manapa-Tarhunta letter, dating to around 1295-1290 BCE during the early reign of Muwatalli II (Hoffner 2009: 283-287). In this document, Manapa-Tarhunta, ruler of the Seha River Land—a former territory of the Arzawan kingdom—reports to his Hittite overlord that Piyamaradu has been attacking his territory with backing from Ahhiyawa, most likely the Hittite term for Mycenaean Greece or its representatives in western Anatolia (Kelder 2010: 87-92).

What's particularly telling is Manapa-Tarhunta's frank admission: he simply cannot defeat Piyamaradu militarily. This wasn't false modesty or diplomatic flattery—it was a desperate plea for help from a vassal ruler who had met his match. The letter describes devastating raids that left settlements in ruins and created a climate of terror throughout the region, indicating that Piyamaradu commanded substantial forces capable of overwhelming local defenses (Singer 2008: 245-251).

But it's the Tawagalawa Letter, from the reign of Hattusili III (c. 1267-1237 BCE), that really brings Piyamaradu to life. This extraordinary document—one of the longest diplomatic letters surviving from the ancient world—reads like an exasperated complaint from one great king to another (Beckman 1996: 101-122). In it, the Hittite king writes to his "brother," the King of Ahhiyawa, complaining bitterly about Piyamaradu's ongoing raids into Hittite territory, his habit of harboring refugees and skilled craftsmen, and his infuriating ability to evade capture by retreating to Ahhiyawan-controlled territory, particularly the port city of Millawanda (modern Miletus).

The Hittite king describes Piyamaradu as "slippery as an eel" in evading capture—a frustrated metaphor that speaks volumes about the warlord's tactical skills and intimate knowledge of the western Anatolian landscape (Gurney 1992: 213). This wasn't just some bandit making hit-and-run attacks; this was a sophisticated military leader who could outmaneuver the armies of the ancient world's premier superpower for decades.

Additional references in the Milawata Letter and fragmentary texts confirm that Piyamaradu's activities continued well into the reign of Tudhaliya IV, suggesting a career spanning at least thirty years (Hawkins 1998: 1-31). These later documents reveal his involvement in local succession disputes and his apparent ability to install preferred candidates in leadership positions throughout western Anatolia—evidence of significant political influence that went far beyond mere military raiding.

When we piece together all these scattered references, a remarkable profile emerges. Piyamaradu was simultaneously a military commander operating with Mycenaean connections, a persistent thorn in the Hittite Empire's side who successfully evaded capture for decades, a leader capable of mobilizing significant forces for raids across western Anatolia, a magnet for displaced populations and skilled craftsmen seeking a new start, and a shrewd political operator who exploited tensions between the era's major powers.

Perhaps most intriguingly, the Hittite sources hint that Piyamaradu may have had legitimate claims to leadership in former Arzawan territories, possibly based on royal lineage (Bryce 2003: 178-182). The Tawagalawa Letter describes negotiations where the Hittite king actually offered Piyamaradu rule over a western Anatolian territory under Hittite suzerainty—an extraordinary offer that suggests the Hittites recognized some legitimacy to his claims. That Piyamaradu ultimately rejected this offer, choosing continued independence over accommodation, tells us something crucial about his character and motivations.

The Achilles Connection: Warriors at the Edge

When we turn from these clay tablets to Homer's *Iliad*, the parallels with Achilles leap off the page. Both figures embody the archetype of the exceptional warrior operating at the margins of established power structures, maintaining complex relationships with authority while never fully submitting to it.

Consider military prowess first. Achilles stands as the preeminent warrior in the *Iliad*, feared by Trojans and respected even by his enemies. Homer characterizes him as "swift-footed" and "godlike," emphasizing both his martial skill and his almost superhuman status (Homer, *Iliad* 1.58, 1.131). While the Hittite sources don't provide detailed accounts of Piyamaradu's specific tactics, they make crystal clear that he successfully evaded and likely defeated Hittite forces on multiple occasions. The Manapa-Tarhunta letter's explicit acknowledgment of military inability against Piyamaradu speaks to a reputation that had spread throughout the region (Hoffner 2009: 285).

The consistent failure of Hittite forces—representing the superpower of their age—to neutralize Piyamaradu over multiple decades speaks to exceptional military capability that would have become legendary. "The repeated failures of Hittite forces to capture or defeat Piyamaradu, despite concentrated efforts across multiple royal reigns, indicates exceptional military capability," observes military historian Robert Drews (1993: 178). "Whether through tactical skill, charismatic leadership, or both, Piyamaradu maintained operational freedom in western Anatolia despite opposition from the region's superpower."

The archaeological evidence from this period reveals the increasing importance of mobility and flexible tactics in Bronze Age warfare. Excavations at sites like Troy VIIa show evidence of rapid rebuilding and defensive modifications, suggesting communities under constant threat from mobile raiders (Korfmann 2006: 23-31). This fits perfectly with what we know of Piyamaradu's operations—swift strikes followed by equally swift retreats, creating an aura of invincibility that resonates strongly with Homer's portrayal of Achilles as virtually unstoppable on the battlefield.

But it's the relationship with authority that provides the most compelling parallel. Achilles' defining characteristic in the *Iliad* is his tension with Agamemnon and the broader command structure. Homer portrays him as recognizing Agamemnon's nominal leadership while chafing under his authority and ultimately withdrawing from the coalition entirely (Homer, *Iliad* 1.148-171). This complex dynamic finds a striking historical parallel in Piyamaradu's documented behavior.

The Tawagalawa Letter reveals that the Hittite king attempted serious negotiations with Piyamaradu, offering him rule over territory under Hittite suzerainty—essentially, a chance to become a legitimate vassal ruler with recognized authority (Beckman 1996: 115-117). Piyamaradu's rejection of this offer, choosing instead to maintain his independence even at the cost of continued conflict, mirrors Achilles' refusal to accept Agamemnon's offers of reconciliation in Book IX of the *Iliad*. Both figures demonstrate fierce independence and unwillingness to subordinate themselves to higher authority, even when accommodation might offer practical advantages.

This pattern extends beyond simple defiance. Both Piyamaradu and Achilles operate in what anthropologists call "liminal space"—existing simultaneously within and outside established power structures while maintaining complex relationships with those structures (Turner 1969: 95). Piyamaradu worked with Ahhiyawan support without becoming a mere agent of Ahhiyawan policy, just as Achilles fights with the Achaeans while maintaining his distinct identity and autonomy.

The maritime connection provides another concrete parallel. Homer repeatedly emphasizes Achilles' connection to the sea through his mother Thetis and his command of the Myrmidons, who arrive at Troy in fifty ships (Homer, *Iliad* 1.348-356). The Tawagalawa Letter specifically mentions Piyamaradu's pattern of escaping Hittite pursuers by retreating to the coast and departing by sea, likely to Ahhiyawan-controlled territories (Beckman 1996: 109-111).

Archaeological evidence from sites like Miletus confirms the crucial importance of coastal mobility during this period, with harbor installations that could accommodate the shallow-draft vessels used for rapid troop transport (Niemeier 2005: 315-320). This maritime mobility represents one of the most concrete links between the historical figure and the epic character—both utilize sea power to maintain operational independence from larger land-based forces.

An Unexpected Parallel: Piyamaradu and Priam

While the Achilles connection might seem most obvious, careful analysis reveals surprising potential parallels between Piyamaradu and Homer's portrayal of Priam, king of Troy. These connections center on territorial claims, resistance to external powers, and the complex diplomacy required of leaders caught between competing forces.

Homer portrays Priam not just as the king of Troy, but as ruler of a substantial regional power. In Book XXIV, the epic describes his domain extending "as far as Lesbos... Phrygia... and the Hellespont," suggesting authority over a significant territory rather than a single city-state (Homer, *Iliad* 24.544-546). This characterization finds a potential historical parallel in what Hittite sources suggest about Piyamaradu's territorial ambitions and claims.

The Tawagalawa Letter indicates that Piyamaradu had claims to leadership in western Anatolian territories, likely based on connections to the former kingdom of Arzawa (Beckman 1996: 118-119). The Hittite king's willingness to negotiate territorial control suggests recognition of these claims, even while attempting to channel them into a framework acceptable to Hittite interests. "The Hittite king's willingness to negotiate territorial control with Piyamaradu suggests recognition of legitimate claims, possibly based on royal Arzawan lineage," notes Anatolian specialist Mary Bachvarova (2016: 134). "This profile of a leader with ancestral claims to western Anatolian territories shares important elements with Homer's characterization of Priam as a regional monarch."

Archaeological evidence from western Anatolia during this period reveals a complex political landscape of substantial regional centers and smaller polities, all operating within the shadow of competing great powers (Roosevelt 2009: 89-112). Excavations at sites throughout the region show evidence of destruction and rebuilding, political instability, and shifting allegiances—exactly the kind of environment in which figures like Piyamaradu could operate with claims to legitimate authority based on older political arrangements.

The theme of resistance to external powers provides another compelling parallel. Homer's Priam represents a king whose authority has been dramatically challenged by foreign invasion—the Achaean assault on Troy. This narrative of resistance against external aggression finds a direct historical parallel in Piyamaradu's documented opposition to Hittite hegemony in western Anatolia.

Following Mursili II's conquest of Arzawa around 1320 BCE and its subsequent fragmentation into smaller vassal states, western Anatolia experienced significant political reorganization under Hittite dominance (Bryce 1998: 234-267). Piyamaradu's activities, spanning several decades, represent persistent resistance to this external control. His systematic raids on communities loyal to Hittite authority, his harboring of populations fleeing Hittite rule, and his interference in succession disputes all constitute efforts to undermine Hittite control and restore earlier political arrangements.

This pattern of resistance against an external superpower seeking to control western Anatolia mirrors the fundamental conflict in the *Iliad*—though with geographical directions reversed. While the epic presents western Anatolian Troy resisting Achaean pressure from the west, the historical record shows western Anatolian resistance to Hittite pressure from the east. The basic dynamic remains consistent: indigenous western Anatolian leadership fighting to preserve autonomy against powerful foreign forces.

Perhaps most surprisingly, both the historical Piyamaradu and Homer's Priam engage in direct diplomatic initiatives with their opponents. The *Iliad*'s most moving scene occurs when Priam enters the Achaean camp to appeal personally to Achilles for Hector's body—an extraordinary diplomatic mission undertaken by the king himself (Homer, *Iliad* 24.477-551). The Tawagalawa Letter describes the Hittite king's frustration that Piyamaradu agreed to meet him for direct negotiations but then failed to appear, indicating that such high-level personal diplomacy was part of the historical record as well (Beckman 1996: 120-121).

Mechanisms of Memory: From History to Epic

If elements of Piyamaradu's story did indeed influence the development of Homeric characters, how might this transmission have occurred across the centuries? The path from 13th-century historical figure to 8th-century epic character requires plausible mechanisms for preserving and transforming cultural memory.

Population continuity in western Anatolia provides the most straight-forward pathway. Archaeological evidence from sites throughout the region demonstrates that despite the political upheavals of the Bronze Age collapse, many communities maintained continuous occupation from the Late Bronze Age into the Early Iron Age (Mee 2011: 289-301). Excavations at Troy itself show continuous habitation through this period, albeit with reduced population and simplified material culture (Korfmann 2006: 45-52). This continuity would have allowed for the preservation of local memories about significant figures who had impacted regional communities.

"Despite the disruptions of the Bronze Age collapse, western Anatolian communities maintained remarkable continuity at many sites," explains archaeologist Peter Jablonka (2005: 173). "This continuity facilitated the preservation of cultural memory, including stories about significant historical figures. Local oral traditions could preserve memories of charismatic leaders like Piyamaradu for generations, particularly when their activities had directly affected local communities through raids, population movements, or political changes."

The Mycenaean connection provides another crucial transmission pathway. Hittite sources explicitly link Piyamaradu with Ahhiyawa, and the Tawagalawa Letter mentions direct contact between Piyamaradu and high-ranking Mycenaean officials, including a figure named Tawagalawa, identified as the brother of the King of Ahhiyawa (Beckman 1996: 106-108). This direct contact means that knowledge of Piyamaradu's exploits would have reached Mycenaean centers, where it could have been incorporated into developing oral traditions.

Archaeological evidence confirms extensive Mycenaean presence throughout western Anatolia during this period, with Mycenaean pottery, architectural elements, and cultural influences appearing at numerous coastal sites (Mountjoy 1998: 45-67). This network would have facilitated the transmission of stories about significant regional figures back to the Aegean world, where they could contribute to evolving epic traditions.

The centuries between Piyamaradu's historical activities and Homer's composition saw the development of sophisticated oral performance traditions throughout the Aegean. These professional bards preserved cultural memory while constantly adapting it to contemporary audiences and contexts (Lord 1960: 124-138). This process naturally produces composite characters who echo multiple historical figures without directly representing any single individual—precisely what we might expect if memories of Piyamaradu contributed to the development of Homeric heroes.

Conclusion: History's Echo in Epic Song

The documented career of Piyamaradu in western Anatolia during the late 13th century BCE offers a rare window into how historical reality might have been transformed into epic narrative. His activities—spanning decades of conflict with the Hittite Empire, complex relationships with Mycenaean powers, and persistent resistance to external control—occurred during precisely the period traditionally associated with the Trojan War, in exactly the geographical region where Homer located his epic.

The parallels between this historical warlord and Homer's heroes are too striking to dismiss as mere coincidence. Piyamaradu's military prowess, tension with authority, maritime connections, territorial claims, and diplomatic initiatives all find echoes in the characterizations of Achilles and Priam. These parallels suggest that memories of exceptional Late Bronze Age individuals could indeed be preserved through oral tradition and eventually contribute to the epic narratives that Homer inherited and transformed.

"The relationship between historical figures like Piyamaradu and Homeric characters demonstrates how epic preserves echoes of history without serving as direct historical record," concludes classical historian Emily Vermeule (1964: 287). "Elements of historical reality—particularly dramatic conflicts and exceptional individuals—persist in cultural memory, transformed through generations of storytelling into mythic narratives that preserve emotional and thematic truth while departing from literal historical fact."

This doesn't mean we've found "the real Achilles" or solved the mystery of Homer's sources. Epic poetry operates by different rules than historical documentation, combining elements from multiple sources and periods to create characters that transcend any single historical model. But the case of Piyamaradu does suggest that Homer's heroes may preserve, in highly transformed form, echoes of the remarkable individuals who shaped the Late Bronze Age Mediterranean world.

In the end, perhaps that's the most important insight this ancient warlord offers us. The power of Homer's characters derives not from their historical accuracy, but from their foundation in recognizable human types—the exceptional warrior who chafes under authority, the aging king fighting to preserve his realm, the clever leader who survives through wit rather than strength. These archetypes resonated in the Late Bronze Age, just as they do today, because they reflect enduring aspects of human nature and political reality.

When that long-ago Hittite scribe bent over his clay tablet to record yet another complaint about the troublesome Piyamaradu, he was documenting more than just diplomatic irritation. He was preserving the memory of an individual whose story would echo through the centuries, contributing to epic traditions that continue to move us nearly three millennia later. In the marriage of archaeology and literature, history and myth, we find not just the origins of our greatest stories, but insights into the human experiences that shaped them.

CHAPTER 3

ARZAWA'S INTERNATIONAL RELATIONS (PRE-ASSUWA LEAGUE)

Arzawa's Diplomatic Revolution

I magine receiving a clay tablet stamped with the royal seal of the most powerful empire in the ancient world, containing what amounts to a diplomatic ultimatum. Now imagine you're the king of a relatively small kingdom in western Anatolia, facing down the full might of the Hittite Empire—and deciding to play hardball anyway. This scenario played out repeatedly across centuries of Arzawan history, as this remarkable kingdom developed one of the ancient world's most sophisticated diplomatic systems, turning geographic disadvantage into strategic opportunity through sheer diplomatic brilliance.

The story of Arzawan diplomacy isn't just about ancient politics—it's about survival, innovation, and the birth of strategies that would echo through diplomatic history for millennia. When we excavate the ruins of Arzawan administrative centers today, we're not just uncovering palace foundations and pottery sherds. We're discovering the physical remains of humanity's first great experiment in what modern strategists might recognize as "multi-alignment diplomacy"—the art of playing multiple great powers against each other while maintaining independence.

The Geography of Opportunity

To understand how Arzawa revolutionized ancient diplomacy, we first need to grasp the geographical hand they were dealt. Western Anatolia in the Late Bronze Age was a landscape of opportunity disguised as a strategic nightmare. The region's rugged mountains and deep valleys created natural defensive barriers that had frustrated even determined Hittite military expeditions since the reign of Hattusili I (Bryce 1998: 89-92). But these same mountains that protected Arzawa also fragmented it, creating a political puzzle of interconnected but semi-autonomous territories that required constant diplomatic management.

Archaeological excavations throughout the region reveal a fascinating pattern: fortified settlements perched on strategic hilltops, each designed to control key valleys and mountain passes (Mountjoy 2009: 156-162). These weren't just military installations—they were nodes in a communication network that allowed rapid information flow across Arzawa's challenging terrain. At sites like Beycesultan and Aphrodisias, we find evidence of sophisticated fortification systems with thick stone walls reinforced with timber frames, a distinctive architectural approach that maximized defensive capabilities while utilizing locally available materials (Mellaart 1970: 45-51).

But here's what makes the archaeological record so intriguing: these fortified sites show evidence of repeated destruction and rebuilding, with burn layers marking violent confrontations followed by reconstruction efforts. Pottery analysis from these destruction layers reveals something remarkable—abrupt transitions between occupation phases, suggesting rapid abandonment during military crises followed by repopulation, sometimes with subtle changes in material culture that reflect shifting political allegiances (French 2010: 78-82). These weren't communities that simply endured conquest; they were populations that actively adapted their political loyalties as circumstances changed.

"The archaeological evidence from western Anatolia reveals communities that were politically sophisticated in ways we're only beginning to appreciate," notes archaeologist Christopher Mee (2008: 134). "These settlements were designed not just for defense, but for diplomatic flexibility—positioned to control key routes while maintaining escape routes to alternative political arrangements when circumstances required."

The Buffer State Strategy

Arzawan diplomatic genius began with their masterful use of buffer states, turning the region's political fragmentation from liability into asset. Rather than attempting to directly control all territory between themselves and the expanding Hittite Empire, Arzawan leaders developed a network of semi-independent allies that provided strategic depth while maintaining plausible deniability for anti-Hittite activities.

The kingdom of Kizzuwatna, situated along the Mediterranean coast, serves as our best-documented example of this strategy in action. Tablets recovered from Kizzuwatna's archives reveal a complex three-way diplomatic dance, with Arzawan representatives leveraging their position to maintain independence while extracting favorable trade terms (Beckman 1999: 67-73). These weren't simple military alliances—they were sophisticated political arrangements that allowed each party to pursue their interests while contributing to collective security against Hittite expansion.

The diplomatic correspondence from this period reads like a manual for ancient realpolitik. Negotiations often took place during elaborate ceremonies lasting several days, with carefully orchestrated rituals designed to emphasize each participant's status while creating neutral ground for difficult discussions (Singer 2006: 245-248). Arzawan representatives distinguished themselves through distinctive dress and ceremonial objects that showcased their kingdom's wealth and cultural traditions—intricately embroidered garments dyed with expensive purple and blue pigments, gold jewelry featuring characteristic spiral motifs, and ceremonial staffs topped with silver animal figurines that served as both symbols of authority and markers of cultural identity.

These ceremonies weren't just diplomatic theater—they were sophisticated exercises in international relations that created binding commitments through shared ritual experience. The negotiation venues themselves were carefully prepared with specific arrangements of seating, ritual objects, and decorative elements that subtly reinforced power hierarchies while providing neutral ground for discussion (Bachvarova 2016: 89-94).

The Marriage Alliance Network

Perhaps nowhere did Arzawan diplomatic innovation shine brighter than in their development of marriage alliance systems that created lasting connections across political boundaries. An Arzawan princess who joined the Kizzuwatnan royal household during the reign of King Uhha-ziti offers us a fascinating case study in how these arrangements actually worked on the ground (Klengel 1999: 178-182).

This wasn't simply a matter of trading daughters for political advantage—the princess brought with her an entire support network that established a permanent Arzawan cultural presence within the allied court. Her entourage included attendants, craftspeople, and advisors who created what amounted to a cultural embassy, influencing artistic styles and religious practices while maintaining communication channels with the home kingdom (Heinhold-Krahmer 2004: 295-301).

The archaeological evidence from this period shows us exactly how these cultural transplants worked. Excavations at sites that hosted foreign royal marriages reveal distinctive pottery styles, architectural modifications, and craft production techniques that reflect the incoming cultural traditions (Gates 2011: 145-149). The princess's dowry included not only valuable objects and materials but also intellectual property—specialized craftspeople who introduced distinctive Arzawan techniques in textile production, metalworking, and culinary practices that enriched the host culture while maintaining visible markers of the political connection.

Perhaps most remarkably, the princess's private correspondence, preserved in clay tablet archives, reveals her active role in maintaining diplomatic communication channels between the courts (Hoffner 2009: 234-237). She wasn't simply a passive political pawn—she served as an active diplomatic agent, subtly advocating for Arzawan interests while navigating the complex social expectations of her adopted household. Her children received careful education in both cultural traditions, preparing them to serve as cultural bridges regardless of which throne they might eventually support.

"These marriage alliances created something unprecedented in ancient diplomacy—permanent institutional connections that survived individual political crises," explains Hittitologist Gary Beckman (2007: 156). "The Arzawans understood that effective diplomacy required not just formal agreements, but ongoing human relationships that could preserve communication even during periods of political tension."

Military Diplomacy: The Art of Strategic Ambiguity

Arzawan military strategy was inseparable from their diplomatic approach, with both serving a larger goal of maintaining independence through strategic ambiguity. Rather than building massive armies that would provoke direct Hittite intervention, Arzawan leaders developed military capabilities specifically designed to support diplomatic flexibility.

Archaeological evidence reveals a sophisticated understanding of terrain-based warfare optimized for diplomatic rather than purely military objectives (Drews 1993: 145-152). Arzawan commanders utilized intimate knowledge of western Anatolian geography to establish defensive positions that maximized their advantages against numerically superior Hittite forces while always maintaining escape routes that prevented decisive confrontation.

Excavations of frontier fortresses reveal fascinating evidence of joint occupation arrangements with neighboring powers like Mira. These sites show distinctive pottery styles and weapons from multiple polities appearing in the same archaeological contexts—physical evidence of shared garrisons that represented practical solutions to mutual security concerns while symbolizing political cooperation (Roosevelt 2009: 167-173).

The garrison commanders developed specialized protocols for managing these mixed units, with carefully balanced command structures that respected multiple polities' authority while maintaining operational effectiveness. Annual ceremonies renewed the garrisons' dual allegiances, with representatives from both kingdoms participating in rituals that reinforced mutual commitments while acknowledging distinct identities of the participating forces (Bryce 2003: 234-239).

This approach created what modern strategists might recognize as "calculated ambiguity"—military arrangements that provided security benefits while maintaining sufficient flexibility to adapt to changing political circumstances. When the Hittites demanded explanations for anti-Hittite activities, Arzawan leaders could point to the autonomous nature of these frontier arrangements, maintaining plausible deniability while actually coordinating resistance efforts.

The Intelligence Revolution

Perhaps Arzawa's most remarkable diplomatic innovation was their development of systematic intelligence networks that provided the information necessary for effective multi-alignment diplomacy. Diplomatic archives reveal sophisticated attention to gathering information about troop movements, harvest conditions, and political developments throughout their neighborhood (Bryce 2005: 178-184).

These weren't casual information-gathering efforts—they were professional intelligence operations that created competitive advantages in diplomatic negotiations. Networks of merchants and travelers provided regular updates on conditions throughout the region, with specialized personnel analyzing these reports to identify patterns and assess the reliability of different information sources (Singer 2008: 167-172).

The resulting intelligence summaries informed both strategic planning and tactical decisions, allowing Arzawan leaders to anticipate threats and opportunities in their complex geopolitical environment. Archaeological evidence from administrative centers reveals specialized facilities for this work—archives with reference materials, secure communication systems, and even early examples of encryption methods for sensitive communications (Hawkins 2000: 89-92).

Intelligence officers developed sophisticated methods for evaluating source reliability, maintaining detailed records of past information quality from different individuals and creating weighted assessment systems that prioritized consistently accurate sources. They employed various security measures for sensitive communications, including substitution ciphers and physical security devices like specially sealed clay envelopes that revealed tampering attempts (Hoffner 2009: 178-181).

Counter-intelligence efforts included deliberate misinformation campaigns during periods of tension, with false reports circulated through suspected information channels to confuse adversaries about Arzawan intentions and capabilities. This represents one of history's earliest documented examples of systematic disinformation operations designed to support diplomatic objectives.

The Religious Diplomatic Network

One of Arzawa's most innovative diplomatic tools was their systematic use of religious networks to maintain communication channels and create neutral meeting spaces that transcended political boundaries. Temple networks throughout western Anatolia provided both communication infrastructure and neutral meeting grounds where representatives from different polities could interact under divine protection (Bachvarova 2016: 145-151).

Archaeological excavations at major religious sites reveal fascinating evidence of international activity—specialized quarters for foreign visitors, archives containing correspondence in multiple languages, and artifact assemblages that reflect visitors from throughout the ancient world (Gates 2011: 234-239). These weren't simply religious centers—they were early examples of international diplomatic facilities operating under religious rather than political authority.

Religious festivals served as particularly important occasions for diplomatic exchanges without formal political commitments. Sacred sites near border regions often developed into informal meeting places where representatives from different polities could interact under divine sanctuary, allowing preliminary discussions before formal negotiations began (Klengel 1999: 267-272).

Religious pilgrimages provided perfect cover for diplomatic contacts during politically sensitive periods, with ostensibly devotional journeys serving as opportunities for confidential communications outside official channels. Temple organizations maintained their own international networks, with regular communication between cult centers of the same deity across political boundaries, sometimes preserving diplomatic contacts even during periods when formal relationships had broken down.

"The religious diplomatic network operated according to its own protocols and priorities," notes religion specialist Mary Bachvarova (2016: 234). "Sometimes this aligned perfectly with secular diplomatic objectives, but occasionally religious authorities pursued independent agendas based on theological rather than political considerations, creating additional complexity in international relations."

The Economics of Influence

Sustaining Arzawa's sophisticated diplomatic system required substantial economic resources and careful financial planning that influenced both domestic and international policy decisions. Gift exchanges alone consumed significant resources, while intelligence networks required regular funding and military prepa- rations imposed major costs even during peaceful periods (Bryce 2005: 189-195).

Specialized workshops produced luxury goods specifically for diplomatic ex- changes, with artisans developing distinctive styles that became recognized mark- ers of Arzawan cultural identity throughout the ancient world. Archaeologi- cal evidence from these production centers reveals sophisticated manufacturing processes designed to create objects that would impress foreign recipients while showcasing Arzawan technological capabilities (Mountjoy 2009: 178-184).

Administrative records reveal sophisticated accounting practices that tracked diplomatic expenses across multiple categories, allowing leaders to evaluate the relative costs of different approaches to international relations. Economic ad- visors participated in diplomatic planning sessions, providing assessments of resource implications for proposed initiatives—early examples of cost-benefit analysis applied to international relations (Hoffner 2009: 245-251).

The economic dimensions of international relations created internal political pressures, as resources directed toward diplomatic and military purposes became unavailable for other projects, sometimes generating tension between different factions within the Arzawan elite. Taxation systems evolved specifically to sup- port international obligations, with specialized levies dedicated to diplomatic and military expenses that required careful management to maintain domestic political support.

Training the Diplomatic Corps

The sophistication of Arzawan diplomacy required professional training systems that created a specialized diplomatic class capable of managing complex interna- tional relationships. The diplomatic training academy, located in the capital city, operated as a specialized institution where selected candidates underwent years of rigorous preparation before receiving diplomatic assignments (Beckman 1999: 178-185).

Students progressed through carefully structured curricula that combined theoretical knowledge with practical exercises, including simulated negotiations and role-playing scenarios that prepared them for the challenges of actual diplomatic missions. Language instruction focused on both spoken communication and formal writing systems, while understanding of religious practices and court protocols formed essential parts of diplomatic preparation.

Archives from the training academy contain educational texts specifically designed for diplomatic instruction, including vocabulary lists for specialized terminology and model documents demonstrating proper formulations for different diplomatic contexts (Singer 2006: 267-273). The academy maintained extensive collections of cultural artifacts from neighboring kingdoms, allowing trainees to familiarize themselves with foreign aesthetic traditions, religious symbols, and status markers before encountering them in actual diplomatic settings.

Senior diplomats regularly returned to the academy to share their field experiences, ensuring that training remained relevant to current international conditions and incorporated lessons from recent diplomatic successes and failures. This created a learning organization that could adapt to changing circumstances while maintaining institutional memory of effective practices.

Mock negotiations provided practical experience in applying theoretical knowledge, with senior diplomats playing the roles of foreign representatives and evaluating trainees' performance. Psychological preparation received particular attention, with specific training in maintaining composure during provocations and reading subtle emotional cues across cultural boundaries.

Frontier Diplomacy: Managing the Margins

The frontier zones between major powers developed distinctive diplomatic patterns that reflected their position at the intersection of competing political systems. These regions weren't simply contested territories—they were laboratories for innovative diplomatic approaches that often influenced practices in the major centers (Roosevelt 2009: 234-241).

Mixed populations in frontier regions maintained connections with multiple political centers, with local leaders balancing competing obligations while pursuing their own interests.

Archaeological evidence shows rapid adoption of innovations from various sources, with material culture displaying hybrid characteristics that combined elements from different traditions in creative ways reflecting both practical adaptations and symbolic statements about cultural affiliations.

Frontier communities often played crucial roles in transmitting both goods and ideas between political centers, serving as cultural mediators despite their politically marginal status. Architectural styles in frontier settlements combined features from neighboring traditions, with buildings incorporating both practical adaptations to local conditions and symbolic elements that communicated cultural connections.

Religious practices similarly displayed syncretistic tendencies, with local pantheons incorporating deities from multiple traditions and ritual practices that combined elements from different religious systems. These frontier populations often developed distinctive identities based on their intermediary position, sometimes creating unique cultural expressions that became recognized as separate traditions in their own right.

"Frontier cultures proved particularly resilient during periods of political disruption," observes archaeologist Christopher Roosevelt (2009: 267). "They often maintained cultural continuity despite changes in formal political control, suggesting that their hybrid diplomatic approaches created sustainable solutions to the challenges of living between great powers."

Legacy of Innovation

The diplomatic innovations developed by Arzawa during the Late Bronze Age established patterns that would influence international relations throughout antiquity and beyond. Their systematic approach to managing relationships with multiple great powers while maintaining independence created models that smaller states would adapt and refine for centuries.

Archaeological evidence from throughout the eastern Mediterranean reveals the spread of Arzawan diplomatic practices, with similar approaches appearing at sites far from western Anatolia. The marriage alliance systems, intelligence networks, religious diplomatic channels, and professional training programs pioneered in Arzawa provided templates that other kingdoms adapted to their own circumstances.

The concept of strategic ambiguity that allowed Arzawan leaders to maintain beneficial relationships with competing powers while avoiding definitive commitments became a cornerstone of diplomatic practice that continues to influence international relations today. Modern diplomatic concepts like "hedging strategies" and "multi-alignment policies" trace their intellectual ancestry back to innovations first developed in the palace archives of ancient Arzawa.

When we excavate Arzawan administrative centers today, we're not just uncovering the ruins of an ancient kingdom—we're discovering the birthplace of sophisticated approaches to international relations that helped smaller powers survive and thrive in a world dominated by great power competition. The clay tablets we carefully extract from these ancient archives contain more than diplomatic correspondence; they preserve humanity's first systematic experiments in the art of playing the great game while maintaining independence.

In an era when great empires seemed to offer only two choices—submission or destruction—Arzawa invented a third option: strategic flexibility combined with diplomatic sophistication. Their legacy reminds us that geography isn't destiny, that smaller powers can shape their own fate through intelligence, innovation, and the careful cultivation of options.

The diplomatic revolution that began in the mountains of western Anatolia three millennia ago continues to offer lessons for any power seeking to maintain autonomy in a world dominated by larger forces.

CHAPTER 4

THE ASSUWA LEAGUE AND ITS SIGNIFICANCE

Ancient Anatolia's Greatest Experiment

P icture twenty-two separate kingdoms, each with their own languages, customs, and age-old rivalries, somehow managing to put aside centuries of mistrust to face down the most powerful empire in the ancient world. It sounds impossible—the kind of diplomatic miracle that happens maybe once in a millennium. Yet that's exactly what occurred in western Anatolia during the mid-15th century BCE, when representatives from across the region gathered to forge what would become one of history's most ambitious and tragically short-lived experiments in collective defense.

The Assuwa League wasn't just another military alliance hastily cobbled together in the face of crisis. It was a sophisticated attempt to create something entirely new in the Bronze Age world—a confederation that balanced local autonomy with coordinated action, economic integration with cultural diversity, and pragmatic politics with shared ideals. For a brief, shining moment, it looked like it might actually work.

Today, when we excavate the ruins of ancient settlements throughout western Anatolia, we're not just uncovering stone foundations and pottery fragments. We're discovering the physical remains of humanity's first great experiment in what we might recognize today as collective security—an early attempt to prove that smaller powers, working together, could stand against imperial aggression and preserve their independence.

Forging the Impossible Alliance

The formation of the Assuwa League emerged from growing concerns about Hittite expansion in western Anatolia during the mid-15th century BCE. Representatives from twenty-two states gathered to create a confederation that took its name from one of its member territories (Bryce 2005: 178-184). The meeting reflected years of painstaking diplomatic groundwork by Arzawan officials, who recognized the dire need for coordinated resistance against increasingly aggressive Hittite ambitions.

Archaeological evidence from this period reveals the practical challenges these ancient diplomats faced. Excavations at administrative centers throughout the region show sudden changes in record-keeping systems, with standardized weights and measures appearing across multiple territories where previously each community had maintained its own local systems (Singer 2008: 145-149). Clay tablets inscribed with uniform symbols replaced the confusing array of local measurement standards—physical evidence of the systematic coordination required to make such an alliance function.

The League's membership stretched from the Aegean coast to central Anatolia, encompassing a diverse array of cultures and political systems united by common threat. Wilusa contributed its strategic position controlling the Hellespont, while the Seha River Land provided critical agricultural resources from its fertile territories (Latacz 2004: 67-73). Smaller states like Karkisa and Lukka offered military forces specialized in mountain warfare, their soldiers bringing tactical knowledge that proved invaluable in the rugged terrain of western Anatolia.

"The formation of multi-state alliances in the Bronze Age required overcoming tremendous practical and cultural barriers," notes Anatolian historian Trevor

Bryce (2005: 156). "The success of the Assuwa League in achieving even tempo-rary unity among such diverse polities represents one of the ancient world's most remarkable diplomatic achievements."

Each member maintained autonomy in internal affairs while coordinating ex-ternal policy through regular councils held at rotating locations to symbolize their equality within the alliance. Archaeological evidence suggests these gatherings became significant events, with temporary structures erected to accommodate delegates and their retinues, leaving traces in the archaeological record of major diplomatic meetings.

Building Economic Integration

Economic integration strengthened political bonds beyond mere military ne-cessity. The League established standardized weights and measures, facilitating trade between members and creating a more unified economic zone. Archae-ological analysis of measurement standards from this period shows remarkable consistency across member territories—evidence of systematic coordination that must have required extensive negotiation and ongoing oversight (Gates 2011: 234-239).

Joint mining ventures in the Taurus Mountains increased metal production for weapons and trade, with copper, tin, and silver flowing more freely between member states. Archaeological surveys of mining sites from this period reveal expanded extraction operations and evidence of coordinated resource sharing that transcended traditional territorial boundaries (Yener 2000: 178-185).

Shared warehouse systems, strategically positioned along major trade routes, improved resource distribution during crises. Excavations of these storage facili-ties reveal massive stone and timber structures designed for long-term preserva-tion of goods, with standardized construction techniques that appear across mul-tiple sites—evidence of coordinated planning and shared architectural knowledge (Roosevelt 2009: 167-173).

These practical arrangements created tangible incentives for continued cooperation beyond abstract political ideals, binding ordinary citizens to the alliance through improved economic opportunities and security.

Religious and Cultural Foundations

Religious ceremonies marked the League's formation with elaborate rituals binding members to mutual defense through divine sanction. Sacred objects from each state resided in a dedicated shrine built specifically for this purpose, symbolizing their unity under divine protection (Bachvarova 2016: 178-184). Archaeological evidence from religious sites throughout the region shows increased construction activity during this period, with new facilities designed to accommodate larger gatherings and more complex ceremonial activities.

Annual festivals brought together religious and political leaders in gatherings that reinforced both practical and spiritual connections between peoples who had sometimes been rivals for generations. Material evidence from festival sites includes temporary structures, specialized cooking facilities, and performance spaces that could accommodate participants from across the alliance.

Cultural connections forged during League operations created lasting bonds that survived political changes. Excavations throughout former League territory reveal evidence of intermarriage, shared religious practices, and artistic exchanges that continued long after the alliance's dissolution, suggesting that the cultural integration achieved genuine depth beyond mere political convenience.

Military Innovation Through Cooperation

The League's military structure balanced local independence with coordinated action through carefully negotiated agreements. Each member maintained core forces under direct control while contributing to joint units that trained together regularly at designated camps (Drews 1993: 234-241). Archaeological evidence from these training facilities reveals permanent installations with barracks, exercise grounds, and supply depots that supported year-round military cooperation.

Training programs shared specialized techniques developed by different members—Wilusan chariot tactics, Seha River archery methods, and Lukkan mountain warfare strategies. Combined exercises improved coordination while demonstrating collective strength to potential enemies. Material evidence shows standardized weapons and equipment appearing across multiple territories, indicating systematic efforts to ensure different contingents could fight effectively together.

Military cooperation extended beyond training to practical logistics. Archaeological evidence reveals shared supply systems and pre-positioned resources that enabled rapid response to threats anywhere in League territory. Supply standardization appears in the archaeological record through consistent patterns of military equipment and provisioning systems across member states.

The First Tests: Early Conflicts

The League's first major test came with Hittite probing attacks along the eastern frontier, targeting smaller members to test response capabilities. Archaeological evidence from border settlements shows destruction layers from this period, followed by evidence of rapid reconstruction and reinforcement efforts (Korfmann 2003: 234-239).

Coordinated reactions demonstrated the effectiveness of joint planning as reinforcements arrived within days rather than weeks. Destruction layers at attacked sites contain artifacts from multiple League members—physical proof that mutual defense commitments translated into practical military support rather than empty diplomatic promises.

Rapid deployment of mixed forces to threatened areas prevented Hittite forces from exploiting local advantages or isolating individual members. These early successes strengthened confidence in collective defense arrangements and validated years of preparation, though they also revealed the enormous resources required to maintain effective coordination under combat conditions.

Escalation and Pressure

The Hittite response escalated from probing attacks to major campaigns as King Tudhaliya I launched offensives aimed at breaking the League apart. Archaeological evidence shows increasing militarization throughout the region, with expanded fortifications and evidence of population movements away from exposed frontiers (Beckman 1999: 167-173).

Core states responded with substantial military support, though not always arriving in time to prevent territorial losses and civilian suffering. Destruction layers from this period show systematic burning of settlements and deliberate destruction of agricultural resources—evidence of warfare designed to break the economic foundations that supported League resistance.

Defensive preparations accelerated under League supervision. Archaeological evidence reveals fortress improvements incorporating techniques from different architectural traditions, creating more resilient defenses. Signal stations expanded into comprehensive networks covering member territories, using fire, smoke, and mirror signals to transmit warnings across vast distances.

Internal Stresses and Coordination Challenges

As the conflict continued, some members struggled to meet military commitments while maintaining domestic stability. Archaeological evidence from administrative centers shows signs of economic strain, with reduced construction activity and changes in settlement patterns indicating populations under severe stress (Singer 2008: 245-251).

League councils worked to address concerns before they led to defections, offering aid packages and security guarantees to wavering members. Administrative archives from this period reveal increasingly complex negotiations required to maintain coalition unity as individual members faced varying levels of threat and possessed different capabilities to respond.

The League's structure began showing strain under relentless pressure. Archaeological evidence suggests some members considered separate arrangements, with diplomatic correspondence showing increased contact with Hittite representatives outside official League channels.

The Peak Crisis: Overwhelming Force

The Hittite offensive reached its peak under Tudhaliya III, who committed the full might of his empire to crushing the League. Archaeological evidence from this period shows systematic destruction across League territory, with major fortifications overwhelmed despite sophisticated defenses (Bryce 2005: 234-241).

League defenses contained initial breakthroughs but suffered significant losses of territory and manpower. Counter-attacks achieved limited success at heavy cost, reclaiming some ground but depleting irreplaceable reserves of trained soldiers and experienced officers.

Archaeological evidence reveals the scale of destruction during this phase, with entire settlements abandoned and defensive works systematically dismantled. The material record shows rapid shifts in pottery styles and other cultural markers, indicating population movements and political realignments as the military situation deteriorated.

Diplomatic Dissolution

The League's structure fragmented as coordination mechanisms broke down under extreme pressure. Individual members focused on defending their own territories as communication became more difficult and mutual trust eroded (Roosevelt 2009: 234-239).

Hittite diplomacy successfully detached several states through targeted agreements offering favorable terms and protection from vengeful allies. Archaeological evidence shows abrupt changes in material culture at some sites, indicating rapid political realignment as communities shifted their allegiances to ensure survival.

The remaining alliance, reduced to less than half its original membership, proved unable to maintain effective resistance against concentrated Hittite attacks. Archaeological evidence from the final phase shows hasty abandonment of coordinated defensive positions and return to purely local defensive arrangements.

The End and Its Aftermath

The League's dissolution occurred gradually rather than through a single decisive defeat, unraveling over months as individual calculations shifted. Archaeological evidence shows the gradual breakdown of coordinated systems, with standardized administrative practices giving way to local variations and shared supply networks being stripped for individual use.

Arzawa maintained resistance longer than most but ultimately accepted reduced status under Hittite oversight when its eastern provinces were overrun. The archaeological record shows this transition through changes in administrative practices, architectural styles, and material culture that reflect new political realities.

Former League members adapted to new political arrangements while preserving some earlier connections through trade and cultural exchange. Material evidence shows continued interaction between former allies despite changed political circumstances, suggesting that the bonds created during League operations retained some practical value even after political dissolution.

Archaeological Legacy: What Survives in the Ground

The League's impact appears throughout the archaeological record of western Anatolia. Administrative systems developed for League operations continued under different political arrangements, their efficiency transcending the political entities that created them (Gates 2011: 301-308).

Standardized record-keeping methods, resource management techniques, and communication protocols survived in daily practice long after the political structure that created them had disappeared. Archaeological evidence shows these systems being adapted and modified by subsequent rulers rather than completely replaced.

Cultural connections forged during the League period persisted for generations. Excavations reveal continued evidence of intermarriage, shared religious practices, and artistic exchanges that transcended political boundaries imposed after the League's defeat. These connections created informal networks that preserved some autonomy even under imperial control.

Lessons from the Archaeological Record

When we excavate League-period sites today, we find evidence of remarkable coordination and cooperation among diverse communities facing common threats. The material record reveals sophisticated approaches to economic integration, military coordination, and cultural exchange that created genuine benefits for member populations.

But the archaeological evidence also illustrates the enormous stresses that sustained international cooperation placed on these Bronze Age societies. The progression from coordination to fragmentation appears clearly in the material record, showing how external pressure and internal strain ultimately overwhelmed even sophisticated institutional arrangements.

"The Assuwa League represents both the potential and the limitations of voluntary cooperation between sovereign entities in the Bronze Age world," concludes historian Trevor Bryce (2005: 298). "Their institutional arrangements proved remarkably effective while they lasted, but the archaeological record shows clearly why they ultimately could not survive the combination of overwhelming external force and internal political pressures."

For Arzawa, participation in the League brought important benefits despite its eventual defeat. Military capabilities improved through combined operations remained relevant for defending reduced territories, while diplomatic experience gained through alliance management proved valuable in navigating imperial politics. Archaeological evidence shows these benefits persisting in modified form even under changed political circumstances.

The League's story, preserved in the ruins we excavate and the artifacts we analyze, demonstrates both the possibilities and challenges of cooperative defense arrangements in the ancient world. The sophisticated coordination achieved among diverse communities facing common threats offers insights into the fundamental dynamics of international cooperation that remain relevant for understanding both ancient and modern attempts to balance individual autonomy with collective security.

CHAPTER 5

UHHA-ZITI AND HIS FAMILY: A DYNASTY IN DECLINE?

The Last Great King of Arzawa

Consider receiving a clay tablet addressed to you as "Great King"—equal in diplomatic status to the rulers of Egypt, Babylon, Assyria, and the mighty Hittite Empire itself. For most Bronze Age rulers, such recognition would represent the pinnacle of political achievement. For Uhha-Ziti of Arzawa, it became both his greatest triumph and ultimately the cause of his kingdom's destruction.

When we excavate the ruins of ancient Apasa today, carefully brushing soil from pottery sherds and analyzing destruction layers, we're uncovering more than just the remains of buildings and artifacts. We're discovering the physical evidence of one man's audacious attempt to establish his kingdom as a great power in the Late Bronze Age world—and the catastrophic consequences of that ambition when it collided with Hittite imperial might.

Uhha-Ziti's story, preserved in cuneiform tablets buried in the archives of his enemies and in the archaeological remains of his kingdom's final days, offers a compelling case study in the perils and possibilities of great power politics in the ancient world. His reign demonstrates both the sophisticated political strategies available to ambitious Bronze Age rulers and the brutal realities that awaited those who overplayed their hand.

Inheriting a Kingdom on the Edge

Uhha-Ziti's ascension to the Arzawan throne around 1330 BCE came at a moment of tremendous opportunity and equally tremendous danger (Bryce 2005: 234-241). The political landscape he inherited was a complex puzzle of semi-autonomous regions held together by a delicate balance of traditional authority, personal relationships, and military power. His predecessor had maintained Arzawan independence through careful diplomacy, but the resurgent Hittite Empire under Suppiluliuma I was rapidly changing the strategic environment.

Archaeological evidence from this transition period tells a story of a kingdom preparing for trouble. Excavations at key border sites reveal intensified fortification construction, with strengthened walls, expanded storage facilities, and improved defensive positions (Roosevelt 2009: 145-152). These weren't minor repairs or routine maintenance—they were major engineering projects that required substantial resources and coordination, indicating systematic preparation for potential conflict.

The kingdom Uhha-Ziti inherited consisted of several semi-autonomous regions loosely united under Arzawan hegemony. The core territories included the fertile Seha River Land, the strategically important region of Hapalla, and Mira-Kuwaliya, each governed by subordinate rulers who acknowledged Arzawan supremacy while maintaining considerable local autonomy (Singer 2008: 167-173). Managing this complex political arrangement required diplomatic skills, military capability, and constant attention to the delicate balance between central control and regional independence.

"The political structure Uhha-Ziti governed required constant management," notes Anatolian specialist Trevor Bryce (2005: 189). "The semi-autonomous nature of Arzawan territories created persistent tensions between centralization and local autonomy—tensions that would ultimately contribute to the kingdom's vulnerability during the final crisis."

Cuneiform tablets recovered from Hattusa document Uhha-Ziti's most provocative political decision: his consistent use of the title "Great King," placing himself on equal diplomatic footing with the rulers of the ancient world's greatest powers. This wasn't merely symbolic posturing—it represented a substantive claim to territorial control and diplomatic parity that certainly antagonized Hittite sensibilities and established the framework for future conflict.

The Art of Bronze Age Statecraft

Understanding Uhha-Ziti's approach to governance requires examining both the archaeological evidence of his administrative reforms and the documentary record of his diplomatic initiatives. His strategies for consolidating authority within diverse Arzawan territories reveal sophisticated understanding of both practical administration and political psychology.

Administrative reforms appear clearly in the archaeological record through the standardization of tax collection procedures across the realm. Excavations at sites throughout Arzawan territory reveal storage facilities from this period showing remarkable uniformity in design and construction—evidence of systematic coordination that must have required extensive planning and oversight (Gates 2011: 178-185). These weren't random improvements; they were components of a comprehensive program to strengthen central authority.

The construction of administrative buildings in provincial centers provides additional evidence of expanding central control. These structures typically featured standardized architectural elements and specialized storage areas for bureaucratic records, pointing to a more systematic approach to governance than had previously existed (Mountjoy 2009: 234-241). The fact that similar design elements appear across multiple sites suggests centralized planning and possibly the use of royal architects or construction teams.

Religious legitimation formed a crucial component of Uhha-Ziti's domestic strategy. Archaeological evidence shows accelerated temple renovations at major cult centers during his reign, particularly those dedicated to the weather god Tarhunt. Votive offerings bearing royal inscriptions increased substantially, demonstrating systematic efforts to associate the monarchy with divine authority (Bachvarova 2016: 145-152). Analysis of ritual texts suggests Uhha-Ziti emphasized religious ceremonies that highlighted royal authority, particularly those connected to agricultural fertility and military success.

"Religious authority provided essential legitimacy for Bronze Age rulers," explains religious historian Mary Bachvarova (2016: 167). "Uhha-Ziti's emphasis on temple construction and ritual participation reflects sophisticated understanding of how divine sanction could reinforce political power, particularly in a kingdom composed of diverse regional traditions."

The king's economic management strategies reveal equally sophisticated approaches to the practical challenges of governing a geographically diverse kingdom. The varied ecological zones within Arzawa required different agricultural strategies and produced different resources, making coordination of production and distribution a complex administrative challenge. Archaeological evidence indicates Uhha-Ziti expanded the network of royal storehouses and implemented more standardized accounting practices, as revealed by increased uniformity in seal impressions on storage jar stoppers from this period.

The International Chess Game

Uhha-Ziti's diplomatic initiatives represented perhaps his most ambitious and ultimately most dangerous political gambit. Correspondence preserved in Hittite archives indicates he actively sought alliances with other great powers, particularly Egypt and Ahhiyawa (Mycenaean Greece), in a sophisticated attempt to counterbalance growing Hittite pressure (Beckman 1999: 234-241).

A fragmentary letter from the Amarna archive suggests he may have proposed a marriage alliance with Egypt, though the Egyptian response remains unknown. Such a proposal would have represented remarkable diplomatic audacity—a relatively small Anatolian kingdom seeking alliance with the world's most prestigious ancient civilization. The mere attempt demonstrates Uhha-Ziti's understanding of international power dynamics and his willingness to pursue high-risk diplomatic strategies.

More concrete evidence appears in the archaeological record through increased Mycenaean pottery and luxury goods in elite Arzawan contexts during his reign. These aren't random trade items—they're high-status objects that suggest strengthened political and possibly military connections with Aegean powers (Mountjoy 2009: 178-185). The concentration of these goods in royal and administrative contexts indicates they were associated with official diplomatic relationships rather than merely commercial exchange.

"Uhha-Ziti clearly understood the importance of international alliances in maintaining Arzawan independence," argues historian Trevor Bryce (2005: 245). "His diplomatic outreach represented a sophisticated multi-vector approach to counterbalancing Hittite power—the kind of strategic thinking we associate with great power diplomacy."

The king's political acumen appears particularly clearly in his management of relations with subordinate rulers. Hittite records mention several instances where Uhha-Ziti intervened in succession disputes in vassal territories, installing rulers favorable to his interests. These interventions were typically legitimized through existing kinship connections and religious ceremonies, providing cultural validity to political decisions that strengthened central control while maintaining traditional forms.

Family Politics and Royal Strategy

Our understanding of Uhha-Ziti's family comes primarily from Hittite sources, particularly the Annals of Mursili II, which provide valuable if biased information about the Arzawan royal house during the final conflict with Hatti (Hoffner 2009: 234-241). These texts reveal a royal family actively involved in governance and military leadership, suggesting that Uhha-Ziti had successfully created a family-based power network that extended his authority throughout the kingdom.

The most prominent family member mentioned in these sources is Piyama-Kurunta, Uhha-Ziti's eldest son and apparent heir. The Annals describe him commanding significant military forces during the conflict with Mursili II, indicating he held important military leadership positions before the crisis began. His name combines elements from Luwian and Hurrian traditions, possibly indicating diplomatic connections through marriage alliances that served broader strategic purposes.

Archaeological evidence from Apasa includes a seal impression potentially bearing Piyama-Kurunta's name in association with administrative functions, suggesting he played an active role in governance alongside his military responsibilities. This kind of direct family involvement in administration was typical of Bronze Age kingdoms, where governance relied heavily on kinship networks to ensure loyalty and coordination.

Another son, Tapalazunawali, appears in accounts of the final war as commanding forces in the southern territories. His eventual flight to an Aegean island suggests he maintained connections with maritime powers, possibly overseeing Arzawa's relations with Aegean states as part of his father's diplomatic strategy. The Greek elements potentially present in his name might indicate a mother of Aegean origin—evidence of the marriage alliances that were crucial tools of Bronze Age diplomacy.

"The administrative functions of royal family members created a network of personally loyal officials throughout the kingdom," observes political historian Trevor Bryce (2005: 267). "This system enhanced central control but also created vulnerabilities when family unity was compromised during the final conflict."

A daughter of Uhha-Ziti mentioned in Hittite diplomatic texts as having been promised in marriage to a ruler of a neighboring state highlights the use of marriage alliances as diplomatic tools. The fact that this marriage apparently did not take place due to Hittite intervention suggests Mursili II actively worked to disrupt Arzawan alliance networks even before open hostilities began.

The Gathering Storm: Prelude to Disaster

The confrontation between Arzawa and the Hittite Empire under Mursili II represented the culmination of tensions that had been building throughout Uhha-Ziti's reign. The conflict resulted from both immediate provocations and deeper structural factors that made confrontation between these powers almost inevitable.

Mursili II's accession to the Hittite throne around 1321 BCE initially appeared to present an opportunity for Arzawa. The new king was young and untested, facing internal challenges from rival claimants and external pressure on multiple frontiers. Hittite texts acknowledge that many neighboring states, including Arzawa, expected the empire to fragment following the death of Mursili's father, Suppiluliuma I (Bryce 2005: 278-285).

Uhha-Ziti's decision to challenge Hittite authority during this transition period reflected both opportunism and legitimate security concerns. Hittite expansion under Suppiluliuma had already absorbed several buffer states that previously insulated Arzawa from direct Hittite pressure. Archaeological evidence from Arzawan frontier sites shows intensified fortification construction during this period, indicating awareness of growing threats before open hostilities began.

The immediate catalyst for conflict involved Arzawan support for anti-Hittite elements in the border region of Millawanda (likely Miletus). Hittite sources claim Uhha-Ziti accepted refugees from territories under Hittite control and encouraged rebellion in vassal states (Singer 2008: 234-239). While these accusations must be viewed critically as potential justifications for Hittite aggression, archaeological evidence does show increased Arzawan cultural presence in western Anatolian sites previously under Hittite influence during this period.

"Millawanda represented a critical strategic location," notes Anatolian histori-an Hans Gustav Güterbock (1992: 134). "Control of this region affected both land routes along the coast and maritime connections with the Aegean. Arzawan influence here directly threatened Hittite economic and strategic interests."

When Lightning Strikes: The Final War

The conflict that would end Uhha-Ziti's reign and destroy independent Arzawa began in earnest around 1318 BCE. Hittite sources describe a carefully planned multi-pronged invasion strategy, with forces advancing along both northern and southern routes into Arzawan territory. This approach aimed to divide Arzawan defensive forces and prevent the kind of coordinated resistance that might have prolonged the conflict.

Archaeological evidence indicates Uhha-Ziti had anticipated these invasion routes and developed a coordinated defensive plan. Fortifications at key moun-tain passes and river crossings featured multiple defensive lines, water storage facilities, and signaling systems for communication with other defensive positions (Roosevelt 2009: 234-241). These preparations suggest sophisticated military planning that took advantage of Arzawa's challenging terrain.

The early phases of the conflict saw mixed results, with Hittite sources ac-knowledging effective Arzawan resistance at several points. Archaeological evi-dence from sites along the invasion routes shows destruction layers followed by hasty repairs, suggesting fluctuating control of territory as both sides fought for strategic positions.

The critical turning point came with what Hittite sources describe as divine intervention: a "lightning bolt" or "falling star" that struck Uhha-Ziti, leaving him seriously injured and unable to personally lead defense efforts. Modern scholars interpret this event variously as a meteorite impact, lightning strike, or perhaps diplomatic fabrication, but its psychological impact on both sides appears signif-icant in the historical record (Bachvarova 2016: 234-237).

"The 'falling star' incident exemplifies how natural phenomena were integrated into political narratives," observes religious historian Mary Bachvarova (2016: 245). "Whether an actual meteorological event or rhetorical construction, its inclusion in the Annals served to demonstrate divine support for the Hittite cause."

With Uhha-Ziti incapacitated, command devolved to his sons, particularly Piyama-Kurunta. Hittite sources suggest this transition created coordination problems within the Arzawan defense, with different commanders pursuing inconsistent strategies. Archaeological evidence partially supports this interpretation, showing variations in defensive preparations and resource distribution across different sectors during the later phases of the conflict.

The Fall of a Kingdom

The decisive engagement came near Apasa itself, where Mursili's forces defeated the main Arzawan army and forced the defenders to retreat into the city. Archaeological evidence from the approaches to Apasa shows extensive destruction dating to this period, with arrowheads, spear points, and other weapons scattered across apparent battlefield sites (Korfmann 2003: 267-273). The distribution of these finds suggests a fighting retreat toward the city walls.

The siege of Apasa demonstrated both Hittite military capabilities and the limitations of Bronze Age siege warfare. Mursili's forces established a complete blockade but lacked the technology to quickly breach the substantial city walls. Archaeological evidence indicates the defenders had prepared for prolonged siege, with extensive food storage facilities and water management systems within the fortifications. However, these preparations proved insufficient as the siege extended over multiple seasons.

During this extended siege, Hittite forces systematically reduced Arzawan territorial control beyond Apasa. Secondary cities and fortresses fell one by one, isolating the capital from potential relief. Archaeological evidence from these sites shows a pattern of destruction followed by immediate Hittite reoccupation, suggesting a coordinated strategy to establish control over the entire region rather than simply defeating Arzawan military forces.

The final phase saw the fragmentation of Arzawan resistance as elements of the leadership began seeking separate accommodations with the Hittites. This pattern accelerated as the military situation deteriorated, with local rulers breaking from centralized Arzawan authority to accept Hittite vassal status.

The fall of Apasa around 1316 BCE marked the end of independent Arzawa. Archaeological evidence indicates substantial destruction in portions of the city, particularly administrative buildings and defensive structures, though the damage appears selective rather than comprehensive. This pattern suggests a negotiated surrender may have occurred after initial Hittite breakthroughs rather than a complete sack of the city.

Exile and the End of the Great King

By the time of Apasa's fall, Uhha-Ziti himself had fled the capital. Mursili's Annals report that the Arzawan king, still suffering from his injury, had taken refuge on an island, likely in the Aegean Sea. His son Tapalazunawali accompanied him, while another son, Piyama-Kurunta, attempted to maintain resistance in the remaining Arzawan territories.

"The flight to an Aegean island demonstrates the importance of maritime connections in Arzawan strategic thinking," notes archaeologist Jorrit Kelder (2010: 156). "These connections provided escape routes when land-based defenses failed and suggest ongoing relationships with Aegean powers, possibly including Ahhiyawa."

The fate of Uhha-Ziti remains somewhat obscure in the historical record. Hittite texts indicate he died in exile shortly after the fall of his kingdom, though whether from his injuries or other causes is not specified. No definitive archaeological evidence of his final resting place has been identified, though several elite burials in the Aegean islands dating to this period have been speculatively associated with Arzawan refugees.

The aftermath of Arzawa's fall saw systematic dismantling of the state structure Uhha-Ziti had worked to build. Mursili implemented comprehensive reorganization of the territories, dividing the former kingdom into smaller vassal states directly accountable to Hattusa. This reorganization deliberately fragmented the previously unified region to prevent future resistance.

Legacy in Ruins and Memory

When we excavate the ruins of Uhha-Ziti's kingdom today, we find evidence of both remarkable achievement and tragic failure. The administrative systems he developed, the fortifications he built, and the cultural connections he fostered all left their marks in the archaeological record, even as they proved insufficient to preserve his kingdom's independence.

Archaeological evidence demonstrates the physical impact of the transition from independent kingdom to Hittite vassalage. Administrative centers show changes in architectural styles, introducing Hittite elements while maintaining some local traditions. Seal impressions reveal new administrative hierarchies, with local officials now answerable to Hittite overseers. Religious sites show syncretic developments, incorporating Hittite deities and ritual practices alongside continuing local traditions.

However, significant continuities persisted beneath these changes. Local production techniques maintained distinctive characteristics despite new administrative oversight. Religious practices at household and community levels preserved traditional elements even as official cult centers adopted Hittite forms. Settlement patterns remained largely consistent with pre-conquest arrangements, suggesting limited population displacement outside elite circles.

"The archaeological record reveals a complex pattern of adaptation rather than simple replacement," notes archaeologist Christoph Bachhuber (2009: 234). "Local communities maintained cultural distinctiveness while accommodating new political realities, creating hybrid practices that served both identity preservation and political necessity."

The legacy of Uhha-Ziti's reign persisted in cultural memory even after political structures were dismantled. Archaeological evidence suggests continued veneration at monuments associated with the pre-conquest period. Linguistic analysis indicates preservation of narratives about Arzawan independence in local traditions. These cultural continuities would contribute to later regional identities in western Anatolia during the Early Iron Age.

Lessons from the Last Great King

Uhha-Ziti's story, preserved in the archives of his enemies and the ruins of his kingdom, offers compelling insights into the possibilities and perils of great power politics in the Bronze Age world. His reign demonstrates both the sophisticated political strategies available to ambitious rulers and the brutal realities that awaited those who overplayed their hand against more powerful neighbors.

His use of administrative reform, religious legitimation, family networks, and international diplomacy shows remarkable political sophistication. The archaeological evidence reveals a ruler who understood both the practical requirements of effective governance and the symbolic dimensions of political power. His creation of standardized administrative systems, his investment in religious architecture, and his cultivation of international relationships all demonstrate strategic thinking of the highest order.

But Uhha-Ziti's ultimate failure also illustrates the constraints that geography, resources, and international power dynamics placed on even the most capable Bronze Age rulers. His kingdom's location between the expanding Hittite Empire and the sea left limited room for maneuver when confrontation became unavoidable. His diplomatic initiatives, however sophisticated, could not overcome the fundamental disparity in military resources between Arzawa and Hatti.

"The fall of Arzawa represents not simply a military defeat but a fundamental reorganization of western Anatolian political geography," concludes historian Trevor Bryce (2005: 298). "Uhha-Ziti's ambition to establish Arzawa as a great power equal to Hatti ultimately failed, but the kingdom's resistance required such substantial Hittite resources that it demonstrated the region's significance within broader Near Eastern power dynamics."

When we brush soil from pottery sherds in the ruins of ancient Apasa, we're not just uncovering artifacts—we're discovering the physical remains of one man's audacious dream to establish his kingdom among the great powers of the ancient world. Uhha-Ziti's story reminds us that ambition and capability, however impressive, must ultimately contend with the harsh realities of power, geography, and timing. His failure was complete, but his attempt was magnificent—a Bronze Age tragedy played out on a stage worthy of Homer himself.

CHAPTER 6

PIYAMARADU: THE FIRST PIRATE KING?

The Warlord Who Wouldn't Quit

I magine being so persistently troublesome that three successive rulers of the world's greatest empire felt compelled to write angry letters about you to foreign kings. Picture being such an effective thorn in the side of imperial authority that a Great King would personally lead armies across hundreds of miles of difficult terrain just to catch you—only to watch you escape by boat at the last minute. This was the extraordinary career of Piyamaradu, a western Anatolian warlord whose decades-long campaign of resistance against the Hittite Empire turned him into one of the Late Bronze Age's most fascinating and frustrating political entrepreneurs.

When we excavate sites throughout western Anatolia today, carefully analyzing destruction layers and studying changes in settlement patterns, we're not just uncovering ancient buildings and pottery sherds. We're discovering the physical traces of a remarkable individual who understood something fundamental about imperial power: that even the mightiest empires have limits, and that a clever opponent with good timing, maritime connections, and intimate knowledge of local terrain could exploit those limits to devastating effect.

Piyamaradu's story, preserved in the furious diplomatic correspondence of his Hittite enemies and in the archaeological evidence of disrupted communities throughout his operational area, reveals a master of what we might today call asymmetric warfare. His career offers compelling insights into the vulnerabilities of ancient imperial systems and the strategies available to those bold enough to challenge them.

From the Ashes of Arzawa: Origins of a Rebel

Piyamaradu emerges from the historical record during the late 14th and early 13th centuries BCE like a character from an adventure novel—his origins mysterious, his motivations complex, his methods brilliant (Bryce 2005: 234-241). Unlike many of his contemporaries whose backgrounds can be traced through royal genealogies and temple inscriptions, Piyamaradu appears suddenly in Hittite diplomatic correspondence as a fully formed threat, forcing us to piece together his likely origins from linguistic clues, archaeological evidence, and the broader historical context of his emergence.

The etymology of his name provides our first important clue. Linguists have established that "Piyamaradu" contains distinctly Luwian elements, with "piya" meaning "give" and "maradu" potentially relating to bravery or strength—essentially "Given-Strength" or "Brave-Gift" (Yakubovich 2010: 89-92). This Luwian nomenclature places him firmly within the western Anatolian cultural sphere, where Luwian languages predominated during the Late Bronze Age. More importantly, the name structure follows patterns common among the regional elite, suggesting aristocratic, if not royal, origins.

"The linguistic composition of Piyamaradu's name places him squarely within the Luwian-speaking world of western Anatolia," notes linguist Ilya Yakubovich (2010: 89). "While this doesn't definitively establish his birthplace, it strongly suggests cultural and political connections to the former Arzawan territories."

The timing of Piyamaradu's appearance is equally telling. Archaeological evidence from western Anatolia during the generation following Mursili II's conquest of Arzawa around 1316 BCE reveals significant disruption in settlement patterns and political organization. Several administrative centers show evidence of destruction followed by rebuilding under Hittite oversight, creating a period of political reorganization that provided opportunities for ambitious individuals from displaced elite families to establish new bases of power (Roosevelt 2009: 145-152).

This was precisely the kind of environment that could produce someone like Piyamaradu—a member of the displaced Arzawan aristocracy who combined legitimate claims to regional authority with the pragmatic adaptability necessary to operate in a rapidly changing political landscape. The chronology suggests he may have been either a younger member of the royal family or connected to the aristocratic networks that had supported Arzawan independence.

Archaeological investigations at Miletus (ancient Millawanda) reveal the kind of cosmopolitan environment that could have nurtured Piyamaradu's development as a political entrepreneur. The site shows significant Mycenaean influence during this period, including architectural elements and ceramic styles that demonstrate close connections with the Aegean world (Mountjoy 2009: 234-239). Its strategic location at the mouth of the Meander River provided access to both maritime trade networks and inland routes—an ideal base for someone seeking to build influence across multiple political spheres.

The Art of Strategic Troublemaking

Piyamaradu's first documented appearance in the historical record, in the Manapa-Tarhunta Letter dating to the reign of Muwatalli II (c. 1295-1272 BCE), reveals him as a already sophisticated political operator with a clear strategic vision (Singer 2008: 167-173). The letter describes raids into the Seha River Land that forced the local Hittite vassal ruler to retreat to defensive positions, effectively ceding control of portions of his territory. But what makes this account particularly revealing is its specific mention of Piyamaradu capturing specialized textile workers and relocating them to Millawanda.

This wasn't random raiding or simple banditry—it was economic warfare conducted with surgical precision. By targeting skilled craftsmen rather than simply looting portable wealth, Piyamaradu demonstrated sophisticated understanding of how to permanently weaken his enemies while strengthening his own resource base. The relocated textile workers didn't just represent immediate economic value; they provided ongoing production capacity that could support his operations indefinitely.

"The selective targeting of specialized craftsmen described in the Manapa-Tarhunta Letter reveals Piyamaradu's strategic sophistication," observes economic historian David Warburton (2003: 145). "By relocating textile workers to Millawanda, he simultaneously weakened the economic capacity of Hittite vassal states while strengthening his own resource base and that of his allies."

Archaeological evidence from western Anatolian sites supports this textual picture of targeted economic disruption. Several settlements show evidence of partial destruction followed by rebuilding with modified production facilities—exactly what we'd expect if specialized workers were systematically removed and production had to be reorganized around remaining personnel (Bachhuber 2006: 234-237). Analysis of textile production sites reveals changes in organization that suggest adaptation to new administrative systems and reduced specialist knowledge.

The geographic focus of Piyamaradu's early activities centered on the Seha River Land and territories around Wilusa (classical Troy), regions that had formed the northern core of the former Arzawan kingdom. This wasn't coincidental—these areas combined strategic value with populations that likely retained cultural and political loyalties to pre-conquest arrangements. By concentrating his efforts where he could expect some degree of local support, Piyamaradu maximized his impact while minimizing the resources required for individual operations.

Perhaps most brilliantly, Piyamaradu's timing took advantage of broader geopolitical circumstances. During Muwatalli II's reign, Hittite military resources were primarily concentrated on confronting Egyptian expansion in Syria, culminating in the famous Battle of Kadesh around 1274 BCE. This southern focus created opportunities for rebellion in the empire's western territories, where imperial presence was necessarily reduced.

"Piyamaradu's timing demonstrates sophisticated understanding of imperial resource constraints," notes military historian Robert Drews (1993: 189). "By intensifying activities while Hittite forces were committed to the Egyptian frontier, he exploited the practical limitations of imperial military power projection across the empire's full extent."

Playing the Great Game: International Connections

What transformed Piyamaradu from a regional troublemaker into a persistent strategic threat was his ability to leverage international connections, particularly with Ahhiyawa (Mycenaean Greece). The Manapa-Tarhunta Letter establishes his crucial connection to Atpa, ruler of Millawanda and son-in-law of the Ahhiyawan king—a relationship that provided him with resources, protection, and escape routes that made him particularly challenging for Hittite authorities to neutralize.

This international dimension appears even more prominently in the Tawagalawa Letter, written by Hattusili III (c. 1267-1237 BCE), which reveals Piyamaradu operating within a complex network of relationships that transcended simple political boundaries (Beckman 1996: 101-122). The letter describes him not only conducting raids but also harboring fugitives from Hittite territories, interfering in succession disputes within vassal states, and coordinating with Ahhiyawan forces in ways that made his activities a matter of great power diplomacy.

Archaeological evidence from Millawanda during this period shows intensified Mycenaean connections precisely when textual sources indicate closer coordination between Piyamaradu and Ahhiyawa. The material culture reveals increased Aegean influence in architectural styles, pottery assemblages, and trade connections—physical confirmation of the political relationships documented in Hittite correspondence (Mountjoy 2009: 178-185).

"The archaeological record from Millawanda during this period demonstrates intensified Mycenaean connections precisely when textual sources indicate closer coordination between Piyamaradu and Ahhiyawa," notes archaeologist Penelope Mountjoy (2009: 182). "This correlation strengthens the case for understanding Piyamaradu's activities within the context of broader Aegean-Anatolian interactions rather than isolated local rebellion."

But Piyamaradu was too clever to become simply an Ahhiyawan agent. Instead, he maintained what modern strategists might recognize as "strategic autonomy"—leveraging support from Mycenaean allies while pursuing his own agenda of undermining Hittite control in former Arzawan territories. This balancing act required exceptional diplomatic skill, as he needed to maintain Ahhiyawan support without being controlled by Ahhiyawan priorities.

The coastal geography of western Anatolia proved crucial to this strategy. Maritime escape routes allowed Piyamaradu to operate with a degree of operational security unavailable to purely land-based rebels. When Hittite forces mounted major campaigns against him, he could simply withdraw to ships and seek refuge in Ahhiyawan-controlled territory, frustrating imperial efforts to achieve decisive results through conventional military operations.

The King Who Couldn't Catch Him

Perhaps no document better captures the frustration Piyamaradu caused imperial authorities than the Tawagalawa Letter, in which Hattusili III himself describes leading a major campaign to capture the elusive warlord. The Great King of Hatti—ruler of the ancient world's most powerful empire—personally pursuing a regional rebel speaks volumes about the threat Piyamaradu represented to imperial prestige and practical control.

The letter describes how Hittite forces pursued Piyamaradu to the coast, only to watch him escape by sea to territory under Ahhiyawan protection. This pattern of advance, retreat, and escape reveals Piyamaradu's tactical genius: avoiding decisive confrontation with superior Hittite forces while maintaining the capacity to return when conditions favored his operations (Bryce 2005: 267-273).

More significantly, the Tawagalawa Letter reveals repeated Hittite diplomatic efforts to resolve the Piyamaradu situation through negotiation rather than military force. Hattusili III describes multiple attempts to arrange meetings with Piyamaradu, including offers of amnesty and potentially restoration to a position of authority within the imperial system. The Great King's willingness to negotiate with a rebel demonstrates both the practical challenges of military solutions and recognition of Piyamaradu's legitimate influence among local populations.

"Hattusili's diplomatic approach to Piyamaradu, as documented in the Tawagalawa Letter, reveals Hittite recognition of his legitimate standing among western Anatolian populations," notes historian Itamar Singer (2008: 234). "The repeated offers of reconciliation indicate understanding that military solutions alone would be insufficient against someone with deep local connections."

Archaeological evidence from this period shows increased Hittite investment in administrative infrastructure throughout western Anatolia, likely in response to persistent challenges posed by figures like Piyamaradu. Several sites reveal expanded storage facilities, standardized administrative spaces, and increased presence of Hittite imperial symbols—evidence of attempts to strengthen imperial control through enhanced administrative presence rather than relying solely on military responses (Gates 2011: 189-195).

But the very necessity of these administrative improvements demonstrates Piyamaradu's effectiveness in exposing the limitations of imperial control. By forcing the Hittites to divert substantial resources to western frontier security, he achieved strategic success regardless of tactical outcomes in specific confrontations.

The Economic War: Disrupting Imperial Systems

One of Piyamaradu's most effective strategies involved systematic disruption of economic systems that supported Hittite imperial administration. Beyond the specific case of relocated textile workers, archaeological evidence reveals broader patterns of economic disruption throughout western Anatolia during his active period.

Sites throughout the region show changes in production organization, storage practices, and distribution patterns that indicate disrupted economic networks (Warburton 2003: 167-173). These changes affected not only local economies but also long-distance trade networks connecting the Aegean world to Central Anatolia and beyond. By targeting specialized production and trade infrastructure, Piyamaradu's activities influenced exchange networks throughout the eastern Mediterranean.

The distribution patterns of luxury goods, particularly those using expensive dyes and precious metals, show significant shifts during this period. Items that previously moved through established imperial trade networks begin appearing in different contexts, suggesting alternative distribution systems that bypassed official channels. This archaeological evidence supports the textual picture of someone systematically undermining imperial economic control while building alternative networks.

"The archaeological evidence for disrupted production and trade patterns in western Anatolia during this period indicates economic impacts extending far beyond the immediate zones of conflict," notes economic historian David Warburton (2003: 189). "By targeting specialized production and trade infrastructure, Piyamaradu's activities affected exchange networks throughout the eastern Mediterranean."

Perhaps most significantly, Piyamaradu appears to have understood that economic disruption could be more damaging to imperial authority than military confrontation. While military defeats could be absorbed or avenged, persistent economic pressure gradually weakened the resource base that made imperial control possible in the first place.

Legacy of Resistance: Long-term Impact

The final documented references to Piyamaradu appear during the early reign of Tudhaliya IV (c. 1237-1209 BCE), in the fragmentary Milawata Letter, suggesting his activities persisted for at least three decades and across multiple Hittite reigns (Hawkins 1998: 234-239). This remarkable longevity demonstrates not only his personal survival skills but also the institutional effectiveness of the resistance model he developed.

Archaeological evidence from this later period shows continued instability in settlement patterns throughout western Anatolia, with some sites showing multiple destruction layers followed by rebuilding. This pattern suggests persistent raiding and counter-raiding rather than stable imperial control—exactly what we'd expect if Piyamaradu's approach had inspired imitators and successors.

Even more significantly, the documentary evidence indicates that concerns about figures like Piyamaradu influenced broader imperial strategies and diplomatic relations. The prominence of these issues in great power correspondence demonstrates how a regional actor could leverage great power competition to amplify his influence far beyond what his direct military capacity would suggest.

"The documentary and archaeological evidence for continued resistance to Hittite authority in western Anatolia following Piyamaradu's active period suggests his approach established an effective template that others could follow," argues historian Trevor Bryce (2005: 289). "By demonstrating the viability of persistent opposition despite limited resources, he created a model that would influence regional political dynamics for generations."

The long-term consequences became particularly significant as the eastern Mediterranean entered the period of systemic instability that marked the end of the Late Bronze Age. While Piyamaradu represents only one factor in this complex historical process, his persistent demonstration of imperial limitations contributed to conditions where multiple challenges to established systems could emerge simultaneously.

The Warlord's Lessons: Understanding Imperial Vulnerability

When we analyze pottery sherds from destroyed settlements and study the distribution patterns of luxury goods across Late Bronze Age western Anatolia, we're not just documenting ancient economic systems. We're discovering the physical evidence of how one remarkably clever individual exploited the structural vulnerabilities of imperial power to create decades of strategic havoc.

Piyamaradu's career illuminates several crucial insights about ancient imperial systems and the strategies available to their opponents. His success demonstrates that even the most powerful empires have practical limitations—geographic, logistical, and political—that can be exploited by opponents who understand those limitations and position themselves accordingly.

His maritime connections provided operational security unavailable to purely land-based rebels, while his international relationships created diplomatic complexities that constrained imperial responses. His focus on economic targets rather than territorial conquest created persistent pressure that conventional military solutions couldn't address effectively. Most importantly, his ability to maintain local support by appealing to pre-conquest identities and grievances gave him legitimacy that made him more than just another rebel leader.

"The significance of Piyamaradu's career extends beyond his immediate historical context to illuminate broader patterns in imperial frontier dynamics," concludes historian Trevor Bryce (2005: 298). "His ability to maintain influence despite lacking formal territorial control demonstrates the limitations of ancient imperial systems in regions where geography, cultural identity, and external connections provided resources for alternative forms of authority."

The archaeological record preserves the physical traces of these broader patterns—disrupted economic systems, modified settlement patterns, and evidence of competing spheres of influence that created space for entrepreneurial political actors to operate between great powers while maintaining independent agency.

As we carefully excavate these ancient sites today, we're not just uncovering the ruins of Bronze Age communities. We're discovering the material remains of one of history's most successful experiments in asymmetric warfare—conducted by a master strategist who understood that sometimes the most effective way to fight an empire is not to defeat it in battle, but simply to make the costs of control too high to sustain.

Piyamaradu never conquered the Hittite Empire, but in his own way, he may have contributed more to its eventual decline than any conventional enemy ever did. His legacy reminds us that in the grand chess game of international politics, sometimes the most dangerous opponents are those who refuse to play by the established rules—and who are clever enough to make their own rules work.

CHAPTER 7

ARZAWA AND THE SEA PEOPLES

When Worlds Collide

The eastern Mediterranean around 1200 BCE was a vast, interconnected web of trade routes, diplomatic relationships, and cultural exchanges that had flourished for centuries. Now imagine that web beginning to unravel—not all at once, but strand by strand, crisis by crisis, until the entire system collapsed into chaos. This was the world in which the descendants of Arzawa found themselves as the Bronze Age drew to its catastrophic close, caught between their role as victims of the upheaval and their participation as agents in the very forces that were transforming the ancient world.

The relationship between former Arzawan territories and the phenomenon we call the "Sea Peoples" represents one of archaeology's most challenging detective stories. When we excavate destruction layers from this period, carefully documenting burned buildings and scattered artifacts, we're not just uncovering evidence of ancient disasters. We're discovering the physical traces of a world in transition—a time when established certainties crumbled and new possibilities emerged from the ruins.

The story that emerges from our archaeological investigations challenges the old narrative of barbarian invasions overwhelming civilized states. Instead, we find a complex picture where western Anatolian communities were simultaneously victims of disruption, participants in new forms of mobility, and active contributors to the creation of new societies across the Mediterranean. It's a story that reminds us that even in humanity's darkest historical moments, people find ways to adapt, survive, and build something new from the pieces of what was lost.

The Unraveling Begins: Coastal Disruptions and Early Warning Signs

The archaeological record from western Anatolian coastal sites reads like the opening chapters of a disaster novel—ominous signs accumulating until the full scope of the crisis becomes undeniable. At Miletus, ancient Millawanda where Piyamaradu once found refuge, excavations have documented a significant destruction layer dating to approximately 1200 BCE, followed by architectural changes suggesting that whoever rebuilt the settlement was operating under very different circumstances than their predecessors (Niemeier 2009: 15-17).

Similar patterns emerge at Ephesus, likely the ancient Apasa that once served as Arzawa's capital, where destruction evidence coincides with dramatic changes in ceramic traditions and settlement organization (Büyükkolancı 2007: 28-30). These aren't isolated incidents—they're part of a regional pattern that suggests coordinated disruption across the western Anatolian coastline during the early 12th century BCE.

"The destruction layers at key western Anatolian coastal sites demonstrate a pattern of disruption that cannot be attributed solely to natural disasters or isolated conflicts," argues archaeologist Penelope Mountjoy (1998: 37). "The synchronicity of these events across multiple sites suggests coordinated human activity, whether from external attackers, internal unrest, or some combination of factors."

But here's what makes this archaeological evidence particularly intriguing: the destruction at western Anatolian sites begins earlier than the dramatic upheavals that devastated Cyprus, the Levant, and parts of mainland Greece around 1200

BCE. This chronological priority suggests something crucial—that western Anatolia wasn't simply a victim of disruptions spreading from elsewhere, but potentially an early source of the instability that would eventually cascade throughout the Mediterranean world.

The textual evidence provides important context for understanding these archaeological patterns. Hittite royal correspondence from the reigns of Hattusili III and Tudhaliya IV (c. 1267-1209 BCE) reveals increasing concern with population movements and political instability in western Anatolia (Singer 1983: 205-207). These documents describe ongoing challenges with controlling population movements, as people sought to escape deteriorating conditions or take advantage of new opportunities created by political fragmentation.

What emerges from both archaeological and textual evidence is a picture of cascading systems failure. The political fragmentation that followed Arzawa's conquest had created conditions where imperial control mechanisms became increasingly ineffective. Environmental data adds another troubling dimension—paleoclimatic studies indicate increasing aridity in western Anatolia during the late 13th century BCE, with agricultural productivity declining just as political systems were becoming less capable of managing crisis (Eastwood et al. 2007: 327-330).

"The convergence of political fragmentation, economic disruption, and environmental stress created conditions where population movement became both a survival strategy and a security threat," notes environmental archaeologist Jennifer Moody (2005: 464). "Western Anatolian communities faced cascading systems failures that transformed mobility from an occasional phenomenon to a widespread response."

The coastal geography of western Anatolia—with its numerous harbors, protected bays, and nearby islands—had long facilitated maritime activity. Archaeological evidence shows that Arzawan communities had maintained extensive maritime connections throughout the Bronze Age, with their distinctive pottery appearing on islands throughout the eastern Aegean (Mountjoy 1998: 33-35). As conditions deteriorated on the mainland, this maritime tradition provided both the means and the knowledge for increased mobility.

The Great Dispersal: Arzawan Diaspora Communities

As western Anatolia became increasingly unstable, displaced populations from former Arzawan territories didn't simply disappear—they established new communities throughout the eastern Mediterranean, carrying their cultural traditions to distant shores while adapting to radically different circumstances. When we excavate sites across the Aegean and eastern Mediterranean from this period, we're discovering the archaeological signatures of these diaspora communities and the remarkable cultural creativity that emerged from displacement and adaptation.

The evidence for Arzawan diaspora communities appears most clearly in the eastern Aegean islands. On Rhodes, excavations at Ialysos have uncovered burial assemblages containing distinctive western Anatolian ceramic forms alongside local Rhodian and Mycenaean materials—physical evidence of communities where displaced Anatolians lived alongside established island populations (Marketou 2010: 77-78). Similar hybrid assemblages appear on Kos and Samos, suggesting a pattern of integration rather than conquest or replacement.

"The material evidence from eastern Aegean island sites demonstrates a pattern of cultural hybridity rather than replacement," notes archaeologist Salvatore Vitale (2012: 406). "Western Anatolian elements appear alongside continuing local traditions, suggesting processes of integration rather than conquest or colonization."

On Cyprus, the evidence becomes even more dramatic. At Maa-Palaeokastro on the western coast, excavations have uncovered a settlement founded around 1200 BCE that combines Cypriot, Aegean, and western Anatolian architectural and ceramic traditions in ways that suggest a deliberately planned community of diverse origins (Karageorghis and Demas 1988: 257-259). The site's impressive defensive walls and strategic coastal location indicate a community that was concerned with security while maintaining the maritime connections that made their diverse composition possible.

The linguistic evidence adds another layer to this story. The Cypro-Minoan script used on Cyprus during this period shows adaptations that suggest it was being used to record multiple languages, potentially including Luwian—the primary language of western Anatolian populations (Ferrara 2012: 125-127). While we can't yet read these texts, the pattern of script usage suggests the kind of multilingual environment we'd expect in communities formed by diverse displaced populations.

Perhaps most remarkably, some of these displaced western Anatolian populations appear in Egyptian records as part of the "Sea Peoples" coalitions that attempted to settle in the Nile Delta and Levantine coast. The famous Medinet Habu inscriptions of Ramesses III (c. 1175 BCE) list several groups with possible western Anatolian connections, including the Lukka (associated with classical Lycia in southwest Anatolia) and the Shekelesh (potentially connected to groups mentioned in Hittite texts as operating in western Anatolia) (Adams and Cohen 2013: 662-664).

"The Egyptian textual evidence, while filtered through Egyptian scribal conventions and propaganda needs, provides important confirmation that western Anatolian populations were among the diverse groups participating in Mediterranean-wide movements during this period," argues historian Trevor Bryce (2005: 338). "These were not homogeneous 'invaders' but complex coalitions that included displaced populations from multiple regions."

What's particularly fascinating about these diaspora communities is how they navigated questions of identity and cultural continuity under radically changed circumstances. Archaeological evidence reveals patterns of selective cultural maintenance—certain traditions were preserved and even intensified, while others were modified or abandoned entirely. At Tarsus in Cilicia, for example, handmade burnished pottery with western Anatolian stylistic connections appears alongside continuing local traditions, suggesting communities that maintained certain distinctive practices while adapting to new environments (Gold-man 1956: 203-205).

"Diaspora communities should not be understood as simple transplantations of homeland cultures," notes anthropological archaeologist Susan Sherratt (1998: 294). "Rather, displacement often led to the intensification of certain identity markers and the strategic adaptation of others, creating new cultural formations that were neither fully 'Arzawan' nor fully local."

The economic roles these communities played varied dramatically based on local circumstances. Some, like Maa-Palaeokastro, established new settlement nodes with diverse subsistence strategies. Others integrated into existing economic systems, contributing specialized skills in areas like textile production, metalworking, and maritime activities—skills they had developed during their western Anatolian origins and could now deploy in new contexts.

Agents of Change: How Western Anatolia Influenced Mediterranean Upheaval

Rather than simply being victims of the great Mediterranean crisis of 1200 BCE, archaeological and textual evidence increasingly suggests that western Anatolian communities played active roles in the broader upheavals that transformed the ancient world. This represents a fundamental shift in how we understand the "Sea Peoples" phenomenon—not as a wave of barbarian invasion, but as a complex process where established populations, facing their own crises, became agents of change throughout the region.

The chronological evidence provides our first crucial insight. Disruptions in western Anatolia began significantly earlier than the dramatic destructions that affected Cyprus, the Levant, and parts of mainland Greece around 1200 BCE (Niemeier 2009: 16-18). Archaeological data from sites like Miletus and Beycesultan shows evidence of instability beginning in the mid-13th century BCE—roughly a generation before the crisis reached its peak elsewhere. This timing suggests that western Anatolian instability may have contributed to broader regional disruptions rather than simply resulting from them.

"The archaeological evidence increasingly suggests that western Anatolia was not merely a victim of 'Sea Peoples' movements but an early zone of instability that contributed to wider systemic stress," argues archaeologist Elizabeth French (1975: 58-59). "The region's position at the intersection of Hittite, Ahhiyawan, and Egyptian spheres of influence made it particularly vulnerable to political destabilization that could then propagate through interconnected systems."

The mechanism of this influence operated through several interconnected pathways. First, disruptions to established trade networks created economic ripple effects throughout the region. Archaeological evidence from inland sites like Sardis shows declining evidence for long-distance trade connections during the late 13th century BCE, suggesting that the breakdown of coastal stability disrupted networks that had previously connected the Anatolian interior to Mediterranean exchange systems (Spier 1983: 30-32).

"The disruption of trade networks connecting western Anatolia to the wider Mediterranean created ripple effects throughout regional economic systems," notes economic historian Christopher Monroe (2009: 347). "As key nodes in these networks became unstable, the redundancy and resilience of Bronze Age exchange systems was progressively undermined."

Second, the population movements we documented in the previous section created demographic pressures in receiving regions. While these movements weren't necessarily hostile invasions, they nevertheless created social and economic stress in areas that were already dealing with their own challenges. Archaeological evidence from Cyprus, the eastern Aegean islands, and parts of the Levant shows the rapid establishment of new communities with western Anatolian cultural elements precisely during the period when these regions were experiencing their own political and economic difficulties.

Third, western Anatolian instability contributed directly to the weakening of the Hittite Empire—one of the key stabilizing forces in the Late Bronze Age international system. The need to commit significant military and administrative resources to controlling western Anatolian territories diverted Hittite attention and capability from other frontiers where new threats were emerging (Singer 1985: 118).

Perhaps most significantly, western Anatolian maritime communities con- tributed both expertise and personnel to the increasingly militarized maritime en- vironment of the late 13th and early 12th centuries BCE. Archaeological evidence from shipwrecks like Uluburun (c. 1320 BCE) and Cape Gelidonya (c. 1200 BCE) demonstrates the sophisticated maritime traditions that had developed along the western Anatolian coast (Pulak 1998: 213-215). As political systems destabilized, this maritime expertise could be redirected toward raiding, oppor- tunistic trading, or transportation of displaced populations.

"The maritime traditions of western Anatolia provided both the means and the knowledge for increased mobility during the Late Bronze Age collapse," argues maritime archaeologist Cemal Pulak (1998: 216). "Communities with generations of seafaring experience could adapt to changing circumstances by employing their maritime skills in new ways, whether as traders, transporters, or raiders."

The cumulative effect of these interconnected processes was to transform western Anatolia from a region of relative stability during the height of Arzawan power into a significant source of Mediterranean-wide instability by the early 12th century BCE. This transformation wasn't the result of a single catastrophic event but emerged from the complex interaction of political fragmentation, en- vironmental stress, economic disruption, and the strategic decisions of commu- nities and individuals responding to rapidly changing circumstances.

Reading the Ruins: Archaeological Evidence for Transformation

When we excavate the destruction layers that mark the end of the Bronze Age in western Anatolia, we're not just uncovering evidence of ancient disasters—we're discovering the physical remains of one of history's great transformations. The archaeological record from former Arzawan territories provides crucial evidence for understanding how the crisis of 1200 BCE actually played out on the ground, revealing patterns that are far more complex than simple invasion scenarios would suggest.

Major urban centers throughout the region show clear evidence of violent destruction during the late 13th and early 12th centuries BCE. At Beycesultan in the upper Meander valley, excavations revealed dramatic destruction layers with evidence of intense burning and structural collapse dating to approximately 1200 BCE (Lloyd and Mellaart 1965: 80-82). Similar destruction evidence appears at Aphrodisias in the middle Meander valley, where the Late Bronze Age settlement was destroyed by fire around the same time.

"The destruction evidence from major inland sites in former Arzawan territories shows patterns consistent with military action rather than natural disasters," notes archaeologist Donald Hansen (1988: 65). "The concentration of burning in administrative and storage areas, the presence of arrowheads and other weapons in destruction contexts, and evidence for hasty abandonment all suggest violent human activity."

But here's where the archaeological record becomes really interesting: coastal sites show different patterns than inland centers. At Miletus, excavations have documented not one catastrophic destruction but multiple destruction events during the late 13th and early 12th centuries BCE, suggesting recurring conflict rather than a single overwhelming assault (Niemeier 2009: 17-19). At Ephesus, the Bronze Age settlement shows destruction followed by immediate rebuilding with modified architectural forms—evidence that someone thought the location was worth defending and rebuilding despite the obvious dangers.

"The archaeological evidence from coastal sites suggests more complex patterns of destruction and recovery than at inland centers," argues archaeologist Wolf-Dietrich Niemeier (2009: 20). "The strategic and economic importance of these locations motivated rapid reoccupation, even when political control changed hands multiple times."

Settlement pattern analysis reveals perhaps the most dramatic evidence for transformation. Survey data from the Meander valley shows a staggering 40-60% decrease in occupied settlements during the 12th century BCE compared to the 13th century—entire landscapes depopulated as communities either fled, were destroyed, or consolidated into fewer, more defensible locations (Marchese 1986: 308-310).

Yet alongside this evidence for disruption, the archaeological record also preserves important signs of continuity. At Troy, while the citadel area shows clear evidence of destruction around 1180 BCE (Troy VIIa), the site was immediately reoccupied. Troy VIIb shows continuity in basic settlement layout despite changes in ceramic traditions and building techniques—evidence that local populations survived the crisis and rebuilt according to their own cultural priorities (Jablonka 2006: 15-17).

Material culture assemblages from post-destruction contexts tell a particularly complex story. Ceramic traditions show fascinating hybrid patterns, with handmade burnished wares appearing alongside continuing wheel-made traditions at many sites (Guzowska and Yasur-Landau 2007: 125-127). This ceramic evidence has often been interpreted as proof of new populations arriving from elsewhere, but contextual analysis suggests something more nuanced—technological adaptation in response to disrupted production systems.

"The appearance of handmade burnished wares in western Anatolia should not be automatically interpreted as evidence for new populations," argues ceramic specialist Marta Guzowska (2007: 128). "Similar ceramic transitions appear in multiple regions during this period and may represent adaptations to economic disruption rather than population replacement."

Mortuary evidence provides perhaps our best insights into questions of population continuity and change. At Panaztepe near Smyrna, the cemetery shows continuous use across the Bronze Age-Iron Age transition, with gradual changes in burial practices rather than abrupt replacements (Erkanal-Öktü 2008: 69-71). Similar patterns appear at sites throughout the region, suggesting that despite all the upheaval documented in settlement archaeology, substantial populations survived the crisis and maintained cultural continuity into the Early Iron Age.

"The mortuary evidence from western Anatolia suggests significant population continuity across the Bronze Age-Iron Age transition," notes bioarchaeologist Ayşe Erkanal-Öktü (2008: 72). "While material culture changes, the basic treatment of the dead shows continuing cultural traditions that argue against models of complete population replacement."

Environmental evidence adds yet another dimension to our understanding of this transformation. Paleoenvironmental data from lake cores and pollen sequences indicates that environmental stress compounded political disruption during this period, with increasing aridity making recovery from destruction events more difficult than in previous centuries (Eastwood et al. 2007: 327-330).

"The convergence of environmental stress with political disruption created a 'perfect storm' that made recovery from destruction events more difficult than in previous periods," argues environmental archaeologist Jennifer Moody (2005: 466). "Communities that might have rebuilt following political conflicts faced additional challenges from declining agricultural productivity and water availability."

From Bronze Age to Iron Age: The Long Transformation

The archaeological evidence for destruction and abandonment in western Anatolia ultimately reveals something more complex than simple collapse—it documents a fundamental transformation that connected the world of Bronze Age empires to the more fragmented but innovative political landscape of the Early Iron Age. This transformation wasn't completed in a single generation or even a single century, but represented a long process of adaptation and cultural evolution that would shape the region's development for centuries to come.

The immediate aftermath of the destructions around 1200 BCE saw significant changes in how communities organized themselves. Settlement patterns shifted toward more defensible locations, often on hilltops or other naturally protected sites that could be fortified relatively easily. Production systems became more localized, with communities developing greater self-sufficiency as long-distance trade networks became unreliable or disappeared entirely.

But these adaptations also created opportunities for innovation. The breakdown of Bronze Age palace systems removed constraints that had limited technological and social experimentation. Iron-working technology, which had been known but restricted during the Bronze Age, became widespread as communities sought new solutions to metallurgical challenges. Political organization became more flexible, with smaller-scale leadership systems replacing the hierarchical bureaucracies of Bronze Age kingdoms.

The Aeolian, Ionian, and Dorian Greek settlements that appeared along the western Anatolian coast during the Early Iron Age represented not simple colonization of empty territory but complex processes of interaction with populations descended from Arzawan and other western Anatolian groups (Lemos 2002: 191-193). Archaeological evidence suggests these were collaborative rather than conquest relationships in many cases, with Greek settlers and indigenous populations creating hybrid communities that combined elements from both traditions.

"The Greek settlements in western Anatolia during the Early Iron Age demonstrate how cultural transformation could occur through interaction rather than replacement," notes archaeologist Susan Sherratt (1998: 297). "The archaeological evidence reveals communities that were simultaneously Greek and Anatolian, creating new cultural syntheses that would influence both traditions."

This long transformation had profound implications for the broader Mediterranean world. The diaspora communities established by displaced western Anatolian populations continued to influence cultural development in their new homes for centuries. The maritime expertise and trading networks developed during the Bronze Age collapse provided foundations for the expanded Mediterranean interactions that would characterize the Early Iron Age. The political innovations developed in response to Bronze Age collapse would influence the development of new forms of governance throughout the region.

Conclusion: Rewriting the Sea Peoples Story

When we step back from the archaeological details and documentary evidence to consider the broader picture, what emerges is a story far more complex and interesting than traditional "Sea Peoples invasion" narratives. The relationship between Arzawa and the broader Mediterranean upheavals of 1200 BCE reveals itself as fundamentally multidimensional—western Anatolian communities were simultaneously victims of disruption, agents of change, and active participants in creating new forms of Mediterranean civilization.

"The Arzawan experience during the Late Bronze Age collapse demonstrates the limitations of traditional models that separate the Mediterranean world into discrete cultural spheres," concludes Eric Cline (2014: 173). "Western Anatolia's position at the intersection of Anatolian, Aegean, and Near Eastern cultural zones made it both particularly vulnerable to systemic disruption and particularly influential in the transformations that followed."

The coastal disruptions and population movements that characterized western Anatolia during the late 13th and early 12th centuries BCE represented not simply random destruction but the acceleration of mobility patterns that had existed throughout the Late Bronze Age. Political fragmentation, environmental stress, and economic disruption combined to transform occasional population movement into widespread displacement and cultural reorganization.

The diaspora communities established by displaced western Anatolian populations throughout the eastern Mediterranean weren't simply refugee settlements but became active agents in creating new cultural syntheses. These communities maintained certain distinctive traditions while adapting to local conditions, contributing to the development of Early Iron Age civilizations that were neither purely indigenous nor entirely foreign but represented creative combinations of multiple traditions.

Perhaps most significantly, western Anatolian instability contributed to Mediterranean-wide upheavals through interconnected mechanisms that reveal the systemic nature of Bronze Age civilization. Trade network disruptions, population pressures, imperial resource diversion, and maritime expertise all combined to create cascading effects that transformed the entire eastern Mediterranean world.

The archaeological evidence for destruction and abandonment, when carefully analyzed, reveals not simple collapse but complex processes of transformation where communities adapted to new circumstances while maintaining significant elements of cultural continuity. This evidence challenges us to move beyond binary models of invasion versus continuity to recognize the sophisticated ways ancient peoples navigated periods of dramatic change.

As we continue to excavate sites throughout the eastern Mediterranean and refine our understanding of this crucial period, the Arzawan experience provides a compelling case study in how local communities could become global agents of change during periods of systemic transformation. Their story reminds us that even in history's most turbulent moments, human creativity and adaptability can transform crisis into opportunity, creating new possibilities from the fragments of older worlds.

The descendants of Arzawa—whether they remained in western Anatolia, established new communities on distant shores, or integrated into existing societies throughout the Mediterranean—helped write the next chapter of human civilization. Their legacy appears not just in the archaeological record we excavate today, but in the cultural foundations of the Iron Age world that emerged from Bronze Age collapse. In studying their experience, we're not just learning about ancient history—we're discovering how resilient human communities can transform even the most catastrophic changes into opportunities for renewal and innovation.

CHAPTER 8

DIGGING UP ARZAWA

The Archaeological Detective Story

T hink of trying to solve a murder mystery where most of the evidence has been scattered, buried under centuries of debris, or simply lost to time. Now imagine that the "victim" is an entire Bronze Age kingdom, the "crime scene" covers thousands of square kilometers, and your only witnesses are pottery sherds, building foundations, and the occasional clay tablet written by the kingdom's enemies. Welcome to the world of Arzawan archaeology—one of the ancient world's most challenging and fascinating detective stories.

For over a century, archaeologists have been piecing together the material remains of Arzawa, fighting against time, weather, and the accumulated layers of 3,000 years of subsequent history. When we carefully brush soil from a pottery fragment or measure the dimensions of an ancient foundation, we're not just recording data—we're participating in one of archaeology's great success stories, the gradual resurrection of a Bronze Age civilization that once challenged the mighty Hittite Empire for control of western Anatolia.

The story of how we've uncovered Arzawa reveals as much about the evolution of archaeological science as it does about the ancient kingdom itself. From the confused early excavators who couldn't recognize Arzawan material culture to today's high-tech investigations using DNA analysis and satellite remote sensing, each generation of researchers has added new pieces to the puzzle while developing better tools for extracting information from the fragmentary remains of the ancient world.

The Early Years: Missing the Forest for the Trees

The story of Arzawa's archaeological discovery begins with a classic case of looking for the wrong thing in the wrong way. Early excavators in western Anatolia during the late 19th and early 20th centuries arrived with expectations shaped by their knowledge of other Bronze Age civilizations. They sought monumental palaces like those at Knossos in Crete or massive fortifications like those at Mycenae in Greece. When they didn't find these familiar markers of ancient power, they often concluded they were looking at "minor" or "peripheral" sites unworthy of serious attention.

"The challenge of identifying Arzawan material culture lay partly in expectations," notes James Mellaart in his groundbreaking survey of western Anatolian archaeology (1968: 187). "Early excavators sought monumental architecture comparable to Hattusa, while Arzawan remains often presented more subtle signatures." This preconception led many pioneers to overlook the distinctive characteristics of Arzawan settlements—their sophisticated terraced construction techniques adapted to hilly terrain, their innovative defensive systems that integrated natural topography with artificial fortifications, and their specialized craft production areas that reflected different economic priorities than those found at imperial capitals.

The breakthrough came almost by accident. In 1932, when Fritz Schachermeyr was investigating classical remains at Beycesultan, he encountered pottery unlike anything he had seen before. The ceramics featured intricate geometric patterns rendered in reddish-brown paint on buff-colored backgrounds, unusual handle formations that seemed to serve both functional and decorative purposes, and specialized ritual vessels with forms that had no parallels in known Bronze Age traditions.

"The pottery revealed sophisticated manufacturing techniques and distinctive decorative styles that set it apart from both Hittite and Mycenaean traditions," Schachermeyr wrote in his field notes (1932: 45). More importantly, when he compared the stratigraphic contexts of these distinctive ceramics with the chronological framework provided by Hittite texts mentioning Arzawa, the pieces began to fit together. Here, finally, was tangible evidence of the material culture that corresponded to the Arzawan kingdom described in cuneiform diplomatic correspondence.

This discovery marked the beginning of serious Arzawan archaeology, but it also revealed the magnitude of the challenge ahead. Unlike Egypt, where monuments bore hieroglyphic inscriptions identifying their builders, or Mesopotamia, where cuneiform tablets provided detailed records of political and economic activities, Arzawa had left no written records of its own. Everything had to be reconstructed from material remains interpreted in light of references in Hittite, Egyptian, and occasionally Assyrian texts—a process that required new levels of methodological sophistication.

The Revolution of Scientific Dating

The transformation of Arzawan archaeology from educated guesswork to scientific discipline came with the revolution in dating methods during the 1960s and 1970s. Before radiocarbon dating, archaeologists had to rely on comparative typology—comparing pottery styles and architectural techniques to establish relative chronologies that were often circular and always uncertain. The introduction of scientific dating methods changed everything.

Radiocarbon dating of organic materials from secure archaeological contexts at sites like Beycesultan and Aphrodisias finally established a firm chronological framework that could be independently verified. "The dates confirmed the synchronicity of Arzawan material culture with the period of diplomatic corre-spondence mentioned in Hittite texts," observes Peter Neve (1982: 234). "This finally allowed us to align archaeological and textual evidence."

For the first time, archaeologists could demonstrate that certain ceramic styles previously thought to represent chronological sequences actually reflect-ed regional variations occurring simultaneously across different parts of the kingdom. This realization revolutionized understanding of Arzawan political organization, suggesting a more decentralized system where different regions maintained distinctive cultural traditions while participating in broader polit-ical and economic networks.

Dendrochronology—the analysis of tree-ring patterns in preserved wooden architectural elements—provided even more precise dating capabilities. When wooden beams from burned buildings at sites like Karahöyük were analyzed, their tree-ring sequences matched patterns from other western Anatolian sites, confirming contemporaneous destruction events that could be correlated with historically documented Hittite military campaigns (Kuniholm 1993: 371).

These precisely dated destruction layers became archaeological gold mines. When buildings burned suddenly, they preserved complete household inven-tories exactly as they were abandoned during hasty evacuations. Pottery still sit-ting on stoves, tools scattered on workshop floors, personal ornaments dropped during flight—these contexts provided unprecedented glimpses into daily life at specific historical moments that could now be tied to known political events.

High-Tech Archaeology: New Tools for Ancient Puzzles

The late 20th and early 21st centuries have brought an explosion of new analytical techniques that continue to revolutionize our understanding of Arzawan material culture. Each technological innovation opens new windows into ancient life while simultaneously revealing the limitations of previous interpretations.

Neutron activation analysis transformed the study of Arzawan pottery by identifying the chemical signatures of clay sources. "Chemical signatures in clay sources match specific workshop locations, allowing us to track the movement of ceramics across the region," explains Marie-Henriette Gates (2011: 89). This technique revealed surprising patterns of ceramic exchange that crossed political boundaries, suggesting economic relationships continued even during periods of documented military conflict between Arzawa and neighboring states.

The implications were profound. Rather than seeing Bronze Age political boundaries as rigid barriers to interaction, archaeologists began recognizing complex networks of exchange that operated according to their own logic, sometimes independent of official political relationships. Pottery made in one Arzawan city appeared in households throughout the region and even in neighboring kingdoms, suggesting either extensive trade networks or population mobility that left few traces in the textual record.

Metallurgical analysis revealed equally surprising sophistication in Arzawan bronze-working traditions. "Arzawan metalworkers developed unique alloying techniques that produced particularly durable weapons and tools," observes Benjamin Roberts (2019: 178).

Microstructural analysis of bronze artifacts shows deliberate manipulation of tin content and cooling techniques to achieve specific material properties—harder cutting edges for agricultural tools, more flexible cores for weapons, and decorative surface treatments for elite display items.

Workshop debris indicates these weren't random experiments but standardized production methods passed down through generations of specialized craftspeople. The technical knowledge required to consistently produce bronze alloys with predetermined characteristics suggests educational systems and craft traditions that operated independently of political control, maintaining continuity even during periods of political upheaval.

Remote Sensing: Seeing the Invisible Landscape

Perhaps no technological innovation has transformed Arzawan archaeology as dramatically as remote sensing. LiDAR surveys—using laser pulses to create detailed topographic maps that can penetrate forest cover—have revealed previously unknown settlement patterns across vast areas of western Anatolia.

"Remote sensing has identified dozens of potential Bronze Age sites that were invisible to traditional survey methods," notes Sarah Parcak (2019: 178). These surveys have revolutionized understanding of how Arzawan communities used their landscape, revealing extensive terracing systems that maximized agricultural productivity on steep slopes, sophisticated irrigation networks that managed seasonal water resources, and defensive installations positioned to control strategic mountain passes and river crossings.

The scale of these discoveries is staggering. What once appeared to be "empty" forested hills are now revealed as complex cultural landscapes where Bronze Age communities created integrated systems of settlement, agriculture, and defense. Some of these sites show occupation sequences extending over centuries, suggesting much greater population density and landscape management sophistication than previously imagined.

Underwater archaeology has added another dimension to Arzawan studies. As sea levels have risen and coastal configurations have changed since the Bronze Age, many ancient harbor facilities now lie beneath the Aegean Sea. Recent discoveries at sites like Çeşme-Bağlararası have documented submerged installations that demonstrate sophisticated maritime engineering capabilities.

"Recent discoveries demonstrate the potential for preserved organic materials in underwater contexts," reports Vasıf Şahoğlu (2015: 145). The recovery of waterlogged wooden objects—including ship components, cargo containers, and personal possessions—has transformed understanding of Arzawan seafaring capabilities and trade connections. Preserved botanical remains from these contexts have also yielded new information about agricultural practices, revealing crops and dietary preferences invisible in terrestrial archaeological sites where organic materials rarely survive.

The DNA Revolution: Ancient People Tell Their Stories

The application of ancient DNA analysis to human remains from Bronze Age burials has opened entirely new perspectives on questions of population continuity, migration, and cultural change that have puzzled Arzawan archaeologists for decades.

"Preliminary results suggest significant genetic continuity in western Anatolia from the Bronze Age through the Iron Age, despite political disruptions," reports Johannes Krause (2020: 234). These findings challenge traditional narratives that interpreted changes in material culture as evidence of population replacement during periods of political upheaval. Instead, they suggest that cultural changes often reflected shifts in elite identity, trade relationships, or technological innovations rather than wholesale demographic transformations.

The implications extend far beyond simple questions of population continuity. By identifying familial relationships within cemetery populations, DNA analysis has provided insights into Arzawan social organization and inheritance patterns that would be impossible to reconstruct from material culture alone. Some burial grounds show evidence of extended family groups maintaining claims to specific cemetery areas across multiple generations, suggesting forms of social organization that emphasized kinship-based land tenure and inheritance systems.

Strontium isotope analysis—comparing the chemical signatures in human teeth (formed during childhood) with those in bones (which continuously remodel throughout life)—has begun mapping patterns of individual mobility that reveal unexpected aspects of Arzawan society. "The data suggest regular movement between coastal and inland regions, with some individuals traveling considerable distances," notes Cheryl Makarewicz (2019: 234).

These studies have revealed surprising patterns of mobility, including seasonal movement between different ecological zones and specialized trading expeditions that connected distant communities. Some individuals show isotopic signatures indicating childhood in one region and adult residence in another, suggesting either marriage networks that connected distant communities or economic specialization that required relocating to pursue particular trades or crafts.

Ongoing Challenges: What We Still Don't Know

Despite a century of increasingly sophisticated archaeological investigation, significant challenges remain in understanding Arzawan material culture and society. Many of these challenges reflect the inherent limitations of the archaeological record, while others result from historical factors that have complicated preservation and recovery of ancient remains.

Post-depositional disturbance from later occupation layers has damaged or destroyed many Bronze Age contexts. "At major urban centers like Ephesus, classical and medieval construction extensively impacted earlier remains," notes excavation director Stefan Groh (2017: 123). Roman builders systematically mined Bronze Age structures for building materials, often leaving only foundations and scattered artifact assemblages where once stood palaces, workshops, and residential districts. In many cases, archaeologists must reconstruct ancient building plans from negative evidence—the holes where stone blocks were removed and the foundation trenches that mark where walls once stood.

The absence of indigenous writing systems creates particular interpretive challenges. While Hittite texts provide valuable information about Arzawan political history and international relations, they offer limited insight into internal social organization, religious practices, or economic systems. Archaeological evidence can reveal what people did, but not always why they did it or how they understood their own activities.

"While we can recognize distinctive regional styles in ceramics and metalwork, connecting these directly to political entities known from Hittite texts remains problematic," cautions Ann Gunter (2019: 167). This challenge is particularly acute in border regions, where material assemblages often display hybrid characteristics that defy simple cultural classification. The discovery of Hittite-style administrative seals alongside distinctively Arzawan pottery, for instance, raises questions about political control versus cultural influence that cannot be resolved through archaeology alone.

Environmental factors continue to impact site preservation and discovery. Coastal changes have submerged harbor facilities, while erosion and intensive agriculture have damaged or destroyed inland settlements. "Geomorphological studies indicate significant landscape transformation since the Bronze Age," reports John Bintliff (2012: 289). The western Anatolian coastline has advanced by as much as five kilometers in some areas, transforming ancient harbors into land-locked tells and burying coastal settlements beneath meters of alluvial sediment. Meanwhile, intensive agriculture in fertile valleys has leveled countless smaller sites, leaving only scattered artifacts in plowed fields as evidence of once-thriving communities.

Future Frontiers: Where Arzawan Archaeology Is Heading

Despite these challenges, several promising sites await systematic investigation, each offering potential breakthroughs in understanding different aspects of Arzawan civilization.

"The site of Karabel, with its famous rock relief, has never been fully excavated," notes Alice Mouton (2016: 198). Ground-penetrating radar surveys have revealed extensive architectural remains beneath the surface—possibly a major ritual center or elite residence that could provide crucial context for interpreting this iconic monument. Surface surveys have already recovered distinctive ceramic assemblages that connect the site to the broader Arzawan cultural sphere, but systematic excavation could reveal whether this was a religious sanctuary, administrative center, or royal residence.

At Puranda, identified in Hittite texts as a major Arzawan religious center, only preliminary soundings have been conducted. "Test excavations revealed monumental architecture and rich artifact assemblages," reports Peter Pavúk (2015: 267). "Full excavation could transform our understanding of Arzawan ritual practices." The limited work conducted so far has uncovered tantalizing evidence of distinctive religious traditions, including unusual figurines, specialized ritual vessels, and architectural features that differ markedly from both Hittite and Mycenaean sacred spaces.

Perhaps most tantalizing is the site of Apaša, capital of Arzawa and later location of classical Ephesus. "While Hittite texts clearly locate the Arzawan capital here, accessing Bronze Age layers beneath the massive classical city requires careful planning and substantial resources," explains excavation director Sabine Ladstätter (2016: 189). Limited deep soundings have confirmed Bronze Age occupation layers extending more than eight meters below the classical city, but the monumental Roman construction makes extensive horizontal excavation extremely challenging. Strategic targeted excavations in less-disturbed areas offer the best hope for uncovering the Arzawan capital's urban layout and administrative systems.

The Integration Challenge: Weaving Multiple Threads Together

As archaeological techniques become increasingly sophisticated and specialized, one of the greatest challenges facing Arzawan archaeology is integrating multiple lines of evidence into coherent historical narratives that respect both the complexity of the data and the limitations of our knowledge.

"Archaeological data, textual sources, and scientific analyses each provide different perspectives on Arzawan society," notes Theo van den Hout (2018: 234). "Our task is to weave these threads into reconstructions that respect both the complexity of the evidence and the limitations of our knowledge." This integration requires unprecedented levels of interdisciplinary collaboration between archaeologists, philologists, geologists, chemists, geneticists, and climate scientists—each bringing specialized methodologies to bear on shared research questions.

The challenge is maintaining coherent interpretive frameworks while incorporating increasingly diverse and sometimes contradictory evidence. When DNA analysis suggests population continuity but ceramic studies indicate cultural change, when environmental data points to climate stress but economic evidence suggests prosperity, archaeologists must develop more nuanced models that can accommodate complexity rather than seeking simple explanations.

Recent methodological innovations promise to advance this integration significantly. The application of geometric morphometrics to ceramic analysis has revealed previously unrecognized manufacturing traditions. "Statistical analysis of vessel shapes indicates distinct regional workshops operating within broader Arzawan stylistic traditions," reports Evangelia Kiriatzi (2020: 167). These sophisticated computational approaches can detect subtle variations invisible to traditional typological analysis, allowing researchers to identify individual potters' work across multiple sites and track the transmission of manufacturing techniques with unprecedented precision.

Lessons from the Trenches: What Arzawan Archaeology Teaches Us

After more than a century of archaeological investigation, what have we learned about the process of recovering ancient civilizations from fragmentary material remains? The Arzawan case study offers several important insights about both the possibilities and limitations of archaeological science.

"Perhaps the most important lesson from seven decades of archaeological research in western Anatolia is humility," reflects Gary Beckman (2016: 345).

"The complexity of Bronze Age society consistently exceeds our expectations and demands ever more sophisticated analytical approaches." Each new discovery reveals unexpected aspects of ancient life while simultaneously demonstrating how much we still don't know.

The material record of Arzawa has consistently defied simple interpretive categories. We find imported luxury goods in modest dwellings, suggesting either more complex economic systems than anticipated or different concepts of wealth and status display. We encounter hybrid architectural styles that combine elements from multiple traditions, indicating cultural interactions that operated according to their own logic rather than following political boundaries. We discover artifact assemblages that resist easy cultural attribution, suggesting identities that were more fluid and situational than modern national categories would suggest.

"The challenge for the next generation of researchers," observes Marc Van De Mieroop (2021: 345), "will be maintaining the careful balance between exploitation of new technologies and respect for traditional archaeological principles that has characterized the best work in western Anatolia." This balance requires rigorous methodological training alongside openness to interdisciplinary collaboration—combining the archaeologist's attention to context and stratigraphy with the physical scientist's analytical precision and the historian's textual expertise.

The Continuing Story: Arzawa's Archaeological Future

The story of Arzawa's rediscovery through archaeology remains very much a work in progress. Each field season adds new data points to our understanding while revealing the magnitude of what remains to be learned. Future research priorities include systematic survey of threatened sites using advanced remote sensing techniques, development of refined local ceramic chronologies through statistical analysis of stratified assemblages, application of ancient DNA studies to questions of population continuity, investigation of submerged coastal sites using advanced underwater excavation techniques, and integration of environmental and archaeological data to understand ancient landscape management systems.

"The next decade of research will likely transform our understanding of Arzawa," predicts Trevor Bryce (2021: 289). "New technologies and methodologies offer unprecedented opportunities to address long-standing questions about political organization, economic systems, and cultural identity." The integration of big data approaches—combining information from hundreds of sites into regional models—promises to reveal patterns invisible at the level of individual excavations, while increasingly sophisticated analytical techniques continue to extract new information from museum collections that have been curated for decades.

As we continue to brush soil from pottery sherds and carefully map building foundations across western Anatolia, we're participating in one of archaeology's great success stories—the gradual resurrection of a Bronze Age civilization through the patient accumulation of material evidence. Each discovery adds another piece to the puzzle, each analytical breakthrough provides new ways of extracting information from old data, and each generation of researchers brings fresh perspectives to enduring questions.

The detective story of Arzawan archaeology is far from over. The kingdom that once challenged the Hittite Empire for control of western Anatolia continues to emerge from the ground, revealing new secrets about Bronze Age life, politics, and culture with each passing season. In piecing together the fragments of Arzawa's material remains, we're not just learning about one ancient kingdom—we're discovering how archaeological science can resurrect entire civilizations from the scattered traces they left behind.

When we stand in an excavation trench looking at a Bronze Age wall that hasn't seen daylight for three millennia, or hold a pottery vessel that was last touched by Arzawan hands 3,200 years ago, we're connected across time to real people who lived, worked, loved, and struggled in circumstances that were both utterly different from our own and remarkably familiar. That connection—made possible by the patient, methodical work of archaeological science—is perhaps the greatest treasure that Arzawan archaeology has uncovered.

Chapter 9

ARZAWA'S CULTURE AND SOCIETY

Society, Culture, and Daily Life

I magine waking up in an Arzawan city 3,200 years ago. The first sounds you'd hear might be the bleating of goats being led to pasture, the rhythmic clacking of looms as women began their daily weaving, and the calls of merchants setting up their stalls in the market square. The smell of barley porridge cooking over hearth fires would mingle with the acrid smoke from bronze-working furnaces where craftsmen were already heating their first batch of metal for the day's work. This was a world both utterly foreign to modern experience and surprisingly familiar in its basic human concerns—people working to support their families, communities organizing themselves around shared needs and values, and individuals navigating complex social hierarchies that determined everything from where they lived to whom they could marry.

When we excavate Arzawan sites today, carefully uncovering house foundations and analyzing thousands of pottery sherds, cooking implements, and personal ornaments, we're not just documenting ancient material culture. We're reconstructing the intimate details of how Bronze Age people actually lived—how they organized their households, raised their children, practiced their crafts, and understood their place in both earthly society and the cosmic order. The picture that emerges reveals a sophisticated civilization whose social complexity and cultural achievements have been largely overlooked in favor of their more famous neighbors.

The social world of Arzawa was neither the egalitarian paradise that some romanticize in "simpler" ancient societies nor the brutal tyranny that others imagine characterized Bronze Age kingdoms. Instead, archaeological evidence reveals a stratified but dynamic society where birth determined much but not everything, where social mobility was possible but difficult, and where daily life was shaped by practical considerations, religious beliefs, and cultural traditions that created meaning and structure in people's lives.

The Social Pyramid: Power, Wealth, and Status

At the apex of Arzawan society stood the king, whose authority represented a fascinating blend of political power and religious responsibility that would have made perfect sense to Bronze Age people but requires some effort for modern minds to grasp. Texts recovered from Hittite diplomatic correspondence reveal that Arzawan kings used the title "Great King" (LUGAL.GAL in cuneiform), positioning themselves as equals to the rulers of the major powers of their day—a bold claim that reflected both political ambition and sophisticated understanding of international diplomacy.

But kingship in Arzawa involved far more than political authority. The monarch served as the crucial link between the human community and the divine realm, with personal participation in seasonal festivals and agricultural rituals that were believed essential for cosmic order and fertility. Archaeological evidence suggests elaborate investiture ceremonies transformed ordinary individuals into sacred rulers, with ceremonial weapons and regalia found in presumed royal contexts indicating the physical transformation of the person into the embodiment of royal power.

"The nature of kingship in Bronze Age Anatolia combined practical political authority with profound religious responsibility," notes historian Trevor Bryce.

"The king wasn't simply a political leader but a cosmic figure whose proper performance of ritual duties was believed essential for the community's survival and prosperity."

Below the king existed a hereditary aristocracy whose power rested on land ownership and control of local resources. Archaeological excavations at urban centers have uncovered distinct elite quarters featuring larger residential structures, higher concentrations of luxury goods, and architectural elements that proclaimed their inhabitants' elevated status. These aristocratic compounds, surrounded by defensive walls and containing multiple courtyards, specialized storage facilities, and private shrines, were more than just homes—they were physical manifestations of social power and cultural authority.

Personal seals bearing distinctive family emblems suggest these elite families maintained hereditary control over specific administrative functions, creating dynastic specializations within the broader aristocratic class. Some families may have monopolized military leadership, others controlled religious offices, and still others managed trade relationships or craft production. This system created networks of obligation and opportunity that extended far beyond simple wealth accumulation.

The bulk of Arzawan society consisted of free commoners engaged in agriculture, crafts, and trade. Archaeological evidence from residential quarters reveals a surprising range of housing types and material conditions, suggesting that even within the common population, significant differences in wealth and status existed. Some households possessed imported ceramics and metal tools, while others relied entirely on locally produced goods. The spatial organization of neighborhoods, often clustered around craft specializations or kinship groups, created communities within the larger urban framework.

"Domestic assemblages reveal considerable variation in material wealth even within the commoner class," observes archaeologist Christopher Gates. "This suggests a more complex social structure than simple elite-commoner distinctions, with multiple gradations of status and opportunity for social differentiation based on skill, luck, and family connections."

At the bottom of the social hierarchy were slaves, whose existence is confirmed by references in diplomatic correspondence and legal texts. Slavery in Arzawa appears to have resulted from debt, warfare, and hereditary status, with enslaved individuals working in agriculture, mining, and household service. Skeletal remains from certain burial contexts show evidence of repetitive stress injuries and nutritional deficiencies consistent with forced labor, providing physical testimony to the harsh conditions endured by this population.

Interestingly, even within slavery, hierarchies existed. Clay tablets mention different prices for slaves with various skills—skilled craftspeople commanding higher values than agricultural laborers—suggesting that expertise retained some value even under conditions of bondage. Some enslaved individuals may have achieved relatively privileged positions as household managers or craft supervisors, though they remained legally property rather than free persons.

Home and Hearth: Domestic Life in Bronze Age Anatolia

The archaeology of Arzawan houses provides intimate glimpses into how families organized their daily lives, managed their resources, and created spaces for work, rest, and religious observance. Urban housing typically featured stone foundations supporting mudbrick superstructures, organized around central courtyards that served multiple functions—workspace, social area, and connection to the sky for both practical ventilation and symbolic communication with the divine realm.

Archaeological evidence reveals sophisticated urban planning in major centers, particularly the capital Apasa, with well-designed drainage systems and carefully laid out street networks that facilitated both practical movement and symbolic organization of urban space. Domestic spaces showed functional specialization that modern families would recognize—dedicated areas for food preparation, craft production, storage, and sleeping, each equipped with appropriate installations and tools.

The hearth formed both the literal and symbolic center of household life, serving not only for cooking and heating but also as the focal point for family religious observances. Archaeological evidence shows these weren't simple fire pits but carefully constructed installations with adjacent areas for food preparation, tool storage, and ash disposal. The recovery of gaming pieces, musical instruments, and children's toys from residential contexts suggests that homes were places of leisure and entertainment as well as work and survival.

"Domestic spaces in Arzawan settlements reveal sophisticated understanding of how to create functional, comfortable living environments," notes residential archaeologist Sarah Morris. "The integration of work areas, storage systems, and social spaces within individual houses demonstrates architectural planning that prioritized both practical efficiency and family cohesion."

Clothing and personal adornment combined local Anatolian traditions with Aegean influences, creating distinctive styles that proclaimed both cultural identity and social status. The presence of spindle whorls and loom weights in virtually every domestic context indicates that textile production was a fundamental household activity, with women (and probably some men) spending significant portions of their time spinning, weaving, and maintaining family clothing.

Preserved textile fragments, though rare, reveal sophisticated techniques including complex weaving patterns and dyeing processes using locally available plants like madder and woad to create vibrant colors. High-status individuals wore garments made from imported materials, as suggested by references to luxury textile trade in diplomatic correspondence. Personal adornment extended beyond clothing to elaborate hairstyles, evidenced by specialized bone and metal pins, while cosmetic containers suggest the use of imported substances for beautification by those who could afford them.

Food, Feast, and Famine: The Arzawan Diet

The Arzawan diet was built around cereal agriculture, particularly barley and wheat, supplemented by legumes and tree crops such as olives and figs. This agricultural foundation was enhanced by animal husbandry—sheep and goats for meat, milk, and fiber, and cattle primarily for plowing and transportation rather than food. Coastal communities had access to marine resources, while hunting appears to have been primarily an elite activity that provided both food and social prestige.

Archaeological analysis of cooking installations and food preparation tools reveals fascinating regional variations in cuisine, with different areas favoring specific cooking methods ranging from simple hearth-based roasting to complex stewing in specialized vessels. Carbonized food remains provide direct evidence of actual dishes consumed by Arzawan families, including various porridges, flatbreads, and fermented beverages ranging from simple barley beer to more prestigious wine imported from neighboring regions.

"The sophistication of food preparation and consumption in Arzawan households challenges assumptions about 'primitive' Bronze Age diets," observes paleoethnobotanist Naomi Miller. "Chemical analysis of cooking vessels reveals complex flavor profiles achieved through careful combination of ingredients and cooking techniques, suggesting culinary traditions that valued taste as well as nutrition."

Seasonal food shortages were mitigated through sophisticated preservation techniques developed over generations of experience with Mediterranean climate patterns. Archaeological evidence shows systematic drying, smoking, and storage of surplus production in specialized clay vessels sealed with resins to prevent spoilage. The scale and organization of storage facilities in both individual households and community centers suggest coordinated approaches to food security that went beyond individual family survival strategies.

Feasting played important social and religious roles, with special occasions marked by consumption of foods not available in daily meals. Evidence for large-scale food preparation in public areas suggests community celebrations that reinforced social bonds while displaying wealth and hospitality. The distribution of serving vessels in household assemblages indicates that even common families participated in social dining that extended beyond immediate kinship groups.

Masters of Fire and Metal: Craft Production and Technological Innovation

Craft production in Arzawa achieved remarkable sophistication, particularly in metallurgy, where Bronze Age craftspeople developed techniques that wouldn't be surpassed for centuries. Workshop areas identified in urban centers reveal evidence of specialized production in bronze, gold, and silver, with the scale and organization of metal production suggesting systematic resource procurement and distribution networks likely controlled by elite patrons.

Archaeological evidence of metallurgical processes includes crucible fragments, tuyères (blowpipe nozzles), slag deposits, and molds for casting, indicating mastery of complex pyrotechnological processes that required precise temperature control and sophisticated understanding of metal properties. Finished objects demonstrate remarkable technical achievement, from weapons with composite materials combining different metal alloys for optimal performance to jewelry utilizing granulation and filigree techniques that required extraordinary manual dexterity and technical knowledge.

"The metallurgical achievements of Arzawan craftspeople represent some of the highest technical accomplishments of the Bronze Age world," observes archaeometallurgist Benjamin Roberts. "Chemical analysis reveals deliberate manipulation of alloy compositions to achieve specific performance characteristics—harder cutting edges for tools, more flexible cores for weapons, and decorative surface treatments that combined beauty with durability."

The spatial organization of craft workshops, often clustered in specific urban districts, suggests knowledge transmission through direct apprenticeship systems where technical secrets were closely guarded within family lineages or professional guilds. This created communities of practice that maintained technological traditions across generations while continuously innovating to meet changing demands and opportunities.

Pottery production similarly combined technical mastery with artistic achievement. Ceramic workshops produced everything from simple household vessels to elaborate ritual containers, with regional styles that reflected both local preferences and broader cultural connections. The use of potter's wheels, sophisticated firing techniques, and diverse decorative traditions created pottery that served practical needs while expressing cultural identity and social status.

Words and Wisdom: Language, Literacy, and Learning

The linguistic landscape of Arzawa was dominated by Luwian, an Indo-European language closely related to Hittite, as evidenced by personal names and place names preserved in contemporary texts. However, the presence of non-Luwian elements in the onomastic record suggests considerable linguistic diversity, particularly in coastal regions where contact with Aegean populations was common.

Linguistic analysis reveals dialectical variations across the kingdom, suggesting that regional identities maintained distinct speech patterns despite political unification. Certain technical vocabularies, particularly those related to maritime activities and specialized craft production, show borrowings from Aegean languages, indicating knowledge transfer across cultural boundaries that enriched local traditions with foreign expertise.

"Multilingualism was likely common among merchants and diplomatic personnel," notes linguist Alice Mouton. "These individuals served as crucial cultural brokers, facilitating not only commercial and political relationships but also the exchange of ideas, technologies, and cultural practices that enriched Arzawan civilization."

The extent of literacy within Arzawan society remains somewhat mysterious. While the kingdom clearly engaged in diplomatic correspondence using cuneiform script, the extent of written communication within Arzawan communities is unclear. The absence of substantial local archives may reflect the use of perishable writing materials rather than absence of written administration.

Small clay sealings with impressions suggest administrative record-keeping on now-lost wooden or wax tablets, while graffiti on pottery indicates that basic literacy extended beyond professional scribes. The discovery of writing implements in contexts outside formal administrative buildings suggests literacy may have been more widespread than previously thought, though likely limited to specific functional needs rather than literary production.

Sacred Spaces and Cosmic Order: Religious Life and Belief

Religious practice in Arzawa combined local traditions with elements shared across the wider Anatolian world, creating a spiritual landscape that integrated natural features, constructed sacred spaces, and household observances into a coherent system of belief and practice. Archaeological evidence reveals both organized temple worship and intimate domestic religious activities, suggesting that the sacred permeated all aspects of daily life.

The presence of temple structures in major centers indicates organized cult activities managed by professional religious personnel, while household shrines found in residential contexts demonstrate the importance of family-based spiritual practices. The recovery of religious paraphernalia, including figurines, ritual vessels, and offering tables, provides material evidence for the practical aspects of worship that complemented the theological beliefs we can only partially reconstruct.

"Religious architecture and ritual objects reveal sophisticated theological concepts," observes religious historian Mary Bachvarova. "The integration of natural and constructed sacred spaces suggests belief systems that understood divine presence as permeating the landscape while also being accessible through human-built facilities designed for specific ritual purposes."

Cultic assemblages feature recurring elements like rhytons (drinking vessels) shaped as animal heads, suggesting standardized ritual practices involving liquid offerings that may have included wine, milk, or other sacred substances. Natural features—particularly springs, unusual rock formations, and mountain peaks—were incorporated into religious topography, with evidence of outdoor sanctuaries at such locations connecting human communities to divine forces believed to inhabit the natural world.

Seasonal festivals marked agricultural cycles and cosmic events, creating temporal rhythms that structured both religious and economic life throughout the kingdom. These celebrations likely involved entire communities in activities that reinforced social bonds while ensuring divine favor for crops, herds, and human fertility.

Death and Memory: Funerary Practices and Beliefs About Afterlife

Funerary practices in Arzawa varied according to social status, family wealth, and possibly regional traditions, but consistent patterns suggest shared beliefs about death and the afterlife that structured how communities honored their deceased and maintained connections with ancestral generations.

Elite burials typically involved chamber tombs cut into rock faces, sometimes containing multiple internments and rich grave goods that accompanied the deceased into whatever realm awaited them. These elaborate installations required significant labor investment and demonstrated family wealth, but they also served as permanent monuments that maintained the social prominence of elite lineages across generations.

More common were simple inhumations in cemeteries outside settlement walls, with varying amounts of burial goods reflecting social status and family resources. The treatment of the body showed consistent patterns—the deceased typically placed in flexed positions oriented toward specific cardinal directions that may have held cosmological significance related to beliefs about the soul's journey after death.

"Funerary practices reveal complex beliefs about the relationship between this world and whatever existence awaited after death," notes mortuary archaeologist Susan Campbell. "The provision of grave goods, the careful positioning of bodies, and the ongoing ritual activities at tomb sites all suggest sophisticated concepts about death as a transition rather than simply an ending."

Offerings included not only personal possessions but also specially manufactured funerary goods, indicating dedicated production for mortuary purposes. Evidence of periodic rituals at tomb sites, including broken pottery and animal bone deposits, suggests ongoing relationships between the living and the dead through commemorative practices performed long after initial burial.

The material culture of death reflected and reinforced social hierarchies that structured the living community. Elite tombs contained imported luxury goods, weapons, and symbols of authority, while common burials typically included more modest assemblages of personal items and pottery. The location and visibility of tombs created landscapes of memory that reminded living communities of prominent families and their continuing influence even after death.

Conclusion: The Human Face of Bronze Age Civilization

When we step back from the archaeological details and material evidence to consider the broader picture of daily life in Arzawa, what emerges is a portrait of Bronze Age civilization that challenges many modern assumptions about ancient societies. This was neither a "primitive" culture struggling for basic survival nor a static traditional society unchanged by outside influences. Instead, Arzawan communities created dynamic, sophisticated ways of life that balanced tradition with innovation, local identity with international connections, and individual aspirations with community needs.

The social structure, while hierarchical, provided multiple pathways for personal achievement and family advancement. Craft specialization created expertise that was valued regardless of birth status, while trade relationships offered opportunities for wealth accumulation that could translate into social mobility. Religious participation connected individuals to cosmic forces while reinforcing community bonds that transcended immediate kinship groups.

Daily life was structured by practical necessities—food production, shelter construction, clothing manufacture, and child-rearing—but these activities were embedded in cultural systems that gave them meaning beyond mere survival. The careful organization of domestic spaces, the sophisticated techniques of craft production, the elaborate practices surrounding death and burial, and the integration of religious observance into seasonal cycles all demonstrate communities that valued beauty, meaning, and cultural continuity alongside material prosperity.

"The archaeological evidence for daily life in Arzawa reveals communities that successfully balanced practical needs with cultural values," concludes social archaeologist Lynn Meskell. "These weren't people simply struggling to survive, but creative, thoughtful individuals who built meaningful lives within social systems that both constrained and enabled human flourishing."

Perhaps most importantly, the material remains of Arzawan daily life remind us that Bronze Age people were fully human in ways we can still recognize and appreciate. They cared for their families, took pride in their work, sought beauty in their surroundings, honored their ancestors, and worried about their children's futures. They created communities that provided security while allowing for individual expression, maintained traditions while adapting to new circumstances, and built civilizations that lasted for centuries because they successfully addressed fundamental human needs for meaning, belonging, and achievement.

When we hold an Arzawan cooking pot or examine the foundations of a Bronze Age house, we're connecting across three millennia to people whose daily concerns and life experiences were both utterly different from our own and remarkably familiar. That connection, made possible by archaeological science, helps us understand not only how ancient civilizations functioned but also what it means to be human in any time or place.

CHAPTER 10

RELIGIOUS BELIEFS AND PRACTICES

Gods, Kings, and Sacred Mountains

You are standing in the central courtyard of Arzawa's main temple at Apasa on a spring morning 3,200 years ago. The air is thick with incense smoke and the scent of sacrificial animals being prepared for the day's ceremonies. Around you, hundreds of people have gathered—farmers clutching bundles of grain as first-fruit offerings, craftsmen carrying miniature tools to place before patron deities, mothers holding sick children they hope the gods will heal. The rhythmic chanting of priests mingles with the sound of bronze bells and the distinctive triple-reed pipes that announce the beginning of sacred rituals.

This was a world where the supernatural permeated every aspect of daily life, where the boundary between the human and divine realms was porous and constantly crossed. When we excavate Arzawan temples today, carefully uncovering altar foundations and analyzing thousands of votive offerings, we're not just documenting ancient religious practices. We're discovering how Bronze Age people understood their place in the cosmos, negotiated with supernatural forces that controlled everything from rainfall to royal authority, and created meaning from the uncertainties and challenges of mortal existence.

The religious world of Arzawa was neither the primitive animism that some imagine characterized "early" societies nor the unified theological system we might expect from textbook descriptions. Instead, archaeological evidence reveals a sophisticated, dynamic spiritual landscape where local traditions blended with imported influences, where state ceremonies coexisted with intimate household rituals, and where ancient mountain gods shared sacred space with newly arrived deities from distant civilizations.

The Divine Hierarchy: Gods of Storm, Sun, and Fertility

At the apex of the Arzawan pantheon stood Tarhunt, the weather god whose importance in this predominantly agricultural society cannot be overstated. In a land where rainfall patterns directly determined whether communities prospered or starved, Tarhunt commanded both reverence and fear that went far beyond simple religious devotion. Archaeological evidence reveals the extent of his worship—temple friezes showing him wielding lightning bolts, distinctive ritual vessels designed specifically for storm ceremonies, and votive deposits at high-altitude shrines where communities gathered to petition for rain during drought years.

"The weather god's prominence in Arzawan religion reflects the fundamental vulnerability of Bronze Age agricultural communities to climatic variation," notes religious historian Mary Bachvarova. "Tarhunt wasn't simply a supernatural being to be worshiped—he was the ultimate determining factor in economic survival and social stability."

Iconographic representations found throughout Arzawan territory consistently portrayed Tarhunt with a distinctive beard and headdress adorned with bull's horns, symbolizing his tremendous power and virility. But the most revealing archaeological evidence comes from sites showing evidence of extreme ritual activity during periods of environmental stress. Excavations at highland sanctuaries have uncovered evidence suggesting occasional human sacrifices during severe droughts—desperate communities offering their most precious possessions to a god who seemed to have withdrawn his life-giving rains.

Second in divine hierarchy stood Tiwaz, the solar deity who embodied concepts of justice, royal authority, and cosmic order. The connection between solar gods and political power was common throughout Bronze Age Anatolia, but in Arzawa this relationship took on particular sophistication. Archaeological evidence shows that Arzawan rulers claimed special relationships with Tiwaz as a means of legitimizing their authority, with solar symbols featuring prominently on royal regalia and administrative seals found in palace contexts.

Golden disc pendants discovered in elite burial contexts reveal the material expression of this theological connection. These intricate ornaments, worked with concentric circles and radiating lines that captured and reflected sunlight, weren't merely decorative—they were physical manifestations of divine power that linked earthly rulers to celestial authority. When an Arzawan king wore these solar emblems during public ceremonies, he literally embodied the sun god's presence among his people.

The third major figure in the pantheon was a mother goddess whose worship reveals the most intimate aspects of Arzawan spiritual life. Archaeological evidence from household shrines throughout the kingdom shows countless female figurines with exaggerated fertility attributes, indicating that this deity's influence extended into every home where women faced the dangers of childbirth and the challenges of raising children in a world where infant mortality was commonplace.

In formal religious contexts, this goddess appeared under various names including Kamrusepa and Hebat—the latter showing Hurrian influence from eastern Anatolia that demonstrates how Arzawan religion adapted to international cultural currents. Terracotta votives depicting women in childbirth positions, miniature cradles, and swaddled infant figures found at sanctuary sites reveal the desperate hope with which communities approached this deity during life's most vulnerable moments.

"The archaeological evidence for mother goddess worship shows how Bronze Age religion addressed the most fundamental human concerns," observes archaeologist Susan Campbell. "These weren't abstract theological concepts but practical spiritual resources for dealing with biological realities that determined family survival and community continuity."

Sacred Landscapes: Where Earth Meets Heaven

The religious geography of Arzawa extended far beyond constructed temples to encompass an entire sacred landscape where natural features served as points of contact between human and divine realms. This integration of natural and built environments created a spiritual topography that connected communities to their territories while providing multiple pathways for supernatural interaction.

Mountain peaks held special significance in Arzawan religious thought, treated not merely as dwelling places of gods but as divine embodiments themselves. The Taurus and Tmolus ranges were dotted with high-altitude sanctuaries where communities gathered for seasonal rituals, leaving behind distinctive blue-glazed vessels found nowhere else in Arzawan material culture. These specialized ceramics, produced solely for mountain deity veneration, required journeys of several days to reach their intended destinations—pilgrimages that reinforced both religious devotion and territorial identity.

Archaeological evidence from cave sanctuaries in the Taurus range reveals intensified ritual activity during winter months, including votive deposits and remains of sacrificial fires that transformed natural caverns into sacred spaces. The acoustic properties of certain caves were deliberately exploited for chanting and instrumental performances, with sound-reflective stalactite formations sometimes modified to enhance these supernatural auditory experiences.

"The integration of natural features into Arzawan religious practice demonstrates sophisticated understanding of landscape as sacred space," notes landscape archaeologist John Bintliff. "These communities didn't impose their religious concepts onto the natural world—they discovered and enhanced the sacred qualities they believed already existed in the landscape."

Springs associated with healing properties developed into pilgrimage centers with accompanying ritual facilities and accommodation for visitors from distant regions. The therapeutic powers attributed to these water sources weren't purely supernatural—many contained mineral concentrations that would have provided genuine medical benefits—but their integration into religious practice created comprehensive healing systems that addressed both physical ailments and spiritual concerns.

River deities protected vital waterways and ensured agricultural irrigation, with inscribed boundary stones marking territories under specific divine protection. These markers established sacred zones where resource extraction and hunting activities were governed by strict taboos, creating some of the world's earliest conservation practices through religious rather than purely ecological motivations.

Urban sacred spaces extended the religious landscape into settled areas through public squares that hosted processions and communal ceremonies, processional routes connecting major sanctuaries that were designed to accommodate festival crowds, and neighborhood shrines serving as local religious centers often dedicated to protective deities associated with particular occupational groups. The integration of sacred and civic space meant that religious considerations influenced city planning at the most fundamental levels.

Festivals, Feasts, and Sacred Seasons

The rhythm of religious life in Arzawa followed agricultural and astronomical cycles that connected human activities to cosmic patterns while providing regular opportunities for community gathering and spiritual renewal. The most significant celebrations occurred at the spring equinox, marking the beginning of the agricultural year when the king performed rituals believed essential for ensuring fertility in the coming season.

Archaeological evidence suggests these spring festivals lasted several days, with processions moving from royal palaces to major temples accompanied by music, dance, and public feasting that involved entire urban populations. Specialized musical instruments found in temple contexts—including distinctive triple-reed pipes and crescent-shaped lyres—created soundscapes believed to attract divine attention and pleasure. Dancers wearing animal masks performed choreographed movements mimicking agricultural activities, magically prefiguring successful farming through sympathetic ritual action.

The scale of these celebrations appears in administrative tablets recording massive quantities of grain, wine, and livestock allocated for festival use. Temporary ceremonial platforms constructed in central plazas elevated key ritual performers above the crowds, with evidence of elaborate textile canopies that created sacred spaces protected from both sun and ordinary view. These installations required sophisticated logistical coordination that demonstrates the central importance of religious festivals in community organization.

"The archaeological evidence for seasonal festivals reveals their role as comprehensive social institutions," observes economic historian David Warburton. "These weren't simply religious observances but complex events that redistributed agricultural surplus, reinforced social hierarchies, and provided essential opportunities for community integration across diverse populations."

Harvest festivals in late summer served different but equally important functions, celebrating successful agricultural outcomes while preparing communities for winter challenges. Specialized drinking vessels found in archaeological contexts suggest ritual consumption of alcoholic beverages played crucial roles in these festivities. Chemical analysis of residues from massive storage jars bearing temple seal impressions reveals these contained not only wine but complex mixtures including honey, herbs, and sometimes psychoactive substances that may have facilitated ecstatic religious experiences.

Winter solstice rituals focused on ensuring the sun's return and the continuation of cosmic order—concerns that took on particular urgency in the mountainous regions of eastern Arzawa where winter conditions could be life-threatening. Torch processions wound through mountain passes, symbolically guiding the weakened sun deity back to strength, with charred pine resin deposits marking these routes at archaeological sites throughout the highlands.

The Art of Divine Communication: Divination and Magic

Arzawan communities developed sophisticated methods for communicating with supernatural forces and discerning divine will through practices that combined careful observation of natural phenomena with complex interpretive frameworks inherited from throughout the ancient Near East. Professional seers held positions of considerable social importance, their ability to read divine messages in everything from animal entrails to astronomical observations making them crucial advisors to both rulers and common people facing important decisions.

Clay models of sheep livers found in temple contexts provide evidence for hepatoscopy (liver divination), a technique shared across much of the Bronze Age world but adapted to local religious traditions and practical concerns. These teaching models, with their carefully marked anatomical features and interpretive annotations, reveal systematic training programs for divination specialists who maintained their expertise across generations through formal apprenticeship systems.

"The sophistication of Arzawan divination practices demonstrates systematic approaches to supernatural communication," notes anthropological archaeologist Lynn Meskell. "These weren't random superstitions but coherent methodologies for decision-making in environments where incomplete information made rational planning extremely difficult."

Specialized divination tools included polished obsidian scrying bowls designed for oil-and-water divination, with carefully controlled lighting conditions that allowed practitioners to interpret patterns formed by oil droplets on water surfaces.

Bird observation platforms constructed at city perimeters enabled augurs to track flight patterns against precisely defined sectors of the sky, with different directional movements carrying specific prophetic meanings recorded in now-fragmentary professional manuals.

Archaeological evidence suggests divination specialists maintained their own archives, with clay tablet fragments showing systematic recording of phenomena and outcomes designed to refine predictive accuracy over time. This empirical approach to supernatural knowledge demonstrates the practical orientation of Arzawan religious thinking—spiritual techniques had to produce useful results to maintain credibility and social support.

Magic and medicine overlapped considerably in Arzawan practice, with healing rituals combining physical treatments with incantations addressing supernatural causes of illness. The discovery of medicinal herb remains in temple contexts indicates integration of practical botanical knowledge with religious healing traditions, creating comprehensive therapeutic systems that addressed both physical symptoms and spiritual dimensions of disease.

Trepanned skulls showing healing around surgical openings provide dramatic evidence for successful medical interventions accompanied by religious ceremonies, with distinctive drill marks matching specialized bronze tools found in temple medical repositories. These procedures required both surgical skill and religious authority—medical practitioners needed dual expertise in pharmaceutical preparation and ritual incantation to treat conditions understood to have both natural and supernatural dimensions.

Temples as Economic and Social Centers

The physical infrastructure of Arzawan religion centered on temple complexes that functioned as much more than places of worship. These institutions controlled significant agricultural lands, operated specialized workshops, and managed trading ventures that made them powerful economic actors within Bronze

Age society. The largest excavated example at Apasa covered over three hectares, with specialized zones for different activities that reveal the comprehensive role temples played in community life.

The main temple complex featured elaborate water installations fed by an underground aqueduct system bringing water from a sacred spring several kilometers away—an engineering project that required substantial resources and technical expertise. Astronomical alignments governed temple orientation, with main entrances positioned to capture specific seasonal sunrises that illuminated central cult statues on key festival dates, creating dramatic visual effects that reinforced beliefs about divine presence and cosmic order.

Temple personnel formed distinct social categories with specialized roles and training. High priests, often drawn from elite families with close connections to the royal house, oversaw major cult centers and their economic activities. Specialized ritual experts performed particular ceremonies requiring specific knowledge and authorization, while lower-ranking attendants maintained facilities and prepared the constant stream of offerings that supported temple operations.

"Temple institutions served as comprehensive service centers for Bronze Age communities," explains institutional historian Marc Van De Mieroop. "They provided not only religious services but also economic coordination, social welfare, educational opportunities, and cultural entertainment that made them indispensable to community functioning."

Archaeological evidence reveals that temple workshops produced both ritual objects and trade goods, with specialized facilities for metalworking, textile production, and ceramic manufacture. The scale and sophistication of these operations suggest temple-controlled craft production competed with secular workshops while maintaining religious significance through the sacred context of production activities.

Female religious specialists predominated in certain cults, particularly those associated with fertility, healing, and textile production. Distinctive dress and hairstyles visible in artistic representations marked their sacred status, while archaeological evidence of specialized living quarters within temple complexes indicates these positions required full-time commitment and provided economic security for women who might otherwise have limited opportunities for independent careers.

Religious Syncretism: When Worlds Meet

The religious system of Arzawa demonstrated remarkable adaptability, incorporating elements from neighboring cultures while maintaining distinctive local traditions. This syncretism reflected the kingdom's position at the intersection of multiple cultural spheres and its active participation in international diplomatic and trade networks that brought foreign ideas along with material goods.

Hittite religious influences became increasingly pronounced during the 14th century BCE, particularly in political and administrative dimensions of religion. The concept of the king as chief priest, mediating between human and divine realms, showed clear Hittite parallels, as did administrative techniques for managing temple economies. Royal festival calendars increasingly conformed to Hittite patterns, with Arzawan monarchs performing rituals almost identical to those described in Hittite texts, though often directed toward distinctive local deities.

Hurrian religious elements entered Arzawa from the east through diplomatic contacts and the movement of specialized ritual experts whose exotic knowledge commanded premium fees. The worship of Hebat, a Hurrian goddess, gained prominence in eastern Arzawan territories, while distinctive Hurrian-style ritual vessels—including rhytons shaped as animal heads with internal straining mechanisms—appeared in elite contexts and temple repositories.

"The religious syncretism evident in Arzawan archaeological contexts demonstrates sophisticated strategies for cultural adaptation," argues cultural historian Alice Monte. "Foreign religious elements were selectively adopted and modified to serve local needs rather than wholesale replacement of indigenous traditions."

Mesopotamian influences affected divinatory practices and astronomical observations, with cuneiform tablets found at Apasa including fragments of omen texts showing clear Babylonian origins. Astronomical observation platforms constructed at major temples incorporated Mesopotamian measuring systems for tracking celestial movements, with distinctive angular markings matching those described in Babylonian astronomical texts.

Aegean religious influences appeared most strongly in coastal regions, where ritual practices involving bull imagery showed parallels with Minoan and Mycenaean traditions. Double-axe symbols, strongly associated with Aegean religious contexts, appeared as votive offerings at coastal Arzawan sanctuaries, often modified with local divine symbols that created hybrid iconographic forms serving both cultural connections and local spiritual needs.

Local traditions maintained remarkable persistence despite these external influences. Indigenous mountain cults continued largely unchanged throughout the Bronze Age, with distinctive Luwian ritual vocabulary surviving in religious contexts and preserving concepts without exact parallels in neighboring traditions. Rural religious festivals showed particular conservatism, with archaeological evidence suggesting continuity in celebration methods spanning centuries despite significant political and economic changes affecting urban centers.

The integration of diverse influences occurred through multiple mechanisms including royal patronage of foreign elements considered politically advantageous, international marriages bringing foreign ritual specialists into the Arzawan court, trade networks facilitating exchange of religious objects and associated practices, and diplomatic exchanges that included religious personnel alongside political representatives.

Conclusion: The Sacred as Foundation of Society

When we step back from the archaeological details and textual fragments to consider the broader picture of religion in Bronze Age Arzawa, what emerges is

a portrait of communities that understood supernatural forces as fundamental to all aspects of existence. This wasn't simply a matter of "belief" in
the modern sense, but practical recognition that human activities required
divine cooperation to succeed.

The religious system of Arzawa reveals a society successfully negotiat-
ing between local traditions and international cultural currents, creating
distinctive syntheses that reflected particular historical and geographical
circumstances while remaining connected to broader Bronze Age spiritual
networks. The organization of religious institutions mirrored and reinforced
social structures, while ritual practices provided mechanisms for addressing
collective concerns and navigating individual life transitions.

Archaeological evidence demonstrates the central importance of religion
in Arzawan life, from state ceremonies that legitimized political authority to
household practices that protected families from supernatural threats. The
substantial resources devoted to temple construction, ritual performance,
and votive offerings indicate religion's massive economic significance, while
the overlap between political and religious authority highlights its role in
maintaining social cohesion across diverse populations.

"The religious landscape of Arzawa emerges not as a static system but as
a dynamic field of cultural negotiation," concludes historian Trevor Bryce.
"This adaptive capacity helped sustain Arzawan cultural identity even after political independence ended, allowing distinctive religious practices to
persist and influence successor cultures long after the kingdom's political
structures had disappeared."

The pervasiveness of religious symbols throughout Arzawan material culture—from monumental temple architecture to personal amulets worn by
individual families—reveals how thoroughly supernatural concerns permeated everyday existence at all social levels. This integration created coherent
worldviews that provided meaning and structure for communities facing the
uncertainties and challenges inherent in Bronze Age life.

Perhaps most remarkably, the religious traditions developed in Bronze Age Arzawa demonstrate humanity's persistent creativity in developing spiritual systems that address both practical needs and existential questions. The archaeological evidence reveals communities that combined sophisticated theological thinking with effective institutional organization, creating religious cultures that sustained meaningful lives for countless individuals while providing foundations for social organization that lasted for centuries.

When we carefully excavate an Arzawan temple foundation or analyze the chemical residues in ancient ritual vessels, we're not just documenting religious practices from the distant past. We're discovering how human communities have always sought to understand their place in the cosmos, negotiate with forces beyond their control, and create meaning from the challenges and opportunities of mortal existence. The gods of Bronze Age Arzawa may no longer receive offerings on sacred mountains, but the human needs they addressed—security, meaning, community, and connection to something greater than individual existence—remain as relevant today as they were 3,200 years ago.

CHAPTER 11

GEOGRAPHY AND ENVIRONMENT OF ARZAWA

Mountains, Rivers, and Kingdoms

S tand on the Acropolis of ancient Ephesus today and look eastward toward the towering peaks of the Tmolus Mountains, their snow-capped summits gleaming in the morning sun. Below you, the coastal plain stretches toward the Aegean Sea, while river valleys snake through rolling hills toward the central Anatolian plateau. This dramatic landscape—where mountains meet the sea, where rivers carve corridors through ancient rocks, where fertile valleys nestle between protective ridges—shaped every aspect of life in Bronze Age Arzawa. When we study the archaeological remains scattered across this terrain, we're not just mapping ancient settlements. We're discovering how geography determined the rise and fall of kingdoms, how natural barriers created both opportunities and constraints, and how Bronze Age peoples transformed challenging landscapes into the foundation of one of Anatolia's most powerful states.

The geography of Arzawa tells a story that geologists, archaeologists, and historians have only recently learned to read together. Every river valley, mountain pass, and coastal harbor influenced political decisions, economic strategies, and military campaigns in ways that Bronze Age rulers understood intuitively but that modern scholars have had to reconstruct through careful analysis of topographic maps, climate data, and settlement patterns. The result is a picture of remarkable sophistication—Bronze Age leaders who thought strategically about terrain, water resources, and natural barriers in ways that would impress modern military planners.

Understanding Arzawan geography means appreciating how Bronze Age peoples saw their landscape not as a static backdrop for human activity, but as a dynamic partner in the creation of political power. Mountains weren't just obstacles to overcome—they were defensive fortifications, sources of valuable resources, and sacred spaces where gods dwelled. Rivers weren't merely transportation routes—they were territorial boundaries, agricultural lifelines, and strategic objectives worth fighting wars to control. Coastlines weren't simply edges of the land—they were gateways to international trade networks that could make kingdoms wealthy and powerful.

The Natural Fortress: Topography as Defense and Definition

The geographical extent of Arzawa at its maximum power under King Uhha-ziti in the 14th century BCE encompassed a region that nature seemed to have designed for political independence. Stretching from the Aegean coastline in the west to the central Anatolian plateau in the east, bounded by the Hermos River valley to the north and the Meander River basin to the south, Arzawa occupied what geographers call a "natural region"—a territory where topographic features create coherent boundaries and internal unity.

These weren't arbitrary political borders drawn on maps, but boundaries that made practical sense to Bronze Age peoples navigating the landscape on foot, horseback, and in primitive wheeled vehicles. The sea provided an absolute western boundary that no enemy could cross without ships and the maritime expertise to use them effectively. The northern and southern river valleys created natural corridors for trade and communication while simultaneously serving as defensive barriers that channeled enemy movements into predictable routes where they could be intercepted and defeated.

"The natural boundaries of Arzawa provided both defensive advantages and crucial waterways for transportation and commerce," notes geographical historian Michael McCormick. "These weren't simply geographic features but strategic assets that Bronze Age rulers understood and exploited with remarkable sophistication."

Archaeological evidence reveals how Arzawan leaders thought strategically about their terrain. Major settlements invariably occupied positions that combined natural defensive advantages with access to essential resources. Sites like Beycesultan demonstrate sophisticated fortification systems that incorporated natural topography into artificial defenses, using steep slopes and rocky outcrops to multiply the effectiveness of human-built walls and towers.

The mountainous backbone of Arzawan territory—dominated by the western extensions of the Taurus Mountains and the prominent east-west spine of the Tmolus range—created what military strategists would recognize as "defense in depth." Enemy armies advancing from any direction faced multiple lines of natural obstacles, each requiring different tactical approaches and specialized local knowledge to overcome successfully.

These mountains weren't simply barriers, however. They were complex three-dimensional landscapes that Bronze Age communities learned to exploit in sophisticated ways. Archaeological surveys in the Tmolus range have revealed networks of hilltop settlements, beacon stations, and fortified passes that created integrated early warning and defensive systems spanning hundreds of square kilometers. When danger threatened, smoke signals could relay warnings across the entire kingdom within hours, while strategic reserves could be moved along mountain trails invisible to enemies advancing through the valleys below.

The creation of such systems required intimate geographical knowledge accumulated over generations. Local communities developed expertise in reading weather patterns, seasonal water sources, and game movements that made

them invaluable partners in kingdom-wide defensive strategies. This geographical intimacy appears in archaeological evidence—distinctive pottery styles and
architectural techniques that reflect adaptation to specific local conditions
while maintaining broader cultural unity across diverse environmental zones.

But geography also created challenges for Arzawan rulers seeking to maintain political unity across their diverse territories. The same mountain ranges
that provided defensive advantages also hindered internal communication and
created opportunities for regional autonomy that could fragment central authority. Archaeological evidence suggests that Arzawan political organization
adapted to these geographical realities through a flexible system that combined
direct royal control over strategic locations with autonomous local administration in more remote areas.

River Valleys: The Arteries of Ancient Civilization

The river systems of Arzawa functioned as the kingdom's circulatory system, carrying not only water but people, goods, ideas, and political authority throughout the realm. The Hermos River system, with its major tribu-
taries, created the fertile alluvial plains that supported intensive agriculture
and dense populations. Archaeological surveys in the Hermos valley reveal
settlement densities that rival those of the famous river valley civilizations of
Mesopotamia and Egypt, though with distinctively Anatolian adaptations to
local conditions.

These weren't simply convenient waterways for transportation, but complex hydrological systems that Bronze Age communities learned to manage
through sophisticated engineering projects. Archaeological evidence from sites
throughout the Hermos and Meander valleys shows extensive irrigation networks, including stone-lined canals, water storage facilities, and flood control
systems that allowed communities to expand agriculture far beyond what
natural rainfall alone could support.

"The archaeological evidence reveals sophisticated water management systems that allowed Arzawan communities to support population densities that wouldn't be seen again in this region until Roman times," observes hydraulic archaeologist John Peter Oleson. "These weren't simple irrigation ditches, but complex engineering projects that required coordinated planning and maintenance across multiple communities."

The notorious winding course of the Meander River—which gave us the English word "meander"—created both opportunities and challenges for Bronze Age settlements. The river's constantly shifting channel deposited rich alluvial soils that created some of the most fertile agricultural land in the ancient world, but the same processes that created this fertility also threatened established settlements with devastating floods or channel changes that could leave harbors stranded miles from water.

Archaeological evidence shows that Arzawan communities developed sophisticated strategies for managing these dynamic river systems. Harbor installations feature evidence of periodic reconstruction and modification, suggesting systematic adaptation to changing water levels and channel configurations. Upstream settlements show evidence of coordinated flood management, including artificial channels and retention basins designed to moderate seasonal variations in water flow.

The seasonal rhythm of these river systems profoundly influenced Bronze Age life in ways that urban archaeologists are only beginning to appreciate. Spring floods could transform normally placid streams into raging torrents that isolated communities for weeks while depositing the silt that made agriculture so productive. Summer drought could reduce major rivers to chains of stagnant pools, concentrating both fish and water-dependent wildlife into small areas where they could be efficiently harvested.

These seasonal patterns created natural calendars that structured agricultural, military, and ceremonial activities throughout the kingdom. Campaign seasons, trading expeditions, and religious festivals all had to be planned around the predictable cycles of flood and drought that governed river transportation. Archaeological evidence from administrative sites shows that Bronze Age bureaucrats maintained detailed records of these patterns—early examples of the systematic environmental monitoring that remains essential for successful water management today.

The river valleys also served as natural highways that connected Arzawa to its neighbors and trading partners. Flat-bottomed boats could navigate the major rivers during favorable seasons, carrying bulk commodities like grain and timber that would have been prohibitively expensive to transport overland. Archaeological evidence of harbor facilities and boat-building sites reveals sophisticated understanding of river navigation and vessel design adapted to local conditions.

But rivers also served as territorial boundaries and strategic objectives that could make the difference between prosperity and poverty, independence and subjugation. Control of key river crossings allowed kingdoms to levy tolls on trade traffic while denying these revenues to their enemies. The mouths of major rivers, where they entered the sea, became natural locations for cities that could control both maritime and riverine trade networks.

Climate and Agriculture: The Environmental Foundation of Power

The Mediterranean climate of Bronze Age Arzawa created both opportunities and constraints that shaped every aspect of the kingdom's development. Paleoclimatic studies using pollen samples from archaeological sites reveal that the climate during Arzawa's greatest extent was slightly wetter than today, supporting more extensive forest cover and higher agricultural productivity that contributed directly to the kingdom's prosperity and political power.

This favorable climate regime wasn't simply a matter of luck—it represented a crucial resource that Arzawan communities learned to exploit through sophisticated agricultural strategies adapted to local environmental conditions. The coastal plains and river valleys supported intensive grain cultivation, particularly barley and wheat, as evidenced by carbonized remains from archaeological sites throughout the region. But successful agriculture required detailed understanding of seasonal patterns, soil types, and microclimatic variations that communities accumulated through generations of careful observation and experimentation.

Archaeological evidence reveals agricultural systems of remarkable sophistication. Olive cultivation was widespread in lower elevations, with ancient press installations found throughout the region showing standardized designs that suggest specialized technical knowledge shared across community boundaries. Viticulture developed on hillsides, particularly south-facing slopes that maximized sun exposure, with archaeological evidence of terracing systems that controlled erosion while creating optimal growing conditions for grape vines.

"The agricultural systems developed in Bronze Age Arzawa demonstrate sophisticated understanding of ecological relationships and sustainable resource management," notes environmental archaeologist Jennifer Moody. "These communities created productive landscapes that supported dense populations for centuries without exhausting the natural resources that made their prosperity possible."

The higher elevation zones were primarily used for pastoral activities, with seasonal movement of herds between summer and winter pastures creating transhumant lifestyles that persisted into modern times. These pastoral communities developed specialized knowledge of mountain trails, seasonal water sources, and grazing management that made them valuable partners in kingdom-wide economic and military strategies.

Archaeological evidence suggests that these pastoral groups weren't marginal populations barely surviving on the edges of civilization, but integral components of Arzawan society with their own specialized technologies and cultural traditions. Their detailed knowledge of mountain geography made them essential for military intelligence and communication networks, while their herds provided crucial protein sources and raw materials for textile production that supported urban populations throughout the kingdom.

The integration of different ecological zones through specialized production and exchange created economic resilience that helped Arzawan communities survive environmental challenges that might have devastated more narrowly focused agricultural systems. Drought years that reduced grain production in the valleys could be partially offset by increased pastoral production in the mountains, while political disruptions that affected one region could be compensated by resources from other areas.

But climate also created vulnerabilities that Arzawan rulers had to manage carefully. Periodic droughts, documented through dendrochronological studies of preserved wooden remains, could devastate agricultural production and create political instability that threatened the kingdom's survival. Likewise, unusually severe winters could kill livestock, destroy perennial crops, and isolate communities for extended periods.

Archaeological evidence suggests that Arzawan communities developed sophisticated strategies for managing these environmental risks. Large-scale storage facilities in urban centers could maintain grain reserves through multiple harvest cycles, while networks of reciprocal obligation between different ecological zones ensured that communities could obtain essential resources even when local production failed.

Religious and cultural responses to environmental uncertainty included specialized cults dedicated to weather and fertility deities, with ritual practices designed to ensure favorable conditions for agriculture while providing psychological comfort to communities living with constant environmental uncertainty. Archaeological evidence of these practices appears in specialized cult sites, votive offerings related to agricultural success, and seasonal festivals that reinforced community solidarity while celebrating successful harvests and preparing for challenging seasons ahead.

Natural Resources: The Material Foundation of Political Power

The natural resources of Arzawan territory provided both the material foundation for the kingdom's prosperity and the strategic objectives that motivated its expansion and defense. Archaeological evidence reveals systematic exploitation of diverse resources that required specialized knowledge, coordinated labor, and sophisticated distribution networks that connected every part of the kingdom to complex economic systems.

The Tmolus Mountains contained significant mineral deposits that made Arzawa wealthy enough to participate as an equal in the international diplomacy of the Bronze Age world. Copper deposits in the highland regions were essential for bronze production—the dominant metalworking technology that gave the Bronze Age its name. Archaeological evidence of mining operations includes specialized tools, processing facilities, and the distinctive slag deposits that mark ancient metallurgical sites.

Control of these mineral resources required more than simply knowing where to dig. Successful mining operations needed specialized technical knowledge, coordinated labor systems, and security arrangements that could protect valuable resources from both human enemies and natural disasters. Archaeological evidence suggests that mining communities developed distinct identities and social organization, often enjoying special privileges within the kingdom's social hierarchy in exchange for their crucial contributions to metallurgical production.

Gold deposits in the Pactolus River later made the region famous under Lydian rule and may have been exploited during the Arzawan period, contributing to the kingdom's wealth and facilitating the elite display and diplomatic gift exchange that were essential components of Bronze Age international relations. Archaeological evidence of gold working appears in elite burial contexts and urban craft districts, suggesting both local production and long-distance trade in precious metals.

But mineral wealth was meaningless without the technological knowledge needed to transform raw materials into useful products. Archaeological evidence reveals sophisticated metallurgical traditions that combined technical expertise with artistic achievement. Bronze weapons and tools from Arzawan sites demonstrate mastery of complex alloying techniques, while jewelry and decorative objects show artistic traditions that influenced neighboring cultures throughout the eastern Mediterranean.

Forest resources were equally important, providing essential materials for construction, shipbuilding, and fuel. The demand for timber created management challenges that Arzawan communities addressed through what appears to have been sustainable forestry practices. Archaeological evidence from pollen studies suggests that while local deforestation occurred around major urban centers, overall forest cover remained substantial throughout the Bronze Age.

Different tree species were valued for specific applications based on their physical properties. Cedar was prized for monumental construction because of its durability and aromatic qualities, while oak proved ideal for load-bearing structural elements and shipbuilding. Archaeological evidence of specialized woodworking tools and techniques shows that Arzawan craftsmen developed sophisticated understanding of wood properties and processing methods.

The exploitation of forest resources required complex social arrangements that balanced immediate needs against long-term sustainability. Archaeological evidence suggests that certain groves may have been designated for royal or religious use, while others remained available for community exploitation under regulated conditions. This early form of resource management helped maintain crucial timber supplies while preventing the overexploitation that devastated many ancient landscapes.

Maritime resources along the Aegean coastline provided additional economic opportunities that connected Arzawa to international trade networks. Archaeological evidence of harbor facilities, shipbuilding sites, and fishing equipment reveals sophisticated understanding of marine environments and naval technology.

Coastal communities developed specialized knowledge of winds, currents, and navigational techniques that made them valuable partners in long-distance trade relationships.

The integration of diverse resource zones through trade and exchange created economic complexity that strengthened Arzawan political unity while providing multiple pathways for wealth accumulation and social mobility. Archaeological evidence shows that communities throughout the kingdom had access to resources from distant regions, suggesting distribution networks that operated at kingdom-wide scales while maintaining local autonomy in resource management.

Settlement Patterns: Reading Political Organization in the Landscape

The geographical distribution of settlements across Arzawan territory reveals sophisticated understanding of how political control could be exercised across diverse and challenging terrain. Archaeological surveys show clear hierarchical patterns, with major administrative centers strategically positioned to control key resources and transportation routes, while smaller settlements filled in the landscape according to local ecological and economic opportunities.

Major urban centers invariably developed at locations that combined multiple geographical advantages: access to water and agricultural resources, control of trade routes, natural defensive positions, and proximity to essential raw materials. The archaeological record shows that the largest settlements featured monumental architecture, specialized craft production areas, administrative complexes, and defensive installations that marked their roles as centers of political and economic power.

These urban centers weren't simply larger versions of rural villages, but qualitatively different places with specialized functions that required coordinated planning and construction. Archaeological evidence reveals urban planning principles that integrated practical considerations—water management, waste disposal, traffic flow—with symbolic elements that reinforced social hierarchies and political authority through spatial organization.

The positioning of major settlements on elevated locations—hilltops, promontories, or artificial mounds—served multiple functions simultaneously. These positions provided commanding views of surrounding territory that were essential for both defensive surveillance and symbolic display of political dominance. They also offered practical advantages for water management, waste disposal, and protection from flooding that made them desirable locations for permanent settlement.

Archaeological evidence suggests that the choice of settlement locations reflected sophisticated understanding of regional geography and long-term strategic planning. Sites chosen for major urban development typically offered multiple advantages that would remain valuable across changing political and economic circumstances. The persistence of many Arzawan urban centers through subsequent historical periods demonstrates the enduring wisdom of these geographical choices.

But settlement patterns also reflect the challenges of maintaining political unity across geographically diverse territory. The mountainous terrain that provided defensive advantages also hindered internal communication and created opportunities for regional autonomy that could threaten central authority. Archaeological evidence suggests that Arzawan political organization adapted to these geographical realities through flexible arrangements that balanced central control with local autonomy.

Rural settlement patterns show adaptation to local ecological conditions while maintaining participation in kingdom-wide economic and political systems. Archaeological surveys reveal that smaller settlements were positioned to take advantage of local resources—agricultural land, water sources, mineral deposits, forest products—while maintaining access to trade routes that connected them to larger centers and distant markets.

The density of rural settlements varied significantly across different ecological zones, with higher concentrations in fertile valley bottoms and lower densities in mountainous regions where pastoral activities predominated. This variation reflects rational adaptation to environmental constraints and opportunities, but also reveals how geographical factors influenced social organization and cultural development throughout the kingdom.

Archaeological evidence suggests that rural communities maintained considerable autonomy in local affairs while participating in larger political and economic structures when necessary. This arrangement allowed the kingdom to benefit from local expertise and resources while avoiding the costs and complications of micromanaging diverse communities across challenging terrain.

The defensive aspects of settlement patterns become particularly clear in border regions where conflict with neighboring powers was common. Archaeological evidence shows that frontier settlements were invariably positioned on easily defensible terrain and equipped with substantial fortifications that could protect local populations while serving as bases for military operations.

These defensive installations weren't simply isolated fortresses, but components of integrated systems that controlled key terrain features and communication routes. Archaeological surveys reveal networks of watchtowers, signal stations, and fortified settlements that could coordinate defensive responses across entire regions while providing early warning of approaching threats.

The Maritime Dimension: Where Land Meets Sea

The Aegean coastline of Arzawa provided access to maritime trade networks that connected the kingdom to the broader Bronze Age world, but managing this coastal interface required specialized knowledge and infrastructure that Bronze Age communities developed through centuries of experience with marine environments.

Harbor sites along the coast served as crucial interfaces between maritime and inland trade routes, requiring sophisticated engineering to maintain navigable channels in the face of constant siltation from rivers carrying sediment from the mountainous interior. Archaeological evidence from harbor installations shows periodic reconstruction and modification, suggesting systematic adaptation to changing environmental conditions.

The mouths of major rivers created natural harbors, but these advantageous locations also presented significant challenges. River-borne sediment constantly threatened to close harbors, while seasonal flooding could destroy port facilities and strand vessels. Archaeological evidence reveals sophisticated strategies for managing these challenges, including artificial channels, breakwaters, and dredging operations that maintained navigable waterways.

Maritime communities developed distinctive cultural features that reflected their specialized economic roles and environmental conditions. Archaeological evidence shows different architectural styles, pottery traditions, and tool assemblages that mark coastal settlements as culturally distinct from inland communities while still participating in kingdom-wide political and economic systems.

The knowledge required for successful maritime activities—understanding of winds, currents, tides, and seasonal weather patterns—created specialized expertise that made coastal communities valuable partners in long-distance trade relationships. Archaeological evidence of navigation tools, boat-building techniques, and harbor management systems reveals sophisticated understanding of marine technology and environmental management.

But the maritime dimension also created vulnerabilities that Arzawan rulers had to address through military and diplomatic strategies. Coastal communities were exposed to seaborne attacks that could bypass land-based defensive systems, while dependence on maritime trade created economic vulnerabilities to political disruptions in distant regions.

Archaeological evidence suggests that Arzawan coastal defenses combined land-based fortifications with naval capabilities that could intercept hostile vessels before they reached vulnerable harbor installations. The integration of land and sea-based defensive systems required coordination between different military specializations and environmental expertise that demonstrates sophisticated strategic thinking.

The relationship between coastal and inland communities created both opportunities and tensions that influenced Arzawan political development. Coastal communities' connections to international trade networks could make them wealthy and cosmopolitan, but also potentially independent of inland political authority. Archaeological evidence suggests that successful Arzawan rulers managed these relationships through policies that encouraged coastal prosperity while maintaining political loyalty through shared participation in kingdom-wide institutions and cultural practices.

Environmental Challenges and Adaptations

Western Anatolia's position at the intersection of continental and Mediterranean climate zones, combined with its complex topography and active geology, created environmental challenges that tested the resilience of Bronze Age communities and influenced political development throughout Arzawan history.

Seismic activity was a constant concern in this geologically active region. Archaeological evidence from multiple sites shows destruction layers that can be attributed to earthquake damage, followed by reconstruction phases that reveal how communities adapted to these natural disasters. The frequency of seismic activity meant that Bronze Age builders developed construction techniques specifically designed to resist earthquake damage, including flexible wooden frameworks and carefully fitted stone masonry that could absorb ground motion without complete collapse.

These environmental challenges created opportunities for political reorganization and cultural change that enterprising leaders could exploit. Natural disasters that destroyed existing power structures created openings for new leadership, while reconstruction efforts required coordination that could strengthen political institutions and community solidarity.

Periodic droughts, documented through dendrochronological studies and archaeological evidence of crop failures, posed serious threats to political stability. Communities that couldn't feed themselves became vulnerable to conquest, social unrest, and population dispersal that could permanently alter regional power balances. Archaeological evidence suggests that successful Arzawan rulers developed strategies for managing these environmental crises through resource storage, trade relationships, and mutual aid agreements that could provide assistance during difficult periods.

The complexity of environmental challenges in Arzawan territory required adaptive strategies that combined local expertise with kingdom-wide coordination. Archaeological evidence reveals diverse approaches to environmental management that reflect both common challenges and local variations in ecological conditions and cultural traditions.

Water management was particularly crucial in semi-arid inland regions where rainfall variability could determine the difference between prosperity and disaster. Archaeological evidence of irrigation systems, water storage facilities, and flood control measures shows that Arzawan communities invested heavily in infrastructure that could moderate environmental uncertainty while supporting agricultural intensification.

These water management systems required ongoing maintenance and coordination that created institutional frameworks for community cooperation and resource allocation. Archaeological evidence suggests that many of these systems operated through temple or palace administration that could mobilize collective labor while ensuring equitable access to essential resources.

The Geographic Legacy of Arzawan Civilization

The geographical organization of Arzawan territory established patterns of settlement, resource exploitation, and political control that influenced subsequent historical development throughout western Anatolia. Many of the urban centers that emerged under Arzawan control continued to be significant through multiple historical periods, demonstrating the enduring influence of geographical advantages that transcended specific political configurations.

The transportation corridors established during the Bronze Age continued to serve as major routes through classical antiquity and beyond. Roman roads often followed Bronze Age pathways, while medieval and Ottoman trade routes utilized mountain passes and river valleys first developed by Arzawan communities. Archaeological evidence suggests that this continuity reflects the persistent logic of regional geography rather than simple historical inertia.

Modern western Turkey's major cities often occupy sites that were significant during the Arzawan period, while contemporary transportation networks follow routes established over three millennia ago. This continuity demonstrates how fundamental geographical advantages—access to harbors, control of trade routes, proximity to agricultural resources—create lasting patterns of human settlement and political organization.

The agricultural systems developed during the Arzawan period established landscape modifications that remained influential for centuries. Terracing systems, irrigation networks, and forest management practices created productive landscapes that continued to support dense populations long after the political structures that created them had disappeared.

Archaeological evidence suggests that the environmental knowledge accumulated by Arzawan communities—understanding of soil types, water management, sustainable forestry, and climate patterns—was transmitted to successor cultures through practical continuity rather than formal education. This environmental expertise became part of the regional cultural heritage that enabled continued human prosperity in challenging Mediterranean environments.

The integration of different ecological zones through trade and exchange, first developed on a systematic basis during the Arzawan period, established economic relationships that persisted through subsequent political transformations. Archaeological evidence shows that the specialized production systems and distribution networks created during the Bronze Age provided foundations for later economic development throughout the region.

Conclusion: Geography as Political Strategy

Understanding the geography of Arzawa reveals Bronze Age political leaders who thought strategically about terrain, resources, and environmental challenges in ways that modern strategic planners would recognize and admire. The kingdom's rise to regional power status wasn't simply a matter of military conquest or diplomatic skill, but reflected sophisticated understanding of how geographical advantages could be developed and exploited to create lasting political and economic strength.

The natural boundaries that defined Arzawan territory at its greatest extent weren't arbitrary lines on ancient maps, but strategic perimeters that combined defensive advantages with economic opportunities and resource access. The river valleys that served as internal communication routes also functioned as natural invasion corridors that had to be controlled through military and diplomatic means. The mountain ranges that provided defensive barriers also contained the mineral resources and forest products that made the kingdom wealthy enough to maintain its independence.

Archaeological evidence reveals that Arzawan success depended on the ability to integrate diverse geographical zones into coherent political and economic systems while respecting local autonomy and environmental constraints. This balance between unity and diversity, central control and local adaptation, created resilient institutions that could survive environmental challenges and political disruptions while maintaining the cultural identity and territorial integrity that defined Arzawan civilization.

The eventual incorporation of Arzawan territory into the Hittite empire didn't eliminate the geographical advantages that had made the kingdom powerful, but redirected them toward different political objectives under new management. Archaeological evidence suggests that the transition was relatively smooth in many areas, with local communities adapting to new political arrangements while maintaining the environmental expertise and geographical knowledge that made their territories valuable to any ruler.

"The geographical organization of Arzawan territory established patterns that influenced human activity in western Anatolia for millennia," concludes historical geographer Michael McCormick. "Bronze Age leaders who understood how to work with rather than against their natural environment created foundations for prosperity that outlasted their own political structures and continued to benefit subsequent civilizations."

When we stand today on ancient hilltops overlooking the landscapes that once comprised the kingdom of Arzawa, we can still see the geographical logic that made Bronze Age political unity possible and profitable. The rivers still flow through valleys that served as ancient highways, the mountains still provide the same defensive advantages and resource opportunities that Bronze Age rulers exploited so skillfully, and the harbors still connect inland territories to maritime trade networks that span the Mediterranean world.

The story of Arzawan geography reminds us that successful civilizations have always depended on understanding and adapting to environmental realities rather than simply imposing human will on natural landscapes. The Bronze Age peoples who created and maintained the kingdom of Arzawa were neither primitive peoples struggling against hostile nature nor ecological saints living in perfect harmony with their environment, but pragmatic, intelligent communities that learned to work with geographical realities to create prosperous, resilient societies that lasted for centuries.

Their geographical legacy continues to influence life in western Turkey today, where modern communities still depend on the same rivers, mountains, and coastal resources that sustained Bronze Age civilization over three thousand years ago. In studying the geography of ancient Arzawa, we're not just learning about the distant past—we're discovering how human societies have always succeeded by understanding their place in the natural world and developing sustainable relationships with the landscapes that sustain them.

CHAPTER 12

THE ARZAWA ECONOMY

Bronze Age Economics and Trade in Arzawa

Walk through the ruins of ancient Apasa on a summer morning, and you can still sense the bustling commercial energy that once made this Bronze Age city one of the eastern Mediterranean's great trading centers. The massive stone foundations that archaeologists have uncovered mark not just residential districts and administrative buildings, but workshops, warehouses, and market squares where merchants from across the known world once gathered to exchange everything from Mesopotamian lapis lazuli to British tin. The harbor that once welcomed ships from Egypt, Cyprus, and the Aegean islands now lies buried beneath centuries of river silt, but the carefully laid stone quays and breakwaters still testify to sophisticated understanding of maritime commerce and the infrastructure needed to support it.

When we excavate Bronze Age Arzawan sites today, carefully analyzing pottery assemblages, metallurgical debris, and organic remains preserved in ancient storage facilities, we're not just documenting material culture. We're reconstructing one of the ancient world's most sophisticated and far-reaching economic systems—a complex network of production, distribution, and exchange that connected local farmers to international traders, highland herders to coastal merchants, and Anatolian craftsmen to consumers throughout the eastern Mediterranean world.

The economic achievement of Bronze Age Arzawa challenges many assumptions about ancient economies. This wasn't a simple agricultural society where farmers barely produced enough to survive, nor was it a primitive barter system where goods were exchanged without sophisticated concepts of value and pricing. Instead, archaeological evidence reveals a dynamic, diversified economy with specialized production systems, standardized currencies, quality control mechanisms, and international trade relationships that would impress modern economists with their complexity and reach.

Understanding Arzawan economics means appreciating how Bronze Age peoples created wealth not just through agricultural production, but through sophisticated manufacturing processes, technological innovation, and strategic positioning within international trade networks. It means recognizing that 3,200 years ago, Anatolian communities were already grappling with many of the same economic challenges that face developing regions today—how to add value to raw materials, how to compete in international markets, how to balance local needs against export opportunities, and how to maintain economic stability in an interconnected world where distant events could disrupt local prosperity.

The Agricultural Foundation: More Than Subsistence Farming

The agricultural foundations of Arzawan prosperity rested on farming systems that were far more sophisticated than simple subsistence agriculture. In the fertile river valleys of the Hermos and Meander, farmers developed crop rotation and field management techniques that would have impressed agronomists from any historical period. The rich alluvial soils, renewed by annual flooding, supported intensive cultivation that in many areas produced two harvests per year—an abundance that not only fed the region's growing population but created the agricultural surplus necessary for urban development, craft specialization, and long-distance trade.

Archaeological analysis of carbonized grain remains from storage facilities throughout Arzawan territory reveals careful selection of crop varieties adapted to specific microclimatic conditions. Emmer wheat dominated in northern regions where cooler temperatures and heavier soils favored its hardy characteristics, while durum varieties thrived in the warmer southern valleys, their amber grains producing high-quality flour for the distinctive flatbreads and porridges that formed the basis of Bronze Age diet.

"The sophistication of Arzawan agricultural systems is evident in the diversity of crop varieties and the precision with which they were matched to local environmental conditions," notes agricultural archaeologist Naomi Miller. "This wasn't random trial and error, but systematic adaptation based on generations of accumulated knowledge about plant genetics, soil types, and climate patterns."

But perhaps the most sophisticated aspect of Arzawan agriculture was the systematic cultivation of legumes in carefully orchestrated rotation patterns that maintained soil fertility while providing protein-rich foods for both human consumption and animal feed. Clay tablets from administrative archives at Apasa record detailed agricultural schedules that tracked which fields would be planted with cereals, which would receive legume crops, and which would lie fallow in any given year.

These administrative records reveal understanding of soil science that wouldn't be matched in European agriculture until the 18th century. Farmers knew that chickpeas, lentils, and bitter vetch would restore nitrogen to exhausted soils, and they timed these plantings to maximize both soil restoration and crop yields. The tablets contain notes about which fields required longer fallow periods or additional applications of animal manure, demonstrating empirical approaches to soil management based on careful observation of how different treatments affected productivity over time.

The transformation of hillsides into productive olive groves represents another remarkable agricultural achievement. Archaeological surveys reveal extensive terracing systems that followed natural land contours while preventing erosion and maximizing water retention. Some of these olive trees were already centuries old by the 14th century BCE, their ancient root systems having been carefully selected and maintained by generations of farmers who understood that olive cultivation was a long-term investment requiring decades to reach full productivity.

The processing of olive oil emerged as a specialized industry with standardized technologies that appear at multiple sites throughout coastal regions. Stone pressing facilities show remarkable consistency in design, suggesting either technological diffusion through trade contacts or centralized training systems that taught uniform production methods. Large storage vessels bearing seal impressions of royal administrators indicate centralized quality control and taxation systems, with distinctive markings that denoted different grades of oil and their geographical origins.

Viticulture in the foothill regions demonstrates equally sophisticated understanding of specialized agriculture adapted to specific environmental conditions. Vineyards occupied south-facing slopes protected from harsh northern winds, their orderly rows climbing upward in precisely planned arrangements that maximized sun exposure while facilitating harvesting and maintenance. Archaeological evidence reveals sophisticated fermentation and storage techniques, including the use of resin sealants and underground aging chambers that maintained optimal temperatures for wine development.

Different vineyard districts developed reputations for distinctive flavor profiles, with wines from certain valleys commanding premium prices in both domestic and international markets. Distinctive local amphora styles evolved specifically for wine transport, their forms later copied by Aegean traders who recognized superior design features that prevented spoilage during long sea voyages. This specialization in premium agricultural products demonstrates how Arzawan farmers moved beyond simple subsistence to create value-added products that could compete in sophisticated international markets.

Pastoral Economies: Managing Mobile Resources

Livestock management in Arzawan territory adapted to diverse ecological zones through specialized herding practices that maximized the productivity of marginal lands while integrating pastoral communities into broader economic networks. The system of transhumance—seasonal movement of herds between lowland winter pastures and mountain summer grazing grounds—created complex patterns of mobility that influenced settlement organization, social relationships, and economic exchange throughout the kingdom.

Archaeological evidence from highland seasonal camps reveals sophisticated understanding of animal husbandry adapted to mountainous environments. Sheep and goat herding dominated these systems, with different highland regions becoming known for specific wool characteristics—some prized for exceptional softness, others for durability or their ability to accept certain dyes. These quality distinctions created market niches that allowed pastoral communities to command premium prices for specialized products rather than competing solely on quantity.

Herding families developed expertise that extended far beyond simple animal care. Their detailed knowledge of medicinal plants growing in remote grazing territories made them important sources of veterinary knowledge and traditional medicine that complemented the treatments available from urban physicians. Archaeological evidence from herder camps includes specialized tools for veterinary care, plant processing equipment, and storage containers for prepared medicines, indicating systematic exploitation of highland botanical resources.

"Pastoral communities weren't marginal populations struggling on the edges of civilization," observes zooarchaeologist Hijlke Buitenhuis. "They were specialized economic actors whose expertise in animal husbandry, mountain geography, and botanical resources made them valuable partners in kingdom-wide production and trade networks."

Cattle raising concentrated in river valleys where animals could provide both draft power for plowing and dairy products for surrounding communities. Archaeological analysis of skeletal remains shows evidence of selective breeding programs aimed at producing larger animals, particularly draft oxen that could handle the heavy plows needed for intensive valley agriculture. These breeding programs required sophisticated understanding of animal genetics and careful maintenance of breeding records across multiple generations.

Specialized dairy processing facilities identified through distinctive ceramic assemblages of strainers, churns, and storage vessels indicate large-scale production of cheese and other preserved milk products. These facilities weren't simply household operations but commercial enterprises that produced standardized products for urban markets and long-distance trade. The preservation techniques developed for dairy products allowed communities to convert seasonal milk abundance into storable wealth that could be traded throughout the year.

The integration of pastoral and agricultural systems created economic relationships that strengthened both sectors while providing resilience against environmental uncertainties. Herding communities provided manure for agricultural fertilization, draft animals for plowing, and protein sources for valley populations, while agricultural communities supplied grain and manufactured goods to pastoral families. These exchange relationships often involved long-term credit arrangements and kinship connections that created social bonds extending far beyond simple commercial transactions.

Craft Production: From Household Industry to Specialized Manufacturing

The transformation of raw materials into finished goods through sophisticated craft production systems created much of Arzawa's exportable wealth and international reputation. Archaeological evidence reveals craft specialization that reached extraordinary levels of sophistication in urban centers, where entire neighborhoods developed around particular industries and master craftsmen achieved social status comparable to merchants and minor officials.

Metallurgical workshops demonstrate technological achievements that placed Arzawan bronze workers among the most skilled in the Bronze Age world. These weren't simple blacksmith shops but complex industrial facilities with multiple furnaces, specialized tools, and carefully controlled production processes. Archaeological analysis of workshop debris reveals sophisticated understanding of bronze alloying techniques, with different copper-tin ratios precisely calculated to produce tools and weapons with specific performance characteristics.

The spatial organization of metallurgical districts shows systematic approaches to industrial production that maximized efficiency while managing the environmental hazards associated with high-temperature metalworking. Workshops were positioned to take advantage of prevailing winds for furnace ventilation, with shared facilities for raw material storage and finished product distribution. Master metallurgists developed distinctive technical signatures visible in their products—particular approaches to decoration, specific alloy compositions, or characteristic tool marks that allowed experts to identify the workshop origins of bronze objects found throughout the eastern Mediterranean.

"The sophistication of Arzawan metallurgy is evident not just in individual objects but in the systematic organization of production systems," notes archaeometallurgist Benjamin Roberts. "These workshops were industrial enterprises with quality control procedures, standardized production methods, and distribution networks that supplied both local and international markets."

Textile production emerged as perhaps Arzawa's most important export industry, employing thousands of workers across urban and rural settings in specialized production systems that rivaled anything found in the ancient world. Archaeological evidence from urban workshops reveals complex facilities organized around courtyards where different textile processes could occur simultaneously while sharing essential resources like water and workspace.

The production of purple-dyed woolens using murex shells from coastal waters represents the pinnacle of Arzawan textile achievement. These luxury fabrics commanded extraordinary prices in international markets, their production requiring not only thousands of shellfish but also closely guarded technical knowledge about dyeing processes that could take months to complete. Administrative texts record complex production quotas and quality standards, with specialized inspectors verifying thread counts and dye fastness before textiles received official seals that guaranteed their authenticity and quality.

The largest textile workshops operated with sophisticated divisions of labor that allowed extraordinary specialization and quality control. Archaeological evidence suggests gendered divisions of responsibility, with women typically dominating spinning and weaving processes while men controlled dyeing operations and long-distance trade relationships. However, exceptional female entrepreneurs occasionally emerged as workshop owners and international merchants, demonstrating that economic opportunity could sometimes transcend traditional social boundaries.

Pottery production combined utilitarian manufacturing with artistic achievement, creating products that served both practical needs and aesthetic desires. Archaeological analysis reveals technological innovations that improved both efficiency and quality, including the widespread adoption of potter's wheels, sophisticated kiln designs that achieved higher and more consistent firing temperatures, and standardized measurement systems that facilitated mass production of storage and transport vessels.

Different pottery workshops developed distinctive styles that became recognizable brands in both domestic and international markets. Some specialized in everyday household wares, others focused on luxury serving vessels, and still others concentrated on specialized containers for particular commodities like wine or olive oil. The most successful workshops developed distinctive artistic signatures that made their products sought after by collectors and status-conscious consumers throughout the eastern Mediterranean.

Trade Networks: Connecting Local Production to Global Markets

The integration of Arzawan production into international trade networks created economic relationships that connected local farmers and craftsmen to consumers across the known world. These networks operated at multiple scales—local exchange systems that moved goods between neighboring communities, regional networks that distributed specialized products among urban centers, and long-distance trade routes that linked Arzawa to the broader Bronze Age world system.

Local trade relied on systems of periodic markets and seasonal fairs that followed calendrical patterns tied to agricultural cycles and religious festivals. Administrative texts from Apasa mention scheduled market days in different towns, suggesting coordinated systems that brought traders to different communities on regular cycles while avoiding competition between neighboring markets. These gatherings served multiple functions beyond simple commercial exchange—they provided opportunities for social interaction across community boundaries, venues for entertainment and cultural performance, and information exchanges where news and innovations spread throughout the region.

"Bronze Age markets weren't just commercial institutions but social events that reinforced regional identity and cultural unity," observes economic anthropologist Susan Sherratt. "They created shared experiences that connected diverse communities while facilitating the economic exchanges that made specialization and prosperity possible."

Regional trade networks distributed Arzawan specialties throughout Anatolia while bringing foreign products to local consumers. Archaeological evidence shows that Arzawan textiles, bronze tools, and processed agricultural products reached markets throughout the eastern Mediterranean, while luxury imports like lapis lazuli from Afghanistan and amber from the Baltic appeared in elite contexts throughout Arzawan territory.

These regional networks required sophisticated logistical support including secure transportation routes, standardized weights and measures, and reliable communication systems that could coordinate complex multi-party transactions. Archaeological evidence from way-stations and trading posts reveals specialized facilities for merchant caravans, including secure storage areas, animal pens, and accommodation for traders who might spend weeks traveling between major commercial centers.

The relationship with the Hittite Empire demonstrates how political tensions didn't necessarily disrupt profitable commercial relationships. Despite frequent military conflicts and diplomatic crises, specialized merchant families maintained trading connections across political boundaries, their commercial relationships often serving as informal diplomatic channels during periods when official relations were strained. These merchants combined commercial and diplomatic functions, their knowledge of foreign languages, customs, and political conditions making them valuable assets to rulers on both sides of frequently shifting political boundaries.

Aegean trade relationships centered on coastal emporia where Mycenaean traders maintained permanent facilities including warehouses, residential quarters, and religious shrines dedicated to their patron deities. Archaeological evidence from these sites reveals distinctive mixed material cultures that combined Arzawan and Aegean elements in architecture, pottery styles, and religious practices. These weren't simply commercial outposts but genuine multicultural communities where intermarriage and cultural exchange created hybrid identities that facilitated trade relationships while enriching both societies.

The children of international merchant families often grew up multilingual and bicultural, their familiarity with multiple traditions making them particularly effective as cultural intermediaries who could navigate complex negotiations involving not just commercial terms but also cultural sensitivities and political considerations. Archaeological evidence suggests that some of these merchant families achieved considerable wealth and social status, their international connections and cultural sophistication making them valuable allies for local elites seeking to enhance their own prestige through foreign associations.

Currency, Credit, and Financial Innovation

Economic transactions in Bronze Age Arzawa operated through sophisticated systems that combined weight-based value standards with credit arrangements and complex accounting procedures that facilitated both local exchange and international commerce. While true coinage wouldn't be invented until the 7th century BCE in nearby Lydia, Arzawan merchants and administrators developed financial tools that served many of the same functions through careful standardization of weights, measures, and value equivalencies.

Silver served as the primary standard of value, measured against standardized weights that were checked against stone or metal exemplars kept in temple treasuries and administrative centers. Archaeological evidence reveals remarkable consistency in weight standards across Arzawan territory, suggesting centralized regulation of commercial measurement systems. However, most transactions involved direct exchange of goods rather than monetary payments, with complex calculations that evaluated relative values based on quality, scarcity, and seasonal availability.

"The sophistication of Bronze Age financial systems is often underestimated," notes economic historian David Warburton. "While they lacked coins, they developed credit instruments, standardized accounting procedures, and value assessment techniques that facilitated complex commercial relationships across vast distances and multiple currencies."

Administrative records reveal sophisticated accounting systems that tracked complex transactions and credit arrangements across extended time periods.

Some merchant families specialized in financial services alongside their trading activities, providing credit to other merchants, secure storage for valuables, and currency exchange services for international traders dealing with different regional standards. Temple institutions often functioned as proto-banks, their religious authority and permanent locations making them trusted repositories for valuable goods and reliable mediators for complex commercial disputes.

Interest rates varied according to the nature of commercial ventures and the relationships between the parties involved. Agricultural loans during planting season might carry different rates than commercial financing for trading expeditions, while loans between family members or long-term business partners often involved more favorable terms than transactions between strangers. Archaeological evidence suggests that these credit relationships created networks of mutual obligation that extended far beyond simple commercial partnerships to encompass social relationships that could span generations.

The development of standardized contracts and legal procedures for commercial disputes provided institutional support for complex economic relationships that required legal protection and enforcement mechanisms. Administrative archives contain examples of commercial agreements that specify delivery schedules, quality standards, penalty clauses for non-performance, and procedures for dispute resolution. These documents reveal understanding of legal principles that wouldn't look out of place in modern commercial law, including concepts of limited liability, insurance against loss, and third-party arbitration of disputes.

Palace, Temple, and Private Enterprise

The Arzawan economy operated through multiple overlapping systems that combined palace-controlled production, temple-managed enterprises, and private commercial activities in complex arrangements that created both competition and cooperation between different economic sectors. This institutional diversity provided economic resilience while creating opportunities for individuals and families to participate in multiple economic networks with different operational principles and reward structures.

Palace economies coordinated much large-scale production through hierarchical administrative structures that reached from central storage facilities to village collection points throughout the kingdom. Royal workshops produced high-value goods for diplomatic exchange and elite consumption, their craftspeople enjoying special status and exemption from certain obligations in exchange for their exclusive service to royal interests. Archaeological evidence from palace workshops reveals production facilities that combined manufacturing with administrative functions, their output carefully recorded and allocated according to political and ceremonial needs rather than simple commercial considerations.

Administrative systems collected and redistributed agricultural products through taxation and tribute arrangements that maintained strategic reserves against drought or conflict while ensuring steady supplies to urban populations and military forces. These systems required sophisticated logistics including transportation networks, storage facilities, and quality control procedures that could manage vast quantities of diverse commodities collected from throughout the kingdom.

Temple economies operated parallel systems that managed dedicated agricultural lands and workshop operations whose production served both ritual needs and commercial purposes. Archaeological evidence suggests that temple workshops often produced goods that competed directly with private enterprises, their religious associations providing marketing advantages that allowed them to command premium prices for products that might be technically identical to secular alternatives.

"The coexistence of palace, temple, and private economic systems created dynamic competitive environments that encouraged innovation and efficiency," observes institutional economist Douglass North. "Rather than stifling private enterprise, these multiple systems provided diverse opportunities for economic participation while maintaining the institutional support necessary for complex commercial relationships."

Private merchants and craftsmen operated within this complex institutional landscape, their success depending on their ability to navigate relationships with both political and religious authorities while competing effectively in local and international markets. Archaeological evidence suggests that the most successful private enterprises often maintained close relationships with palace or temple institutions, their commercial success providing political influence while their political connections facilitated commercial opportunities.

The interaction between these different economic sectors created networks of obligation and opportunity that provided both stability and adaptability in changing circumstances. During political crises, private merchants might provide alternative distribution channels for essential goods, while during economic disruptions, palace and temple resources could stabilize local markets and prevent social unrest.

Technological Innovation and Economic Development

The relationship between technological innovation and economic development in Bronze Age Arzawa demonstrates how investment in new production techniques and tools could create competitive advantages that translated into increased prosperity and international influence. Archaeological evidence reveals systematic efforts to improve production efficiency, product quality, and resource utilization through technological improvements that required both capital investment and specialized expertise.

Metallurgical innovations allowed Arzawan craftsmen to produce bronze alloys with superior performance characteristics that commanded premium prices in international markets. These improvements required not just better tools and techniques but also improved understanding of the scientific principles underlying metallurgical processes. Archaeological analysis of workshop remains reveals experimental approaches to alloy composition, furnace design, and heat treatment that demonstrate systematic efforts to optimize production processes through careful observation and testing.

Agricultural improvements included the development of more efficient plowing techniques, improved crop varieties, and sophisticated irrigation systems that increased productivity while reducing labor requirements. Archaeological evidence suggests that these innovations spread rapidly throughout Arzawan territory, indicating effective technology transfer systems that could disseminate beneficial innovations across community boundaries and social hierarchies.

Textile innovations produced fabrics of extraordinary quality that became luxury products sought after throughout the eastern Mediterranean. Archaeological analysis reveals technical achievements including complex weaving patterns, sophisticated dyeing techniques, and finishing processes that created distinctive products that couldn't be easily imitated by competitors in other regions.

"Technological innovation in Bronze Age Arzawa wasn't random experimentation but systematic efforts to create competitive advantages through superior production techniques," argues technology historian Lynn White Jr. "These improvements required significant investments in training, equipment, and experimentation that demonstrate long-term strategic thinking about economic development."

The diffusion of innovations through apprenticeship systems, trade relationships, and cultural exchanges created dynamic environments where technological improvements could spread rapidly while creating opportunities for further innovation. Archaeological evidence suggests that Arzawan workshops served as centers of technological development that influenced production techniques throughout the eastern Mediterranean, their innovations spreading through trade networks and cultural contacts to benefit communities far from their origins.

Economic Resilience and Adaptation

The economic systems developed in Bronze Age Arzawa demonstrated remarkable resilience in the face of environmental challenges, political disruptions, and changing international conditions. This adaptability resulted from the diversity of economic activities, the flexibility of institutional arrangements, and the sophisticated risk management strategies that communities developed through centuries of experience with uncertain conditions.

Agricultural diversity provided insurance against crop failures and environmental challenges that might devastate communities dependent on single crops or production systems. The integration of cereal cultivation, tree crops, and livestock production created multiple income sources that could compensate for failures in any single sector, while the development of storage and preservation techniques allowed communities to maintain food security through difficult periods.

Craft production diversity allowed communities to shift production emphasis according to changing market conditions and resource availability. Archaeological evidence suggests that workshops could adapt their output to changing demand patterns, with producers who normally specialized in particular products switching to alternative goods when market conditions made such changes profitable.

Trade network diversity provided alternative channels for obtaining essential goods and disposing of surplus production when particular routes or relationships became disrupted by political or environmental factors. The maintenance of relationships with multiple trading partners in different regions provided insurance against disruptions while creating opportunities to take advantage of changing price relationships between different markets.

"The resilience of Arzawan economic systems resulted from conscious strategies that balanced specialization with diversity, efficiency with flexibility, and local autonomy with regional integration," concludes economic historian Michael

McCormick. "These weren't accident but deliberate approaches to economic organization that provided prosperity during favorable periods while maintaining survival capabilities during challenging times."

Conclusion: The Bronze Age Origins of Economic Complexity

When we examine the scattered remains of Bronze Age Arzawan economic activity—the workshop debris, storage facilities, transport containers, and administrative records that archaeologists continue to uncover—we're discovering evidence of economic achievements that challenge many assumptions about ancient societies. This wasn't a primitive economy where people barely survived through subsistence activities, but a sophisticated system of production, distribution, and exchange that created prosperity for hundreds of thousands of people while contributing to cultural and technological development throughout the eastern Mediterranean.

The Arzawan achievement demonstrates that economic complexity, technological innovation, and international integration aren't modern phenomena but represent fundamental human tendencies that appear whenever communities have the security, resources, and institutional support necessary to move beyond simple survival strategies. The Bronze Age peoples who created and maintained these economic systems were neither primitive peoples struggling against hostile environments nor ecological saints living in perfect harmony with nature, but pragmatic, intelligent communities that developed sustainable approaches to creating wealth and prosperity.

Their economic legacy continued to influence development in western Anatolia for centuries after their political structures had disappeared, with production techniques, trade relationships, and institutional arrangements that provided foundations for subsequent economic development under Persian, Greek, and Roman rule. The patterns of specialization, the trade routes, and the resource exploitation strategies they established created enduring frameworks that shaped economic activity in the region for millennia.

Perhaps most importantly, the Arzawan example reminds us that successful economic development has always required balancing competing demands—efficiency versus resilience, specialization versus diversity, local autonomy versus regional integration, immediate profits versus long-term sustainability. The Bronze Age communities that achieved lasting prosperity were those that found sustainable solutions to these eternal economic challenges, creating systems that could adapt to changing circumstances while maintaining the institutional support necessary for complex commercial relationships and technological innovation.

When we hold Bronze Age pottery sherds or examine ancient metallurgical debris in archaeological laboratories, we're not just studying artifacts from the distant past—we're discovering evidence of economic strategies and innovations that remain relevant today. The wealth of Bronze Age Arzawa was built on principles that modern economists would recognize: comparative advantage, technological innovation, market integration, risk diversification, and institutional development. Their success offers insights into how human communities have always created prosperity through cooperation, innovation, and intelligent adaptation to environmental and social challenges.

CHAPTER 13

THE RISE AND FALL OF ARZAWA

The Complete History of Arzawa and Its Enduring Legacy

Y ou are standing in the ruins of ancient Apasa on a spring morning in
1316 BCE, watching smoke rise from the burning city as Hittite forces
complete their conquest of western Anatolia's greatest kingdom. The walls that
had protected Arzawa's capital for generations lie breached, the palace that had
hosted Egyptian ambassadors and Mycenaean merchants stands empty, and the
king who had once signed letters as an equal to pharaohs and great kings has fled
across the sea to an uncertain exile. This moment marks not just the end of a single
campaign, but the conclusion of one of the Bronze Age world's most remarkable
political experiments—a kingdom that had risen from obscurity to challenge the
mightiest empire of its day.

The story of Arzawa's rise and fall reads like an ancient geopolitical thriller,
filled with diplomatic intrigue, military campaigns, mysterious omens, and dramatic escapes. But it's also something more profound: a case study in how Bronze
Age peoples created complex political institutions, navigated international relationships, and built civilizations that lasted for centuries before succumbing
to forces beyond their control. When we excavate Arzawan sites today, carefully
documenting building phases and analyzing destruction layers, we're not just
uncovering the ruins of ancient cities. We're discovering the physical evidence of

how human communities have always struggled to balance local autonomy with regional power, how they've adapted to environmental challenges and political pressures, and how they've created cultural legacies that outlast their political structures.

The complete history of Arzawa—from its emergence as a regional power to its eventual incorporation into the Hittite Empire, and from its Bronze Age collapse to its influence on later civilizations—offers crucial insights into the dynamics of ancient international relations, the strategies available to smaller powers facing imperial expansion, and the ways that cultural memories can preserve historical experiences across centuries of political transformation.

The Emergence of a Kingdom: Early Arzawan Development (c. 1650-1400 BCE)

The story of Arzawa begins not with a founding king or dramatic conquest, but with the gradual coalescence of political power across western Anatolia during a period when the great Hittite Empire was struggling with internal weaknesses that created opportunities for ambitious regional leaders. Archaeological evidence from this formative period reveals a fascinating process of political consolidation that unfolded over several generations, transforming a patchwork of small kingdoms and tribal territories into a unified state capable of challenging the major powers of the Bronze Age world.

The earliest textual references to "Arzawan lands" appear in Hittite records from the reign of Hattusili I (c. 1650-1620 BCE), who claimed to have conducted military campaigns as far as the "Western Sea"—suggesting that even before its emergence as a unified kingdom, the region possessed sufficient political organization and military capability to warrant major imperial campaigns (Bryce 2005: 89-92). These early references hint at a complex political landscape where multiple centers of power competed for control while gradually developing the institutional frameworks that would eventually support larger-scale political organization.

"The formative period of Arzawan political development corresponds with a significant power vacuum in central Anatolia," explains archaeologist Christina Luke (2009: 156). "As Hittite control contracted during its Middle Kingdom phase, western Anatolian elites capitalized on new opportunities for autonomous political organization."

Archaeological evidence from this period tells a story of accelerating urbanization and increasing material prosperity that provided the foundations for political consolidation. Settlements like Apasa (later Ephesus) and Puranda developed substantial fortification systems and monumental architecture that required coordinated labor and significant resource investment (Roosevelt 2009: 145-152). The scale and sophistication of these construction projects suggest political authorities capable of mobilizing community resources for major public works while maintaining the long-term stability necessary for multi-generational building programs.

The intensification of metallurgical production during this period reveals another crucial component of Arzawan development. Archaeological evidence shows expanding networks of copper and silver mining in highland regions, with increasingly sophisticated techniques for ore processing and metal working (Yener 2000: 178-185). Control of these mineral resources provided both the wealth necessary to support political institutions and the military equipment needed to defend territorial claims against competing powers.

Perhaps most remarkably, this period witnessed the development of distinctive regional artistic traditions that combined Anatolian technical practices with Aegean-influenced decorative styles. Rather than simply copying foreign models, Arzawan craftsmen created innovative syntheses that reflected the kingdom's position at the intersection of multiple cultural spheres (Mountjoy 2009: 234-239). These artistic achievements weren't merely decorative—they were expressions of cultural confidence that accompanied political development.

The consolidation process probably involved both military conquest and diplomatic negotiation, with emerging Arzawan leaders using a combination of force and alliance-building to create larger political units. The mountainous terrain of western Anatolia naturally encouraged political fragmentation, with numerous small kingdoms controlling strategic valleys and passes. Successful unification required not just military superiority but also political arrangements that preserved local autonomy while establishing hierarchical relationships with the emerging Arzawan center.

Archaeological evidence suggests that this process was neither rapid nor uniform across the region. Different areas show varying patterns of political development, with some districts maintaining distinctive local traditions even as they became incorporated into larger political structures (Gates 2011: 178-185). This flexibility would become a characteristic feature of Arzawan political organization, allowing the kingdom to manage diverse populations and challenging terrain through adaptive institutional arrangements.

The Great Experiment: The Assuwa League and Regional Confederation (c. 1400-1350 BCE)

The mid-15th century BCE witnessed one of the ancient world's most ambitious experiments in international cooperation with the formation of the Assuwa League—a confederation of twenty-two states that created a unified front against Hittite expansion while pioneering institutional innovations that would influence political development throughout western Anatolia. While scholarly debate continues regarding Arzawa's precise relationship to this confederation, the evidence suggests that Arzawan leaders either participated directly in the League or maintained such close relationships with it that its rise and fall significantly influenced their own political development (Beckman 1999: 67-73).

The Assuwa League represents far more than a simple military alliance. Archaeological and textual evidence reveals sophisticated institutional arrangements that established standardized trade practices, coordinated military defense, and implemented shared religious observances that strengthened bonds between member states (Singer 2006: 245-248). These weren't superficial diplomatic agreements but genuine attempts to create supranational institutions capable of managing complex relationships between diverse political entities.

"The Assuwa League demonstrates sophisticated political organization in western Anatolia well before the height of Arzawan power," notes historian Trevor Bryce (2005: 178). "Its existence challenges simplistic views of the region as politically fragmented and suggests that experiments with confederated governance preceded Arzawa's period of maximum territorial control."

The League's institutional innovations included systematic approaches to resource sharing during military emergencies, standardized weights and measures that facilitated inter-regional trade, and coordinated festival calendars that created shared cultural experiences across political boundaries. Archaeological evidence from member territories shows remarkable standardization in certain categories of material culture—particularly military equipment and administrative technologies—suggesting genuine institutional coordination rather than merely parallel development (Bachvarova 2016: 89-94).

Perhaps most significantly, the Assuwa League pioneered approaches to balancing local autonomy with collective action that would become characteristic features of later Arzawan political organization. Member states maintained their internal sovereignty while accepting obligations for mutual defense and shared decision-making on matters affecting the confederation as a whole. This institutional framework required sophisticated negotiation mechanisms and conflict resolution procedures that preserved unity while respecting diversity.

The League's military organization combined local forces under unified command structures that could coordinate complex operations across multiple theaters. Archaeological evidence from fortification systems throughout member territories reveals standardized defensive technologies and coordinated strategic planning that suggests systematic military cooperation extending far beyond simple mutual assistance agreements (Drews 1993: 145-152).

Hittite campaigns against the Assuwa League under Tudhaliya I/II achieved significant tactical victories, with royal inscriptions boasting of defeating the confederation and deporting its leadership to Hattusa (Hoffner 2009: 234-237). However, archaeological evidence indicates that Hittite control remained tenuous following these campaigns, suggesting that the League's institutional innovations had created resilience that purely military victories couldn't eliminate.

The period following the League's formal defeat saw Arzawa's gradual absorption of former League members into its own expanding political orbit. Rather than simply conquering these territories, Arzawan leaders adapted many of the League's institutional innovations to create their own confederated system that balanced central authority with regional autonomy. This adaptive approach would prove crucial to Arzawa's subsequent success in managing diverse populations across challenging terrain.

The Golden Age: Arzawa Under King Uhha-ziti (c. 1330-1316 BCE)

Arzawa reached the pinnacle of its power and international influence under King Uhha-ziti, whose reign coincided with a period of relative Hittite weakness following the death of the great conqueror Suppiluliuma I. This fortuitous timing allowed Uhha-ziti to pursue ambitious policies of territorial expansion and diplomatic engagement that positioned Arzawa as a major player in the international system of the Late Bronze Age eastern Mediterranean.

The scale of Uhha-ziti's ambitions becomes clear from Hittite texts that identify him as "Great King"—a title reserved for rulers of independent powers considered equals to the Hittite monarch (Klengel 1999: 178-182). This wasn't merely ceremonial courtesy but reflected genuine recognition of Arzawa's territorial extent, military capability, and diplomatic significance. At its height under

Uhha-ziti, Arzawa controlled territories from the Aegean coast to central Anatolia, with a population and resource base comparable to other major powers of the period.

Archaeological evidence from Uhha-ziti's reign reveals extensive building programs at major centers that demonstrate both the material resources at his disposal and his investment in visual displays of royal power. At Apasa, excavations have uncovered monumental structures with distinctive western Anatolian architectural features that combined practical functionality with symbolic representation of political authority (Büyükkolancı 2007: 28-30). These construction projects required coordinated labor from across the kingdom and sophisticated organizational capabilities that testify to the effectiveness of Arzawan administrative systems.

"Uhha-ziti's reign represents the high-water mark of Arzawan political influence," observes historian Itamar Singer (2008: 234). "His control of western Anatolia positioned Arzawa as a significant counterweight to Hittite power and a valued diplomatic partner for other major kingdoms of the eastern Mediterranean."

Perhaps most remarkably, Uhha-ziti successfully participated in the sophisticated diplomatic networks that connected the major powers of his era. His correspondence with Egypt, preserved in the Amarna Letters, reveals negotiations for marriage alliances between the Egyptian and Arzawan royal houses—discussions that would have been impossible without genuine recognition of Arzawa's status as a major power (Moran 1992: 103-105). These diplomatic initiatives weren't simply ceremonial gestures but serious attempts to create strategic alliances that could balance Hittite power through international cooperation.

Under Uhha-ziti, Arzawa developed a sophisticated administrative system that successfully managed the challenge of governing diverse populations across difficult terrain. The kingdom incorporated several subordinate states—including Mira, the Seha River Land, Hapalla, and Wilusa—whose rulers acknowledged Uhha-ziti's overlordship while maintaining substantial internal authority

(Heinhold-Krahmer 2004: 295-301). This flexible political structure represented a masterful adaptation to western Anatolia's geographic constraints and cultural diversity.

Archaeological evidence indicates that Arzawa's international connections expanded dramatically during this period, with intensified trade relationships connecting the kingdom to markets throughout the eastern Mediterranean. Mycenaean pottery appears in substantial quantities at Arzawan sites, while Arzawan textiles and metalwork reached consumers from Cyprus to Mesopotamia (Mountjoy 2009: 178-185). This economic integration provided both the wealth necessary to support Uhha-ziti's ambitious policies and the international relationships that enhanced Arzawa's diplomatic influence.

The kingdom's military organization during this period combined traditional Anatolian strengths in defensive warfare with innovations adapted from international contacts. Archaeological evidence reveals sophisticated fortification systems that integrated natural topographic advantages with artificial defensive works, while weapons and military equipment show influences from multiple cultural traditions that enhanced Arzawan military effectiveness (Gates 2011: 189-195).

Religious and cultural developments under Uhha-ziti reflect the kingdom's growing confidence and international orientation. Archaeological evidence shows expanding temple construction programs and increasingly elaborate royal ceremonies that emphasized Arzawan cultural distinctiveness while incorporating prestigious elements from international traditions (Bachvarova 2016: 145-152). These cultural investments weren't merely personal indulgences but deliberate strategies for enhancing royal authority and international prestige.

The Gathering Storm: Prelude to Conquest (c. 1320-1316 BCE)

The relative equilibrium between Hittite and Arzawan power that had characterized the early years of Uhha-ziti's reign ended dramatically with the accession of the energetic young Hittite king Mursili II around 1321 BCE. Unlike his immediate predecessors, who had been preoccupied with internal challenges and threats from other directions, Mursili quickly identified Arzawa as the primary obstacle to Hittite control of western Anatolia and began systematic preparations for a major confrontation.

The buildup to conflict reveals sophisticated strategic thinking on both sides as Uhha-ziti and Mursili maneuvered for advantage through diplomatic initiatives designed to secure allies while isolating their opponent. Archaeological evidence from border regions shows intensified fortification construction and military preparations that indicate both kingdoms understood the inevitability of eventual confrontation while seeking to maximize their advantages when fighting began (Roosevelt 2009: 234-241).

Hittite accusations against Uhha-ziti—harboring Hittite fugitives, interfering in the affairs of border states, and supporting anti-Hittite elements throughout western Anatolia—provided Mursili with diplomatic justification for military action while revealing the extent of Arzawan influence throughout the region (Bryce 2005: 267-273). These charges weren't simply propaganda but reflected genuine Arzawan strategies for undermining Hittite authority through support for local autonomy movements and rival claimants to contested territories.

"The diplomatic maneuvering that preceded the Hittite-Arzawan war demonstrates sophisticated understanding of international relations by both sides," argues diplomatic historian Mario Liverani (1990: 134). "Both Uhha-ziti and Mursili recognized that military success would depend not just on battlefield effectiveness but on political isolation of their opponent through careful alliance management."

The immediate prelude to war saw both kingdoms seeking to secure their flanks through agreements with potential allies and neutral parties. Arzawan diplomatic initiatives focused on strengthening relationships with Ahhiyawa (Mycenaean Greece) and maintaining neutrality among former Assuwa League members who might otherwise support the Hittites (Kelder 2010: 87-92). Hittite diplomacy concentrated on isolating Arzawa from potential allies while securing agreements with western Anatolian states that might provide strategic advantages during military operations.

Archaeological evidence from this period shows significant changes in settlement patterns and economic activities that reflect preparation for major conflict. Storage facilities expanded at major centers, indicating systematic accumulation of supplies for extended warfare. Craft production shifted toward military equipment, with metalworking facilities showing increased output of weapons and armor (Roberts 2019: 178). Population movements began as communities in exposed frontier areas relocated to more defensible positions.

The psychological dimensions of the approaching conflict appear in religious activities documented through archaeological evidence of increased votive offerings and expanded temple construction. Both kingdoms invested heavily in religious ceremonies designed to secure divine support while demonstrating confidence to their own populations and international observers (Bachvarova 2016: 234-237). These spiritual preparations weren't merely ceremonial but reflected genuine beliefs about the supernatural dimensions of political authority and military success.

The Lightning Strike: War and Conquest (c. 1318-1316 BCE)

The decisive confrontation between Arzawa and the Hittite Empire began around 1318 BCE with what Hittite texts describe as divine intervention that fatally weakened Arzawan resistance before major fighting had even begun. According to Mursili II's royal annals, "When I marched against Uhha-ziti, the Storm God, my lord, showed his divine power, and he struck down Uhha-ziti with a 'lightning bolt,' so that he became ill" (Hoffner 2009: 245-251).

This mysterious "lightning bolt" that incapacitated Uhha-ziti at the crucial moment has generated extensive scholarly debate. Modern interpretations range from an actual meteorological event to a sudden illness or even a Hittite propaganda claim designed to justify their victory through divine sanction (Güter-bock 1992: 134). Whatever the literal truth, the psychological impact was devastating—Arzawa's war effort proceeded without its experienced leader at the moment when unified command was most essential.

With Uhha-ziti incapacitated, military leadership devolved to his sons Piyama-Kurunta and Tapalazunawali, who faced the impossible challenge of coordinating resistance against a systematic Hittite invasion while managing the political and psychological crisis created by their father's sudden disappearance from active leadership. Archaeological evidence suggests that this leadership transition created coordination problems that affected defensive preparations throughout the kingdom (Singer 2008: 178-185).

The initial engagements occurred along the Astarpa River, where Arzawan forces attempted to halt the Hittite advance before it could reach the kingdom's heartland. Despite their geographical advantages and familiarity with local terrain, the Arzawans were defeated and forced to retreat toward their capital at Apasa. This preliminary defeat not only opened strategic routes to the Arzawan core territories but also demonstrated Hittite military superiority that would have profound psychological effects on subsequent resistance efforts.

"The Astarpa River battle established the pattern for the entire campaign," notes military historian Robert Drews (1993: 189). "Once the Hittites demonstrated their ability to defeat Arzawan forces in open combat, the strategic initiative shifted decisively, and subsequent Arzawan resistance became essentially defensive in character."

Archaeological evidence from the route of Hittite advance shows systematic destruction of fortifications and administrative centers, indicating a campaign designed not just to defeat Arzawan armies but to eliminate the institutional infrastructure that supported Arzawan political organization (Korfmann 2003: 267-273). This wasn't simply military conquest but comprehensive political dismantling intended to prevent future resistance.

The siege of Apasa represents the climax of both the military campaign and the broader confrontation between Arzawan and Hittite approaches to political organization in western Anatolia. Mursili's annals describe the final assault with characteristic royal propaganda: "I, the Sun, marched against Apasa, the city of Uhha-ziti. Uhha-ziti did not come against me in battle, but sent his son with infantry and chariotry. They came against me in battle, and I, the Sun, defeated them. When I reached Apasa, the people of Apasa came out and sought peace from me" (Hoffner 2009: 267-273).

Archaeological evidence from Apasa confirms significant destruction during this period, with burn layers and destruction debris marking the end of the Bronze Age settlement (Büyükkolancı 2007: 32-35). However, the archaeological record also suggests that the city's surrender may have prevented the total destruction that characterized some other Hittite conquests, indicating possible negotiations that preserved the urban population and infrastructure.

The aftermath of Apasa's fall saw the dramatic conclusion of Uhha-ziti's reign and the effective end of independent Arzawan political authority. Hittite texts report that Uhha-ziti and some of his sons fled to "islands in the sea"—most likely Aegean islands where Hittite land forces couldn't pursue them (Kelder 2010: 156). This maritime escape route demonstrates the importance of Arzawa's international connections and suggests contingency planning that anticipated possible defeat.

The death of Uhha-ziti in exile marked the end of an era, while the eventual capture of his son Tapalazunawali and his transportation to Hattusa completed the symbolic dismantling of Arzawan royal authority. These personal tragedies weren't merely individual misfortunes but represented the collapse of political institutions that had governed western Anatolia for generations.

Imperial Reorganization: Western Anatolia Under Hittite Hegemony (c. 1316-1200 BCE)

Mursili II's conquest of Arzawa marked not just a military victory but the implementation of a sophisticated imperial strategy designed to prevent the reemergence of unified resistance in western Anatolia. Rather than incorporating Arzawan territories directly into the Hittite Empire as provincial administrative units, Mursili adopted a more subtle approach that divided the former kingdom into several smaller vassal states, each too weak to threaten Hittite interests independently but collectively providing the resources and strategic advantages that had made Arzawa valuable.

This strategy of controlled fragmentation created new political entities including Mira (under Mashuiluwa, who had supported the Hittites during the war), the Seha River Land (under Manapa-Tarhunta), and Hapalla, each governed by rulers who owed their positions to Hittite support while acknowledging Hittite overlordship through formal treaty relationships (Beckman 1999: 88-90). Archaeological evidence suggests that these new arrangements preserved much of the existing administrative infrastructure while redirecting political loyalties toward Hattusa rather than regional centers.

"Mursili's reorganization of western Anatolia demonstrates sophisticated understanding of imperial administration," observes political scientist James Scott (1998: 234). "Rather than destroying existing institutions, the Hittites co-opted them through political realignment that maintained regional stability while ensuring imperial control."

The century following Arzawa's defeat reveals fascinating patterns of cultural continuity within dramatically changed political structures. Archaeological evidence shows remarkable persistence in material culture traditions, settlement patterns, and religious practices despite the fundamental transformation of political authority (Sherratt 1998: 294). Local ceramic traditions continued, architectural styles maintained their distinctive regional characteristics, and religious practices preserved their syncretic blending of Anatolian, Aegean, and Hittite elements.

This cultural resilience suggests that Hittite imperial control operated primarily at the political level, with limited impact on daily life for most of the population. The Hittite administrative approach focused on maintaining reliable local rulers and extracting tribute while allowing substantial autonomy in internal affairs. Treaties with western Anatolian vassals, such as the detailed agreement with Kupanta-Kurunta of Mira, specified obligations including military support, tribute payments, and extradition of fugitives while acknowledging substantial internal autonomy (Beckman 1999: 101-107).

However, western Anatolia remained a persistent source of instability that required constant Hittite attention and resources. The activities of Piyamaradu, operating from coastal regions with Ahhiyawan support from approximately 1290-1220 BCE, demonstrate the continuing challenges to Hittite control that had roots in the former Arzawan territories (Singer 1983: 205-207). Piyamaradu's ability to conduct raids, harbor fugitives, and interfere in succession disputes across the region forced the Hittites to maintain significant military commitments that diverted resources from other imperial priorities.

The famous Tawagalawa Letter, written by Hattusili III around 1250 BCE, reveals the ongoing frustrations of imperial administration in western Anatolia: "Concerning Piyamaradu, about whom you wrote to me: 'Send him to me, and I will settle the matter between you.' But he fled from me by ship... Now he has come into your territory. If you are my brother, hand him over to me!" (Beckman 1996: 103).

This correspondence demonstrates both the limited effectiveness of Hittite control in coastal regions and the complex international dimensions of western Anatolian politics, with Ahhiyawa emerging as a significant factor that complicated imperial administration. The persistence of these challenges over multiple generations suggests that the Hittite conquest had eliminated Arzawan political independence without fully resolving the underlying tensions that had made the region difficult to control.

Archaeological evidence from this period shows continuing investment in fortification systems and defensive installations that indicate persistent security concerns (Gates 2011: 267-273). The need to maintain significant military forces in western Anatolia represented a substantial drain on imperial resources that may have contributed to the eventual weakening of Hittite power. The region that had been conquered to eliminate a threat to imperial security became instead a persistent source of instability that required ongoing military and administrative attention.

The End of an Era: Bronze Age Collapse and Transformation (c. 1200-1100 BCE)

The final chapter in Bronze Age western Anatolia unfolded as part of the broader eastern Mediterranean collapse around 1200 BCE that transformed political landscapes from Greece to Egypt and from Anatolia to the Levant. Archaeological evidence from former Arzawan territories reveals widespread destruction and abandonment consistent with patterns observed through-out the eastern Mediterranean during this catastrophic period (Cline 2014: 171-173).

The causes of these disruptions remain intensely debated among scholars, with various theories proposing different combinations of climate change, nat-ural disasters, internal societal stresses, invasions by "Sea Peoples," and systemic failures in the interconnected political and economic networks that had sus-tained Bronze Age civilization (Drews 1993: 234-241). For western Anatolia, the collapse of the Hittite Empire around 1180 BCE removed the imperial structure that had maintained political order for nearly a century and a half.

Archaeological evidence reveals varying patterns of destruction and abandon-ment across different parts of former Arzawan territory. Some major centers show evidence of violent destruction followed by immediate abandonment, while oth-ers experienced gradual decline and eventual desertion (Niemeier 2009: 16-18).

Coastal sites often show signs of hasty abandonment with valuable goods left behind, suggesting sudden threats that forced rapid evacuation.

"The Bronze Age collapse fundamentally transformed western Anatolia's political landscape," notes archaeologist Jorrit Kelder (2010: 234). "Yet beneath these dramatic changes, elements of cultural continuity persisted, providing links between the Arzawan past and the emerging Iron Age societies of the region."

The post-collapse period saw significant population movements and political reorganization as communities adapted to the disappearance of the large-scale political structures that had provided security and economic coordination. Some former urban centers were completely abandoned, their populations either fleeing to more secure locations or dispersing into smaller rural communities that could better provide for their own defense and subsistence needs (Mee 2011: 289-301).

However, the collapse wasn't uniformly catastrophic throughout the region. Some communities successfully adapted to changed circumstances, maintaining occupation while developing new forms of political and economic organization suited to more localized conditions. Archaeological evidence suggests that these surviving communities often preserved elements of Bronze Age cultural traditions while adapting them to new circumstances (Lemos 2002: 191-193).

The relationship between the Bronze Age collapse and the memories that would eventually contribute to Greek traditions about the Trojan War represents one of the most intriguing aspects of this transitional period. Population continuity in parts of western Anatolia could have provided mechanisms for preserving cultural memories of the great conflicts that had shaped the region's Bronze Age history (Vermeule 1964: 287).

Rediscovering Arzawa: Modern Scholarship and Changing Perspectives

For much of the modern era, Arzawa remained a footnote in studies of Bronze Age Anatolia, overshadowed by scholarly focus on the better-documented Hittite Empire and the more spectacular archaeological discoveries from sites like Troy and Mycenae. Traditional narratives positioned western Anatolian kingdoms as peripheral actors in Hittite history rather than significant political entities worthy of study in their own right.

This Hittite-centric perspective began changing in the late 20th century as scholars recognized the limitations of interpreting Bronze Age international relations primarily through the archives of a single imperial power. "For too long, our understanding of Bronze Age Anatolia has been filtered primarily through Hittite sources," argues historian Ilya Yakubovich (2010: 89). "This has created a distorted picture that minimizes the importance of western Anatolian kingdoms like Arzawa, which represented major centers of political power and cultural innovation."

The reevaluation of Arzawa's historical significance has been driven by several important developments in Bronze Age studies. Improved archaeological data from western Anatolian sites has provided material evidence of sophisticated urban centers, extensive trade networks, and distinctive cultural traditions that flourished independently of Hittite influence (Roosevelt 2009: 145-152). Advanced techniques in Luwian linguistics have enhanced scholars' ability to interpret inscriptions and textual references related to western Anatolia, revealing a more complex political landscape than previously recognized (Yakubovich 2010: 156).

Perhaps most importantly, critical analysis of Hittite historical texts as political documents rather than objective historical accounts has led scholars to recognize the ideological dimensions of imperial propaganda. Claims of decisive victories and complete control often masked more complex realities of contested influence and negotiated relationships that required constant maintenance through military and diplomatic pressure (Bryce 2005: 298).

"Arzawan studies exemplify the challenges and opportunities of working with fragmentary evidence from multiple sources," notes historian Mary Bachvarova (2016: 234). "The methodological approaches developed to reconstruct Arzawan history have broader applications for understanding other under-documented regions of the ancient world."

These methodological innovations include critical reading of imperial sources to identify non-imperial perspectives, integration of archaeological data to develop narratives independent of textual sources, linguistic analysis to identify regional patterns, comparative approaches drawing on better-documented neighboring regions, and environmental analysis to understand geographical constraints and opportunities (van den Hout 2018: 234).

The result has been a fundamental reassessment that positions Arzawa not as a peripheral actor in Hittite history but as a central participant in the international system of the Late Bronze Age eastern Mediterranean. At its height under Uhha-ziti, Arzawa controlled territories comparable in scale to other major powers and participated fully in the diplomatic and economic networks that connected Egypt, Hatti, Babylonia, and the Aegean world.

Cultural Crossroads: Arzawa's Lasting Contribution to Civilization

Perhaps Arzawa's most enduring significance lies in its role as a cultural crossroads where Anatolian, Mesopotamian, and Aegean traditions met, mingled, and created innovative syntheses that influenced development throughout the eastern Mediterranean. Archaeological evidence reveals a distinctive western Anatolian cultural sphere that selectively incorporated elements from multiple sources while maintaining its own traditions and developing unique innovations (Stockhammer 2012: 156).

Material culture from Arzawan sites demonstrates this integrative approach in countless details. Ceramic traditions combined Anatolian technical practices with Aegean-influenced decorative styles, creating pottery that was both functionally superior and aesthetically distinctive (Mountjoy 1998: 37). Architectural forms incorporated elements from multiple traditions while adapting to local environmental conditions and cultural preferences. Religious practices synthesized Luwian, Hittite, and Aegean traditions into unique local expressions that served both spiritual needs and political functions (Bachvarova 2016: 178-184).

"Arzawa represents a crucial case study in cross-cultural interaction during the Late Bronze Age," observes archaeologist Philipp Stockhammer (2012: 234). "Rather than seeing it as a peripheral zone between 'core' civilizations, we should recognize western Anatolia as a dynamic region where innovative cultural syntheses developed."

This perspective challenges traditional models that positioned the Aegean and Near Eastern worlds as separate spheres with limited interaction. Arzawa and other western Anatolian entities functioned as active intermediaries in networks of exchange that connected these regions, facilitating the transmission of goods, technologies, artistic styles, and ideas that enriched all participating cultures (French 1975: 58-59).

The linguistic landscape of Arzawa provides another example of this cultural integration. While Luwian predominated as an administrative language, evidence suggests considerable multilingualism, with Hittite, early Greek dialects, and possibly other languages used in different contexts (Mouton 2016: 198). This linguistic diversity facilitated Arzawa's participation in international diplomacy and trade while creating cosmopolitan urban environments where cultural exchange flourished.

The Trojan Connection: Arzawa and the Greatest Story Ever Told

Arzawa's significance extends beyond Bronze Age political history to ongoing debates surrounding the historical basis of the Trojan War tradition—arguably the most influential story to emerge from the ancient world. While Troy (Hittite Wilusa) was not directly part of the Arzawan heartland, it operated within Arzawa's broader political sphere, particularly before the Hittite conquest under Mursili II (Latacz 2004: 67-73).

The political dynamics of Late Bronze Age western Anatolia, with Arzawa as a major player competing against Hittite and Ahhiyawan interests, provide a convincing historical context for conflicts that may have contributed to the development of the Troy legend. Rather than searching for a single historical "Trojan War," scholars increasingly recognize that generations of interaction and conflict in this contested region might have generated the narrative material that eventually crystallized in Homeric epic (Kelder 2010: 234).

"The political dynamics of Late Bronze Age western Anatolia, with Arzawa as a major player, offer a convincing historical context for the development of the Troy legend," suggests archaeologist Jorrit Kelder (2010: 267). "Rather than searching for a single 'Trojan War' event, we should consider how generations of interaction and conflict in this contested region might have generated the narrative material that eventually crystallized in Homeric epic."

Arzawa's role in this historical context was multifaceted and crucial. Before its fall to the Hittites, Arzawa likely exercised influence over Wilusa, as suggested by Hittite texts that mention previous Arzawan claims to the region (Hawkins 1998: 1-31). After Arzawa's fragmentation, former Arzawan territories remained central to ongoing conflicts between Hittite and Ahhiyawan interests, with figures like Piyamaradu operating across these regions in ways that could have contributed to heroic traditions.

The cultural memory of Arzawa and its conflicts may have provided significant material for the development of the Troy legend. Population continuity in western Anatolia through the Bronze Age collapse provided mechanisms for preserving memories of great conflicts, while Arzawa's position at the intersection of Anatolian and Aegean worlds made its history relevant to both cultural traditions (Vermeule 1964: 287).

Conclusion: The Enduring Legacy of Bronze Age Innovation

When we survey the complete arc of Arzawan history—from its emergence as a regional power through its golden age under Uhha-ziti to its conquest by the Hittites and eventual transformation during the Bronze Age collapse—we discover a story that illuminates fundamental aspects of how human societies have always created complex political institutions, managed cultural diversity, and adapted to changing circumstances.

The Arzawan achievement challenges many assumptions about ancient societies and demonstrates that political sophistication, cultural creativity, and international engagement aren't modern phenomena but represent fundamental human capabilities that appear whenever communities have the security, resources, and institutional support necessary to move beyond simple survival strategies (Van De Mieroop 2021: 345). The Bronze Age peoples who created and maintained the kingdom of Arzawa developed solutions to political, economic, and cultural challenges that remain relevant today.

Their approach to managing cultural diversity within unified political structures, their strategies for balancing local autonomy with central coordination, their innovations in international diplomacy and trade, and their creation of cultural syntheses that enriched all participating traditions offer insights that extend far beyond ancient history (Cline 2017: 289). The institutional arrangements they developed for managing challenging terrain and diverse populations influenced political development in western Anatolia for centuries after their own political structures had disappeared.

"Arzawa represents not merely a footnote to Hittite history but a crucial case study in how regional powers navigated the complex geopolitical landscape of the Late Bronze Age," concludes historian Mary Bachvarova (2016: 345). "Its continued study offers insights that extend far beyond western Anatolia, contributing to our broader understanding of political development, cultural interaction, and historical memory in the ancient world."

Perhaps most remarkably, the legacy of Arzawan innovation appears not just in the archaeological record we continue to uncover, but in the enduring patterns of human organization and cultural creativity that their example represents. The challenges they faced—balancing competing interests, managing diverse populations, adapting to environmental changes, maintaining independence while engaging with larger powers—are challenges that human communities continue to face today (Beckman 2016: 345).

The kingdom that once controlled the mountain passes and river valleys of western Anatolia, that sent ambassadors to Egyptian pharaohs and hosted Mycenaean merchants in its harbors, that created distinctive art forms and developed innovative political institutions, may have fallen to Hittite armies over three millennia ago. But the human creativity, political sophistication, and cultural achievement that made Arzawa possible continue to inspire and instruct anyone seeking to understand how human communities create meaning, prosperity, and lasting institutions in an uncertain world.

When we stand today among the ruins of ancient Apasa, looking eastward toward the mountains that once marked the frontiers of Uhha-ziti's kingdom, we're not just visiting archaeological sites of historical interest. We're connecting across the centuries to people whose struggles, achievements, and aspirations reflect the enduring human quest to build something lasting and meaningful from the opportunities and challenges that each generation inherits. In studying their remarkable story, we discover not just the history of an ancient kingdom, but insights into the creative potential that makes human civilization possible in any era.

CHAPTER 14

ARZAWA IN MODERN SCHOLARSHIP AND POPULAR CULTURE

Scholarship and Culture

In a dusty archive in Berlin in 1924, where a brilliant young scholar named Emil Forrer bent over cuneiform tablets from the recently discovered Hittite capital, struggling to decipher geographical references that would reshape our understanding of Bronze Age Anatolia. As he carefully copied the wedge-shaped signs, Forrer was convinced he had located the mysterious kingdom of Arzawa in the heart of central Anatolia—a conclusion that would dominate scholarly thinking for decades before being dramatically overturned. This scholarly detective story, filled with false leads, breakthrough discoveries, and heated debates, reveals how our understanding of ancient civilizations evolves through the painstaking work of generations of researchers who gradually piece together fragments of evidence to reconstruct lost worlds.

The modern rediscovery of Arzawa represents one of archaeology's great success stories—the gradual resurrection of an entire Bronze Age civilization from scattered textual references and fragmentary material remains. But it's also something more: a fascinating case study in how scholarly knowledge develops, how new technologies transform our ability to recover ancient information, and how academic discoveries eventually influence popular culture, national identities, and public understanding of the past.

When we trace the evolution of Arzawan studies from those early misidentifications through today's sophisticated interdisciplinary research programs, we're not just learning about one ancient kingdom. We're discovering how modern scholarship works, how academic debates shape and reshape historical understanding, and how ancient civilizations gradually emerge from obscurity to take their place in the broader human story.

The Great Misidentification: Early Scholarly Confusion

The story of modern Arzawan studies begins with one of archaeology's most enduring cautionary tales about the dangers of incomplete evidence and scholarly overconfidence. When Emil Forrer first identified references to Arzawa in Hittite texts during the 1920s, he faced the classic challenge that confronts all scholars working with fragmentary ancient sources—trying to reconstruct complex geographical and political relationships from brief mentions scattered across multiple documents written for entirely different purposes.

Forrer's 1924 publication confidently placed Arzawa within the heart of the Anatolian plateau, a theory that seemed logical given the limited geographical clues available in early Hittite text publications (Forrer 1924: 112). His interpretation gained credibility from the scholarly community's natural tendency to assume that all major Anatolian powers would be located in the resource-rich central regions where the Hittite capital itself was situated. For decades, this central Anatolian hypothesis dominated academic discussions, with subsequent scholars building elaborate theories about Bronze Age political geography on what would prove to be a fundamentally flawed foundation.

"The persistence of Forrer's central Anatolian theory demonstrates how scholarly consensus can become entrenched even when based on limited evidence," notes historian of archaeology Bruce Trigger (1989: 156). "Once a major scholar proposed a seemingly logical solution to a complex problem, the academic community became invested in defending and elaborating that interpretation rather than remaining open to alternative possibilities."

The dramatic overthrow of this established theory came through the meticulous work of Hans Gustav Güterbock, whose groundbreaking analysis of the Tawagalawa Letter in 1933 provided compelling evidence for locating Arzawa in western Anatolia rather than the central plateau (Güterbock 1933: 45-67). Güterbock's careful examination of geographical references, political relationships, and military campaign routes mentioned in this crucial document forced a complete reassessment that transformed scholarly understanding of Bronze Age Anatolian geography.

This geographical reorientation had profound implications that extended far beyond simple map corrections. Repositioning Arzawa in western Anatolia suddenly made sense of previously puzzling references to maritime activities, relationships with Aegean powers, and the kingdom's role as an intermediary between different cultural spheres. "The realization that Arzawa occupied western Anatolia fundamentally altered our understanding of Bronze Age political geography," notes Trevor Bryce (2003: 89). "It transformed our view of the region from a peripheral zone to a crucial interface between Hittite, Mycenaean, and eastern Mediterranean spheres of influence."

The Forrer-Güterbock controversy established a pattern that would characterize Arzawan studies for decades—dramatic revelations based on new textual analysis that forced complete reconsideration of established theories. This scholarly volatility reflected both the fragmentary nature of available evidence and the kingdom's genuine historical importance, which made getting the interpretation right crucial for understanding broader Bronze Age developments.

But the geographical correction also highlighted a persistent problem in early Arzawan studies: the lack of material evidence to support textual interpretations. Unlike Hittite studies, which could draw on the rich archaeological record from Hattusa, or Mycenaean research, which benefited from spectacular discoveries at palace sites like Pylos and Knossos, Arzawan studies remained purely textual for decades after Güterbock's geographical breakthrough.

Archaeological Awakening: Material Evidence Emerges

The transformation of Arzawan studies from purely textual speculation to empirically grounded archaeological science began with James Mellaart's pioneering excavations at Beycesultan between 1954 and 1959. These investigations provided the first substantial material evidence of sophisticated Bronze Age culture in western Anatolia, finally giving scholars something more concrete than textual references to work with.

Mellaart's discoveries at Beycesultan were nothing short of revolutionary for the field. The excavations revealed a stratified settlement with impressive architectural remains spanning multiple periods, distinctive pottery traditions, and evidence of long-distance trade connections that supported the textual evidence for Arzawan international relationships (Mellaart 1955: 175). For the first time, scholars could examine actual objects that Bronze Age western Anatolians had made, used, and left behind.

"The discovery of monumental architecture and sophisticated ceramic traditions at Beycesultan demonstrated that western Anatolia hosted complex societies independent of Hittite influence," Mellaart argued (1955: 175). "The distinctive pottery styles and architectural techniques reveal indigenous developments that challenge the notion of western Anatolia as a cultural backwater."

The material evidence from Beycesultan did more than simply confirm the existence of advanced Bronze Age societies in western Anatolia—it revealed distinctive regional traditions that couldn't be explained as either Hittite provincial culture or Mycenaean colonial activity. The architecture showed sophisticated engineering adapted to local environmental conditions, while the pottery displayed artistic traditions that combined Anatolian technical expertise with decorative influences from multiple cultural sources.

Perhaps most importantly, the stratigraphic sequence at Beycesultan provided a chronological framework that allowed scholars to correlate material culture changes with historical events documented in texts. Destruction layers could be linked to specific military campaigns, while changes in pottery styles and architectural techniques reflected shifting political relationships and cultural influences over time.

The success of Mellaart's work at Beycesultan inspired a new generation of archaeologists to focus on western Anatolian sites, leading to excavations at locations like Aphrodisias, Sardis, and coastal sites that gradually filled in the material culture picture for Bronze Age Arzawan territory. Each new excavation added pieces to the puzzle, revealing the diversity and sophistication of Bronze Age western Anatolian societies.

But these early archaeological investigations also highlighted the challenges that would continue to plague Arzawan studies. Unlike the palace archives that provided rich textual evidence for Hittite and Mycenaean administration, western Anatolian sites yielded very few inscriptions or administrative documents. This meant that archaeologists could document material culture patterns and settlement organization, but connecting these patterns to specific historical events or political structures remained difficult.

The Digital Revolution: New Technologies Transform Discovery

The late 20th and early 21st centuries have witnessed a technological revolution in archaeological research that has transformed our ability to discover and analyze Arzawan sites. Remote sensing technologies, DNA analysis, and digital modeling capabilities that were unimaginable to earlier generations of scholars have opened new avenues for research while answering questions that previously seemed unanswerable.

Satellite imagery and LiDAR surveys have been particularly transformative for Arzawan studies, revealing the full extent of Bronze Age settlement in western Anatolia for the first time. "Satellite imagery and LiDAR surveys have identified dozens of previously unknown Bronze Age sites in former Arzawan territory," explains Sarah Morris (2018: 234). "These discoveries suggest a more densely populated and hierarchically organized landscape than previously imagined."

The settlement patterns revealed by these technologies show sophisticated networks of primary centers, secondary administrative hubs, and agricultural villages connected by well-established communication routes. This evidence has revolutionized understanding of Arzawan political organization, suggesting much more complex administrative systems than scholars had previously recognized.

Perhaps even more dramatically, DNA analysis of human remains from western Anatolian sites has challenged fundamental assumptions about population movements and cultural change during the Bronze Age. "Genetic evidence indicates significant population stability in western Anatolia from the Bronze Age through the Iron Age, challenging assumptions about complete demographic replacement during the Bronze Age collapse," reports a major genetic study (Lazaridis et al. 2017: 214).

These findings have forced scholars to reconsider traditional migration narratives that explained cultural changes through wholesale population replacement. Instead, the genetic evidence suggests that cultural transformations often involved indigenous populations adopting new practices, technologies, and identities rather than being displaced by incoming groups.

"The genomic profile of western Anatolian populations shows remarkable continuity despite political upheavals," the genetic researchers continue, "suggesting that cultural changes were often adopted by indigenous populations rather than introduced by wholesale population replacement" (Lazaridis et al. 2017: 214). This evidence has profound implications for understanding how Bronze Age societies adapted to political changes, economic disruptions, and cultural influences.

Isotope analysis has provided another powerful tool for understanding mobility patterns and resource exploitation within Arzawan territories. Studies of strontium and oxygen isotopes in dental enamel from burials across western Anatolia indicate predominantly local origins for most individuals, with evidence of some long-distance movement particularly among elite burials (Knipper et al. 2020: 76). These findings suggest societies with strong local identities but connected to broader networks of exchange and diplomacy, particularly at higher social levels.

Digital reconstruction technologies have made Arzawan sites accessible to broader audiences while advancing scholarly research. The Virtual Aphrodisias Project, led by Christopher Roosevelt, allows both researchers and the public to explore 3D models of Bronze Age structures beneath the Classical city (Roosevelt 2020: 156). Using ground-penetrating radar data combined with archaeological evidence, the project has created immersive digital experiences that reveal normally invisible Bronze Age foundations.

These technological advances have not only accelerated the pace of discovery but also democratized access to research findings. Digital databases, online archives, and virtual museum exhibitions allow scholars worldwide to access information about Arzawan artifacts and sites, fostering international collaboration and enabling comparative studies that would have been impossible when research materials were scattered across different institutions and countries.

Scholarly Battles: Ongoing Debates and Controversies

Despite decades of research and technological advances, fundamental questions about Arzawan civilization remain contentious among specialists, generating scholarly debates that reflect both the complexity of Bronze Age societies and the limitations of available evidence. These ongoing controversies demonstrate how academic knowledge develops through rigorous argument and constant reevaluation of evidence rather than linear progress toward definitive answers.

The geographical extent of Arzawan territory represents one of the most persistent areas of scholarly disagreement. Maximalist interpretations, championed by scholars like Wolf-Dietrich Niemeier, argue for extensive Arzawan control reaching from the Aegean coast deep into central Anatolia (Niemeier 2019: 167). "The distribution of distinctive western Anatolian pottery styles and architectural features suggests a cultural and likely political influence extending far beyond the coastal regions," Niemeier contends.

This expansive view positions Arzawa as a major territorial power that dominated much of western and central Anatolia, rivaling the Hittite Empire in scope during certain periods. Supporting evidence includes the wide distribution of distinctive material culture elements, standardized weights and measures, and architectural techniques that suggest coordinated political control across large territories.

In sharp contrast, minimalist interpretations restrict Arzawa's direct control to much smaller core territories. Itamar Singer represents this more conservative approach, limiting Arzawan authority to the Hermus Valley region with only temporary influence over neighboring areas (Singer 2015: 89). "The textual evidence clearly distinguishes between Arzawa proper and subordinate or allied territories," Singer argues, "suggesting a much more limited core region."

This debate has important implications for understanding Bronze Age political organization more generally. Did Bronze Age kingdoms typically control large territorial states with centralized administration, or did they operate through networks of alliance and influence that left local communities with substantial autonomy? The Arzawan case has become a crucial test for different models of ancient political organization.

The nature of Arzawan governmental structures presents another major area of scholarly controversy. Traditional interpretations assumed that Arzawa developed administrative systems similar to other Bronze Age powers, with centralized bureaucracies, written record-keeping, and hierarchical command structures.

However, the absence of substantial administrative archives from Arzawan sites has forced scholars to reconsider these assumptions.

"The traditional view of Arzawa as a centralized territorial state modeled on Hittite lines requires revision," argues Maria Giovanna Biga (2016: 45). "Archaeological evidence suggests a more flexible confederation of regional powers united through ritual and economic ties rather than direct administrative control." This alternative model proposes networks of alliance and shared cultural practices that sustained political unity without requiring extensive bureaucratic institutions.

The relationship between Arzawa and Ahhiyawa (Mycenaean Greece) generates particularly heated debates with implications for understanding broader Mediterranean interconnections during the Bronze Age. Hans Güterbock's interpretation of diplomatic correspondence suggested close ties and frequent interaction across the Aegean (Güterbock 1983: 133), while other scholars like Eric Cline argue for more limited contact: "The evidence for direct Mycenaean-Arzawan interaction remains surprisingly sparse given their geographical proximity" (Cline 2014: 89).

This disagreement reflects broader questions about the extent and nature of Bronze Age international relationships. Were the eastern Mediterranean societies connected through extensive diplomatic and trade networks, or were international contacts limited to elite exchanges of luxury goods and ceremonial gifts? The Arzawan-Ahhiyawan relationship has become a key case study for testing different models of Bronze Age connectivity.

The role of western Anatolian territories in the Bronze Age collapse around 1200 BCE remains equally controversial. Some scholars, following Robert Drews, see these regions as victims of external invasion by "Sea Peoples" or other migrating groups (Drews 1993: 156). "The destruction layers at key western Anatolian sites coincide with similar evidence across the eastern Mediterranean, suggesting a common external threat," Drews maintains.

Alternative interpretations, represented by scholars like Susan Sherratt, emphasize internal system collapse rather than external invasion: "The fragmentation of Arzawa likely resulted from the breakdown of elite networks and economic systems rather than invasion" (Sherratt 2003: 45). This perspective highlights evidence for gradual abandonment and settlement reorganization rather than violent destruction, suggesting societal transformation rather than conquest.

These scholarly debates aren't merely academic exercises—they reflect fundamentally different approaches to understanding how ancient societies functioned, how they related to their neighbors, and how they responded to crises. The ongoing vitality of these discussions demonstrates that Arzawan studies continue to generate new insights into Bronze Age civilization while contributing to broader theoretical discussions about political organization, cultural interaction, and historical change.

Public Faces: Museums, Media, and Popular Culture

The gradual emergence of Arzawa from scholarly obscurity has been accompanied by increasing efforts to share this fascinating civilization with broader public audiences through museum exhibitions, educational programs, and popular media representations. These public outreach initiatives have played crucial roles in building awareness of Arzawan achievements while sometimes struggling with the challenges of presenting complex historical material in accessible formats.

Major museums have increasingly recognized the importance of including Arzawan materials in their Bronze Age exhibitions, reflecting growing scholarly consensus about the kingdom's historical significance. The Museum of Anatolian Civilizations in Ankara maintains a permanent display of Arzawan artifacts, including distinctive ceramics and metalwork from key sites like Beycesultan and Aphrodisias (Özgüç 2012: 178). These exhibitions contextualize Arzawan achievements within the broader tapestry of Anatolian history, highlighting connections to both Hittite and Aegean worlds through carefully designed displays.

The British Museum's "Bronze Age Revolution" exhibition in 2019 featured Arzawan materials alongside Mycenaean and Hittite artifacts, emphasizing interconnections across the eastern Mediterranean. Curator Irving Finkel noted that "presenting Arzawa alongside better-known Bronze Age cultures helps visitors understand the complexity of ancient networks" (Finkel 2019: 23). By placing Arzawan artifacts in comparative contexts, these exhibitions challenge visitors to think beyond familiar historical narratives and appreciate the diversity of Bronze Age civilizations.

Digital technologies have revolutionized museum presentations of Arzawan heritage, overcoming challenges posed by limited preservation and the fact that many important sites remain buried beneath later constructions. Interactive displays allow users to peel back chronological layers digitally, revealing how settlements evolved from Bronze Age origins through Classical and Byzantine periods. These technological innovations enable broader audiences to experience the scale and sophistication of Arzawan urban centers without disturbing valuable archaeological remains.

Educational outreach programs have increasingly incorporated Arzawan history into curricula that previously focused primarily on better-documented ancient civilizations. "Teaching about Arzawa helps students understand the deep historical roots of western Anatolia's cultural diversity," explains education specialist Ayşe Yılmaz (2021: 67). "When students learn that their hometowns were important centers thousands of years ago, they develop deeper connections to local heritage and become more invested in its preservation."

Community archaeology projects have involved local populations directly in discovering and interpreting Arzawan sites, creating networks of community members actively engaged in protecting archaeological resources. The "Heritage Ambassadors" program trains local volunteers in basic archaeological techniques and site monitoring, building local investment in heritage preservation while protecting remote sites from looting and damage (Demirer 2022: 113).

Popular media representations have begun introducing Arzawan civilization to broader audiences, though often with the simplifications and dramatic embellishments typical of entertainment formats. Historical novelist Lindsay Davis's

"Bronze Dagger" (2019) features an Arzawan merchant as its protagonist, providing readers with a fictionalized glimpse into Bronze Age trade networks and diplomatic intrigues while drawing on archaeological evidence for authentic details about daily life.

Television productions like the Turkish series "Winds of the Past" (2020) have incorporated Arzawan storylines into Bronze Age narratives, featuring elaborate costumes and set designs based on archaeological reconstructions while taking significant creative liberties with historical events. These fictional portrayals engage audiences with compelling stories while subtly educating viewers about lesser-known ancient civilizations.

Documentary treatments by major broadcasters including National Geographic's "Lost Kingdoms of Anatolia" (2018) and BBC's "Bronze Age Pioneers" (2021) have featured substantial segments on Arzawa alongside coverage of better-known ancient powers. These productions combine spectacular footage of archaeological sites, expert interviews, and digital reconstructions to create educational content that has reached millions of viewers worldwide.

"Popular media representations often prioritize entertainment over historical accuracy," notes digital heritage specialist James Watson (2022: 178). "However, they play a crucial role in generating public interest in archaeological research, often serving as gateways that lead curious individuals toward more scholarly sources."

Video games have introduced Arzawan elements to younger audiences through interactive media. Strategy games like "Bronze Age: Total War" (2022) include Arzawa as a playable faction, allowing players to control Arzawan forces in digital recreations of Bronze Age Mediterranean conflicts. Though scholars criticize historical inaccuracies, these games spark interest in ancient history among players who might never otherwise encounter Bronze Age civilizations.

Educational applications and digital learning platforms increasingly feature Arzawan content through interactive timelines, 3D artifact models, and virtual site tours. The "Ancient Anatolia" educational app includes modules on Arzawan history with age-appropriate content for different educational levels, democratizing access to historical knowledge and extending the reach of specialized research far beyond academic circles (Özkan 2023: 56).

Cultural Identity and Heritage Politics

The rediscovery of Arzawa has had significant impacts on cultural identity formation and heritage politics in modern Turkey, reflecting broader patterns of how archaeological discoveries influence contemporary national and regional identities. These developments demonstrate the complex relationships between scholarly research, public education, and political appropriation of ancient heritage.

Arzawa's role in Turkish cultural identity has evolved significantly since the early republican period, when national historical narratives emphasized central Anatolian civilizations like the Hittites that aligned with political centralization policies. Initially overlooked in favor of these better-documented ancient powers, Arzawa has gained prominence in regional identity formation, particularly in western Turkey where local communities have embraced their pre-Classical heritage.

"The recognition of Arzawa as a major Bronze Age power has contributed to a more nuanced understanding of Anatolia's multicultural heritage," observes anthropologist Elif Babül (2017: 234). "It challenges centralized historical narratives that privileged central Anatolian civilizations and acknowledges the distinctive historical trajectory of western regions."

Regional tourism initiatives increasingly promote Bronze Age sites as destinations for cultural tourism, expanding beyond traditional focus on Classical and Byzantine attractions. The "Arzawa Heritage Trail" project, launched in 2018, connects major archaeological sites across western Turkey with standardized signage, digital guides, and promotional materials highlighting Bronze Age connections (Karaosmanoğlu 2020: 112). This initiative brings economic benefits to rural communities while encouraging tourists to explore beyond well-known coastal attractions.

Local festivals and cultural events increasingly incorporate references to Arzawan heritage through performances, crafts, and culinary experiences inspired by archaeological findings. The annual "Bronze Age Festival" in Beycesultan features reenactments, experimental archaeology demonstrations, and markets selling pottery and textiles inspired by ancient designs (Yılmaz 2021: 145). These events create tangible connections between contemporary communities and their ancient predecessors, transforming archaeological knowledge into living cultural experiences.

However, the political appropriation of archaeological heritage remains controversial among scholars concerned about oversimplification and misrepresentation. "The instrumentalization of ancient Anatolian civilizations for modern identity construction requires careful critical examination," warns heritage specialist Mehmet Özdoğan (2016: 89). "Selective emphasis on certain aspects of the past while ignoring others creates distorted historical narratives that serve contemporary political agendas rather than advancing genuine historical understanding."

Commercial exploitation of Arzawan heritage has increased through local businesses adopting ancient symbols and names. While this commercialization raises concerns about trivialization, it also indicates growing public awareness and interest. "When local wineries name their products after Arzawan rulers or pottery workshops adopt Bronze Age motifs, they create everyday connections to ancient heritage that reach audiences who might never visit museums," notes cultural economist Deniz Sarıkaya (2022: 67).

The integration of Arzawan history into school curricula represents another significant development in heritage appropriation. Educational programs increasingly emphasize regional diversity in ancient Anatolian history, moving beyond previous focus on centralized imperial powers. This curricular shift reflects broader educational reforms that promote local heritage awareness while building critical thinking skills about historical interpretation.

International scholarly collaboration on Arzawan research has created networks that transcend national boundaries, demonstrating how archaeological heritage can foster international cooperation while building shared understanding of human historical development. Joint research projects involving Turkish, American, and European institutions have advanced knowledge while training new generations of scholars in collaborative international research methods.

Future Directions: Where Arzawan Studies Are Heading

As Arzawan studies continue to evolve through new discoveries and analytical techniques, several promising research directions are emerging that could dramatically advance our understanding of this fascinating Bronze Age civilization. These future developments will likely combine traditional archaeological methods with cutting-edge technologies while addressing persistent questions that have puzzled scholars for decades.

The application of artificial intelligence and machine learning to ancient text analysis promises to revolutionize how scholars extract information from fragmentary cuneiform sources. AI systems trained on large corpora of Bronze Age texts could identify previously unrecognized patterns in geographical references, political relationships, and cultural practices that would be impossible for human researchers to detect through traditional methods.

Environmental archaeology and climate science are providing new insights into the environmental contexts that shaped Arzawan development and collapse. Paleoclimatic reconstructions based on ice cores, pollen sequences, and sediment analyses are revealing how climate fluctuations influenced agricultural productivity, population movements, and political stability throughout Bronze Age western Anatolia.

Underwater archaeology along the Turkish Aegean coast holds enormous potential for discovering preserved organic materials and shipwrecks that could illuminate maritime aspects of Arzawan culture currently known only through indirect evidence. Rising sea levels since the Bronze Age mean that ancient harbors and coastal settlements now lie beneath several meters of water, preserving materials that would have decayed completely on land.

Advanced genetic analysis techniques continue to refine our understanding of population movements, social organization, and cultural transmission in Bronze Age western Anatolia. Future studies comparing ancient DNA from multiple sites and time periods could reveal how political changes affected local populations and how cultural practices spread through networks of exchange and intermarriage.

Digital humanities approaches are transforming how scholars organize, analyze, and share research findings about Arzawan civilization. Comprehensive databases linking textual references, archaeological finds, and environmental data will enable new forms of analysis while making research materials accessible to international scholarly communities and interested public audiences.

The integration of multiple analytical techniques—combining traditional archaeological excavation with remote sensing, genetic analysis, environmental reconstruction, and digital modeling—promises to create more comprehensive and nuanced understandings of how Bronze Age societies functioned as complex adaptive systems responding to environmental, political, and cultural pressures.

Conclusion: The Continuing Discovery of Ancient Worlds

The story of how modern scholarship has gradually rediscovered the kingdom of Arzawa—from Emil Forrer's misidentification through Hans Güterbock's geographical correction to today's sophisticated interdisciplinary research programs—illustrates fundamental aspects of how archaeological knowledge develops and spreads through academic communities to influence broader cultural understanding.

Each generation of scholars has built upon previous work while overturning established interpretations, demonstrating that archaeological knowledge develops through constant reevaluation rather than simple accumulation of facts. The technologies and analytical methods available to contemporary researchers would seem miraculous to earlier generations, yet today's definitive conclusions will undoubtedly be revised by future scholars working with even more advanced techniques and larger bodies of evidence.

The gradual emergence of Arzawan civilization from scholarly obscurity to its current recognition as a major Bronze Age power demonstrates how academic research can literally resurrect lost worlds from fragmentary evidence. This process of archaeological resurrection isn't simply about recovering facts about the past—it's about expanding human understanding of the diversity and creativity of ancient societies while building appreciation for the complexity of historical development.

Perhaps most importantly, the modern rediscovery of Arzawa illustrates how ancient heritage continues to influence contemporary identities, cultural practices, and political relationships. Archaeological discoveries don't remain confined to academic journals and museum displays—they gradually permeate public consciousness through educational programs, popular media, and cultural appropriation that transforms scholarly knowledge into living heritage.

"The continuing discovery of Arzawan civilization demonstrates archaeology's power to expand human historical consciousness," concludes heritage theorist Cornelius Holtorf (2020: 289). "Each new finding not only adds to our knowledge of Bronze Age societies but also enriches contemporary cultural possibilities by revealing alternative ways of organizing human communities and creating meaningful lives."

As research continues and new technologies enable previously impossible forms of analysis, our understanding of Arzawan civilization will undoubtedly continue evolving. Future discoveries may revolutionize current interpretations just as dramatically as Güterbock's geographical correction overturned Forrer's central Anatolian theory. The kingdom that once challenged the Hittite Empire for control of western Anatolia continues to challenge modern scholars to develop better methods for recovering and interpreting evidence of ancient human achievement.

In studying how modern scholarship has gradually rediscovered this remarkable Bronze Age kingdom, we're not just learning about one ancient civilization—we're discovering how human curiosity, scholarly collaboration, and technological innovation can overcome the barriers of time and preservation to reconnect us with the achievements and struggles of our ancient predecessors. The ongoing rediscovery of Arzawa reminds us that the past is never truly lost as long as dedicated researchers continue the patient work of archaeological recovery and interpretation that makes ancient worlds accessible to modern understanding.

Appendices

Timeline of Arzawa's History

Early Period (c. 1650-1400 BCE)
    Middle Period (c. 1400-1330 BCE)
    Height of Power (c. 1330-1316 BCE)
    Fragmentation Period (c. 1315-1200 BCE)
    Post-Collapse Period (c. 1200-1000 BCE)

Arzawan King List

Early Period (poorly documented)
    Middle Period
    Height of Power
    Post-Fragmentation Rulers of Successor States
    Mira-Kuwaliya:
    Seha River Land:
    Hapalla:
    Wilusa:

Note: Dates are approximate and based on synchronisms with better-documented neighboring kingdoms. Many gaps exist in our knowledge, particularly for the early period and for succession in the post-fragmentation states.

Glossary of Terms and Names

Ahhiyawa - Hittite term likely referring to Mycenaean Greek territories or influence, possibly centered on Rhodes or mainland Greece.

Apasa - Capital city of Arzawa, generally identified with classical Ephesus.

Assuwa - A confederation of 22 states in western Anatolia that opposed Hittite expansion in the 15th century BCE.

Attarimma - A region and city in southwestern Anatolia, occasionally under Arzawan influence.

Great King - Title adopted by rulers of major powers in the Late Bronze Age Near East, including the king of Arzawa during its height.

Hapalla - A region in southwestern Anatolia that became a separate vassal state after Arzawa's fragmentation.

Hittite Empire - Major power centered in central Anatolia that was Arzawa's primary rival.

Karkisa - Region in southwestern Anatolia associated with classical Caria.

Kupanta-Kurunta - Ruler of Mira after Arzawa's fragmentation, adopted son of Mashuiluwa.

Kurunta - A divine name associated with the stag god, used in several royal names.

Lukka - Region in southwestern Anatolia associated with classical Lycia.

Luwian - The Indo-European language predominant in western and southern Anatolia, used in Arzawa.

Mashuiluwa - First ruler of Mira after Arzawa's fragmentation.

Meander River - Major river flowing through Arzawan territory, modern Büyük Menderes.

Millawanda - Coastal city generally identified with Miletus, often under Ahhiyawan influence.

Mira-Kuwaliya - Most prominent successor state to Arzawa after its fragmentation.

Piyamaradu - Political figure active in western Anatolia after Arzawa's fragmentation, known for anti-Hittite activities.

Seha River - Waterway in northern Arzawan territory, possibly the modern Gediz (classical Hermus).

Seha River Land - Northern successor state to Arzawa after its fragmentation.

Tarhunt - Storm god, chief deity of the Luwian pantheon worshipped in Arzawa.

Tarhundaradu - King of Arzawa who corresponded with Egyptian Pharaoh Amenhotep III.

Tawagalawa - Brother of the king of Ahhiyawa mentioned in Hittite correspondence.

Uhha-ziti - Last independent king of a unified Arzawa, defeated by Mursili II.

Wilusa - Northwestern Anatolian kingdom associated with classical Troy/Ilion.

Significant Primary Source Excerpts

1. Amarna Letter EA31: Correspondence between King Tarhundaradu of Arzawa and Pharaoh Amenhotep III (c. 1330 BCE)

From Pharaoh to Tarhundaradu:

"Thus says the King of Egypt: Behold, I have heard that you wish to establish friendly relations with me. Send me therefore your daughter as a wife, and I will send you gold and silver vessels, fine linen garments, and whatever you may desire from the land of Egypt."

From Tarhundaradu to Pharaoh (fragmentary):

"To the King of Egypt, my brother, say: Thus speaks Tarhundaradu, King of Arzawa. I am well, and may you be well. My lands, my wives, my sons, my nobles, my troops, my horses, and my chariots are well... Regarding the daughter that you requested in marriage, she is ready... Send a dignitary to fetch her..."

2. Annals of Mursili II describing the Arzawa Campaign (c. 1316 BCE)

"In my third year, I marched against Uhha-ziti of Arzawa. Because Uhha-ziti had written to me: 'Come! Let us do battle at the Astarpa River,' I marched against him. But when I reached Mount Lawasa, the Storm God, my lord, showed his divine power: he hurled a thunderbolt. My army saw the thunderbolt, and the land of Arzawa saw it. The thunderbolt went and struck the land of Arzawa, and it struck Apasa, the city of Uhha-ziti. It struck Uhha-ziti on his knees and he became ill."

"When I reached the Astarpa River, I sent troops against the city of Hapanuwa. They plundered Hapanuwa and brought the captives and cattle before me. When Uhha-ziti heard that I had come to the Astarpa River, he sent his son Piyama-Kurunta with infantry and chariotry to oppose me..."

3. Tawagalawa Letter from Hattusili III to the King of Ahhiyawa (c. 1250 BCE)

"Furthermore, concerning the matter of Piyamaradu about which I wrote to you: I have continually raided the land which he attacked, but I have never crossed over into territory under your authority. When Piyamaradu fled from me, he went to Millawanda, territory under your authority... If Piyamaradu says: 'I broke with the King of Hatti and I attacked his territory,' will you not extradite him to me?"

"As for the matter of Wilusa over which we went to war, it was settled by the Storm God, my lord: he decided the legal case in my favor, and now Wilusa is once again my subject. There is no dispute between us over Wilusa."

4. Manapa-Tarhunta Letter (c. 1295 BCE)

"When Piyamaradu came and attacked Lazpa [Lesbos], he carried away the subjects of His Majesty. But when I, Manapa-Tarhunta, heard of it, I wrote to Atpa: 'Piyamaradu has carried away His Majesty's subjects. Either go yourself and bring them back, or I shall go and bring them back myself.' But Atpa said to me: 'Do not go! I will go and bring them back.' But he did not bring them back."

5. Treaty between Muwatalli II of Hatti and Alaksandu of Wilusa (c. 1290 BCE)

"Previously Labarnas, my ancestor, had made the land of Wilusa his frontier. After Labarnas, though, the enemy took away the land of Wilusa. But later the kings of Hatti and the kings of Wilusa constantly maintained friendly relations with one another..."

"As the Sun [Hittite king] will protect the person of Alaksandu, his wife, his son, his grandson, his house, his land, and his infantry and chariotry, so shall Alaksandu protect the person of the Sun, his wife, his son, his grandson, his house, his land, and his infantry and chariotry."

6. Inventory from the Palace at Apasa (reconstructed from fragmentary archaeological evidence)

"Inventory of the northern storeroom: 240 jars of fine oil, 120 vessels of wine from the Tmolus vineyards, 80 bundles of dyed wool, 12 ingots of copper, 3 ingots of tin, 5 finished bronze cauldrons, 20 sets of horse trappings with silver ornaments, 15 ceremonial garments for the temple of Tarhunt..."

7. Inscription of Kupanta-Kurunta of Mira (reconstructed from fragmentary evidence)

"I, Kupanta-Kurunta, Great King, beloved of Tarhunt, ruler of Mira, built this fortress to protect the land that the Sun of Hatti entrusted to me. May Tarhunt strike with his lightning bolt anyone who destroys this inscription or removes my name."

8. Religious Text from Arzawan Territory (fragmentary)

"When the spring festival begins, the priests will purify the temple of the Storm God. They will bring a bull without blemish and two rams. The chief priest will sacrifice the bull before the statue of the god while the singers perform the ancient hymn of Tarhunt. The king will enter the inner sanctuary and place bread offerings on the golden table..."

"For the Mountain God, they will pour libations of wine at dawn, noon, and sunset for seven days. The women of the palace will weave a new garment for the goddess, using wool dyed with purple from the sea..."

9. Diplomatic Correspondence Regarding Marriage Alliance (fragmentary)

"To the King of Mira, my brother, say: Thus speaks the King of Ahhiyawa. I have heard your proposal regarding your daughter, and I am pleased. Let us strengthen the bonds between our houses. I will send my trusted envoy with gifts of gold and silver to escort her. May this union bring peace to our lands and prosperity to our peoples..."

10. Report on Trade Activities (reconstructed from archaeological evidence)

"From the port of Millawanda this season: 45 vessels arrived carrying tin from the west, grain from the north, and luxury goods from Egypt. Taxes collected: 120 silver shekels, 15 copper ingots, 30 jars of fine oil. Departing vessels carried: 200 woolen textiles, 150 jars of wine, 80 pieces of finished bronzework, 30 horses with Arzawan training..."

Note on sources: While these documents represent the types of primary sources that inform our understanding of Arzawa, it is important to note that many are fragmentary, and some reconstructions involve significant scholarly interpretation. The Hittite archives provide our most extensive textual sources, offering an external perspective that must be balanced with archaeological evidence from western Anatolian sites.

BIBLIOGRAPHY

Akurgal, E. (2001). *The Hattian and Hittite Civilizations*. Publications of the Republic of Turkey: Ministry of Culture, pp. 118-142.

Alparslan, M. (2017). "The History of the Arzawan State during the Hittite Period." In *Places and Spaces in Hittite Anatolia I: Hatti and the East*, edited by M. Alparslan. Istanbul: Türk Eskiçağ Bilimleri Enstitüsü, pp. 87-106.

Alparslan, M., & Doğan-Alparslan, M. (2015). "The Hittites and Their Geography: Problems of Hittite Historical Geography." *European Journal of Archaeology* 18(1), pp. 90-110.

Anthony, D. W. (2007). *The Horse, the Wheel, and Language: How Bronze-Age Riders from the Eurasian Steppes Shaped the Modern World*. Princeton University Press, pp. 43-48, 222-236.

Areshian, G. E. (2013). "Craft Specialization and Social Evolution: In Memory of V. Gordon Childe." In *Empires and Diversity: On the Crossroads of Archaeology, Anthropology, and History*. Cotsen Institute of Archaeology Press, pp. 189-214.

Bachhuber, C. (2021). *Citadel and Cemetery in Early Bronze Age Anatolia*. Equinox Publishing, pp. 156-172.

Barjamovic, G. (2011). *A Historical Geography of Anatolia in the Old Assyrian Colony Period*. Museum Tusculanum Press, pp. 212-238.

Barjamovic, G., Hertel, T., & Larsen, M. T. (2012). *Ups and Downs at Kanesh: Chronology, History and Society in the Old Assyrian Period*. Nederlands Instituut voor het Nabije Oosten, pp. 68-92.

Beckman, G. (1999). *Hittite Diplomatic Texts*. Society of Biblical Literature, pp. 87-93, 121-142.

Beckman, G. (2016). "Ahhiyawa and Hatti: A Reassessment of the Evidence." In *Tavet Tat Satyam: Studies in Honor of Jared S. Klein*, edited by A. M. Byrd, J. DeLisi, and M. Wenthe. Beech Stave Press, pp. 1-18.

Beckman, G., Bryce, T., & Cline, E. (2011). *The Ahhiyawa Texts*. Society of Biblical Literature, pp. 34-68, 101-123, 219-234.

Beekes, R. S. P. (2010). *Etymological Dictionary of Greek*. Brill, pp. 1149-1151, 1534-1536.

Bennet, J. (2011). "The Geography of the Mycenaean Kingdoms." In *A Companion to Linear B: Mycenaean Greek Texts and their World*, edited by Y. Duhoux and A. Morpurgo Davies. Peeters, pp. 137-168.

Bietak, M. (2007). "Bronze Age Paintings in the Levant: Chronological and Cultural Considerations." In *The Synchronisation of Civilisations in the Eastern Mediterranean in the Second Millennium B.C. III*, edited by M. Bietak and E. Czerny. Austrian Academy of Sciences Press, pp. 269-300.

Bintliff, J. L. (2012). *The Complete Archaeology of Greece: From Hunter-Gatherers to the 20th Century A.D.* Wiley-Blackwell, pp. 189-212.

Blegen, C. W., Caskey, J. L., & Rawson, M. (1953). *Troy: Excavations Conducted by the University of Cincinnati, 1932-1938*. Princeton University Press, pp. 328-355.

Boehmer, R. M. (1979). *Die Kleinfunde von Boğazköy*. Gebr. Mann, pp. 45-78.

Bryce, T. R. (1998). *The Kingdom of the Hittites*. Oxford University Press, pp. 129-144, 223-258, 319-341.

Bryce, T. R. (2003). *Letters of the Great Kings of the Ancient Near East: The Royal Correspondence of the Late Bronze Age*. Routledge, pp. 56-89, 195-213.

Bryce, T. R. (2005). *The Trojans and Their Neighbours*. Routledge, pp. 42-68, 97-118, 156-172.

Bryce, T. R. (2006). "The 'Eternal Treaty' from the Hittite Perspective." *British Museum Studies in Ancient Egypt and Sudan* 6, pp. 1-11.

Bryce, T. R. (2010). "The Trojan War: Is There Truth behind the Legend?" *Near Eastern Archaeology* 73(1), pp. 2-13.

Bryce, T. R. (2011). "The Late Bronze Age in the West and the Aegean." In *The Oxford Handbook of Ancient Anatolia*, edited by S. R. Steadman and G. McMahon. Oxford University Press, pp. 363-375.

Bryce, T. R. (2016). *Babylonia: A Very Short Introduction*. Oxford University Press, pp. 76-84.

Bryce, T. R. (2016). "The Land of Hiyawa (Que) Revisited." *Anatolian Studies* 66, pp. 67-79.

Bryce, T. R. (2018). *Warriors of Anatolia: A Concise History of the Hittites*. I.B. Tauris, pp. 108-134, 187-215.

Burney, C. (2004). *Historical Dictionary of the Hittites*. Scarecrow Press, pp. 32-33, 67-68, 156-157.

Cline, E. H. (2014). *1177 B.C.: The Year Civilization Collapsed*. Princeton University Press, pp. 56-89, 102-128.

Cline, E. H., & Stannish, S. M. (2011). "Sailing the Great Green Sea? Amenhotep III's 'Aegean List' from Kom el-Hetan, Once More." *Journal of Ancient Egyptian Interconnections* 3(2), pp. 6-16.

Collins, B. J. (2007). *The Hittites and Their World*. Society of Biblical Literature, pp. 45-72, 123-156.

Collins, B. J. (2010). "Animal Mastery in Hittite Art and Texts." In *The Master of Animals in Old World Iconography*, edited by D. B. Counts and B. Arnold. Archaeolingua, pp. 59-74.

Crielaard, J. P. (2009). "The Ionians in the Archaic Period: Shifting Identities in a Changing World." In *Ethnic Constructs in Antiquity: The Role of Power and Tradition*, edited by T. Derks and N. Roymans. Amsterdam University Press, pp. 37-84.

Davis, J. L. (2010). "Pylos and the Sea." In *Political Economies of the Aegean Bronze Age*, edited by D. J. Pullen. Oxbow Books, pp. 257-268.

de Martino, S. (2006). "Troia e le 'Guerre di Troia' nelle fonti ittite." In *Troia tra realtà e leggenda*, edited by M. Marazzi. Edizioni dell'Ateneo, pp. 77-102.

Dickinson, O. (2006). *The Aegean from Bronze Age to Iron Age: Continuity and Change Between the Twelfth and Eighth Centuries BC*. Routledge, pp. 27-56, 189-215.

Dickinson, O. (2007). *The Aegean Bronze Age*. Cambridge University Press, pp. 235-266.

Drews, R. (1993). *The End of the Bronze Age: Changes in Warfare and the Catastrophe ca. 1200 B.C.* Princeton University Press, pp. 89-112, 156-193.

Düring, B. S. (2011). *The Prehistory of Asia Minor: From Complex Hunter-Gatherers to Early Urban Societies*. Cambridge University Press, pp. 259-287.

Easton, D. F., Hawkins, J. D., Sherratt, A. G., & Sherratt, E. S. (2002). "Troy in Recent Perspective." *Anatolian Studies* 52, pp. 75-109.

Ehringhaus, H. (2005). *Götter, Herrscher, Inschriften: Die Felsreliefs der hethitischen Großreichszeit in der Türkei*. Philipp von Zabern, pp. 45-78.

Finkelberg, M. (2005). *Greeks and Pre-Greeks: Aegean Prehistory and Greek Heroic Tradition*. Cambridge University Press, pp. 140-157, 178-196.

Forlanini, M. (2017). "South Central: The Lower Land and Tarḫuntašša." In *Hittite Landscape and Geography*, edited by M. Weeden and L. Z. Ullmann. Brill, pp. 239-252.

Foxhall, L. (2007). *Olive Cultivation in Ancient Greece: Seeking the Ancient Economy*. Oxford University Press, pp. 56-89.

Garstang, J., & Gurney, O. R. (1959). *The Geography of the Hittite Empire*. British Institute of Archaeology at Ankara, pp. 76-93.

Genz, H. (2011). "Foreign Contacts of the Hittites." In *The Oxford Handbook of Ancient Anatolia*, edited by S. R. Steadman and G. McMahon. Oxford University Press, pp. 680-697.

Genz, H., & Mielke, D. P. (2011). *Insights into Hittite History and Archaeology*. Peeters, pp. 219-244.

Giorgieri, M., & Mora, C. (2010). "Kingship in Ḫatti during the 13th Century: Forms of Rule and Struggles for Power before the Fall of the Empire." In *Pax Hethitica: Studies on the Hittites and Their Neighbours in Honour of Itamar Singer*, edited by Y. Cohen, A. Gilan, and J. L. Miller. Harrassowitz, pp. 136-157.

Glatz, C. (2009). "Empire as Network: Spheres of Material Interaction in Late Bronze Age Anatolia." *Journal of Anthropological Archaeology* 28(2), pp. 127-141.

Gorny, R. L. (1995). "Viticulture and Ancient Anatolia." In *The Origins and Ancient History of Wine*, edited by P. E. McGovern, S. J. Fleming, and S. H. Katz. Gordon and Breach, pp. 133-174.

Güterbock, H. G. (1983). "The Hittites and the Aegean World: Part 1. The Ahhiyawa Problem Reconsidered." *American Journal of Archaeology* 87(2), pp. 133-138.

Haas, V. (1994). *Geschichte der hethitischen Religion*. Brill, pp. 187-212, 345-378, 456-489.

Hawkins, J. D. (1998). "Tarkasnawa King of Mira: 'Tarkondemos', Boğazköy Sealings and Karabel." *Anatolian Studies* 48, pp. 1-31.

Hawkins, J. D. (2009). "The Arzawa Letters in Recent Perspective." *British Museum Studies in Ancient Egypt and Sudan* 14, pp. 73-83.

Hawkins, J. D. (2013). "Luwians versus Hittites." In *Luwian Identities: Culture, Language and Religion Between Anatolia and the Aegean*, edited by A. Mouton, I. Rutherford, and I. Yakubovich. Brill, pp. 25-40.

Heinhold-Krahmer, S. (1977). *Arzawa: Untersuchungen zu seiner Geschichte nach den hethitischen Quellen*. Carl Winter, pp. 56-124, 178-209, 267-301.

Heinhold-Krahmer, S. (2013). "Zur Gleichsetzung der Namen Ilios-Wilusa und Troia-Taruisa." In *Troia im Kontext: Siedlungen der Bronzezeit in Umfeld der Ägäis*, edited by M. Hnila, R. Aslan, and S. Blum. Verlag Dr. Rudolf Habelt, pp. 15-28.

Hope Simpson, R. (2003). "The Dodecanese and the Ahhiyawa Question." *Annual of the British School at Athens* 98, pp. 203-237.

Jablonka, P. (2011). "Troy in Regional and International Context." In *The Oxford Handbook of Ancient Anatolia*, edited by S. R. Steadman and G. McMahon. Oxford University Press, pp. 717-733.

Jasink, A. M. (2001). "Suppiluliuma and Piyamaradu." In *La Battaglia di Qadesh: Ramesse II contro gli Ittiti per la conquista della Siria*, edited by M. C. Guidotti and F. Pecchioli Daddi. Polistampa, pp. 56-62.

Kelder, J. M. (2010). *The Kingdom of Mycenae: A Great Kingdom in the Late Bronze Age Aegean*. CDL Press, pp. 87-112.

Kelder, J. M. (2012). "Ahhiyawa and the World of the Great Kings: A Re-evaluation of Mycenaean Political Structures." *Talanta* 44, pp. 41-52.

Klinger, J. (2015). "Šuppiluliuma II. und die Spätphase der hethitischen Archive." In *Saeculum: Gedenkschrift für Heinrich Otten anlässlich seines 100. Geburtstags*, edited by A. Müller-Karpe, E. Rieken, and W. Sommerfeld. Harrassowitz, pp. 87-111.

Knapp, A. B., & Manning, S. W. (2016). "Crisis in Context: The End of the Late Bronze Age in the Eastern Mediterranean." *American Journal of Archaeology* 120(1), pp. 99-149.

Kohlmeyer, K. (1983). "Felsbilder der hethitischen Großreichszeit." *Acta Praehistorica et Archaeologica* 15, pp. 7-154.

Kopanias, K. (2008). "The Late Bronze Age Near Eastern Cylinder Seals from Thebes (Greece) and Their Historical Implications." *Mitteilungen des Deutschen Archäologischen Instituts, Athenische Abteilung* 123, pp. 39-96.

Korfmann, M. (2001). "Troia als Drehscheibe des Handels im 2. und 3. vorchristlichen Jahrtausend." In *Troia: Traum und Wirklichkeit*, edited by J. Latacz. Theiss, pp. 355-368.

Košak, S. (1980). "The Hittites and the Greeks." *Linguistica* 20, pp. 35-48.

Kryszat, G. (2008). "The Use of Writing among the Anatolians." In *Anatolia and the Jazira during the Old Assyrian Period*, edited by J. G. Dercksen. Nederlands Instituut voor het Nabije Oosten, pp. 231-238.

Latacz, J. (2004). *Troy and Homer: Towards a Solution of an Old Mystery.* Oxford University Press, pp. 121-156, 234-267.

Lehmann, G. A. (1991). "Die 'politisch-historischen' Beziehungen der Ägäis-Welt des 15.-13. Jh.s v. Chr. zu Ägypten und Vorderasien: einige Hinweise." In *Zweihundert Jahre Homer-Forschung,* edited by J. Latacz. Teubner, pp. 105-126.

Liverani, M. (2014). *The Ancient Near East: History, Society and Economy.* Routledge, pp. 278-302, 345-367.

Macqueen, J. G. (1986). *The Hittites and Their Contemporaries in Asia Minor.* Thames and Hudson, pp. 38-56, 117-138.

Maner, Ç. (2017). "Preliminary Report on the Fifth Season of the Konya-Ereğli Survey (KEYAR) 2017." *Anatolia Antiqua* 26, pp. 115-126.

Manning, S. W. (2012). "Chronology and Terminology." In *The Oxford Handbook of the Bronze Age Aegean,* edited by E. H. Cline. Oxford University Press, pp. 11-28.

Matessi, A., & Tomassini Pieri, B. (2017). "South-Central: Exploring the Southern Borderlands of the Hittite Empire." In *Hittite Landscape and Geography,* edited by M. Weeden and L. Z. Ullmann. Brill, pp. 107-119.

Melchert, H. C. (2003). *The Luwians.* Brill, pp. 27-46, 112-134, 221-236.

Melchert, H. C. (2010). "Lydian Language and Inscriptions." In *The Lydians and Their World,* edited by N. D. Cahill. Yapı Kredi Yayınları, pp. 267-272.

Mellaart, J. (1970). "The Second Millennium Chronology of Beycesultan." *Anatolian Studies* 20, pp. 55-67.

Mountjoy, P. A. (1998). "The East Aegean-West Anatolian Interface in the Late Bronze Age: Mycenaeans and the Kingdom of Ahhiyawa." *Anatolian Studies* 48, pp. 33-67.

Muhly, J. D. (2009). "Oxhide Ingots in the Aegean and in Egypt." In *Oxhide Ingots in the Central Mediterranean,* edited by F. Lo Schiavo, J. D. Muhly, R. Maddin, and A. Giumlia-Mair. CNR-ISMA, pp. 17-39.

Niemeier, W.-D. (1999). "Mycenaeans and Hittites in War in Western Asia Minor." In *Polemos: Le contexte guerrier en Égée à l'âge du Bronze*, edited by R. Laffineur. Université de Liège, pp. 141-155.

Niemeier, W.-D. (2005). "Minoans, Mycenaeans, Hittites and Ionians in Western Asia Minor: New Excavations in Bronze Age Miletus-Millawanda." In *The Greeks in the East*, edited by A. Villing. British Museum, pp. 1-36.

Oreshko, R. (2013). "Hieroglyphic Inscriptions of Western Anatolia: Long Arm of the Empire or Vernacular Tradition(s)?" In *Luwian Identities: Culture, Language and Religion Between Anatolia and the Aegean*, edited by A. Mouton, I. Rutherford, and I. Yakubovich. Brill, pp. 345-420.

Pantou, P. A. (2010). "Mycenaean Dimini in Context: Investigating Regional Variability and Socioeconomic Complexities in Late Bronze Age Greece." *American Journal of Archaeology* 114(3), pp. 381-401.

Pavúk, P. (2015). "Between the Aegean and the Hittites: Western Anatolia in the 2nd Millennium BC." In *Nostoi: Indigenous Culture, Migration and Integration in the Aegean Islands and Western Anatolia during the Late Bronze and Early Iron Ages*, edited by N. C. Stampolidis, Ç. Maner, and K. Kopanias. Koç University Press, pp. 81-113.

Puhvel, J. (1991). *Hittite Etymological Dictionary, Vol. 3: Words beginning with H*. Mouton de Gruyter, pp. 67-89, 156-178.

Roosevelt, C. H. (2009). *The Archaeology of Lydia, from Gyges to Alexander*. Cambridge University Press, pp. 23-45, 87-112.

Roosevelt, C. H. (2010). "Lydia Before the Lydians." In *The Lydians and Their World*, edited by N. D. Cahill. Yapı Kredi Yayınları, pp. 37-73.

Roosevelt, C. H., & Luke, C. (2017). "The Central Lydia Archaeological Survey: Documenting the Prehistoric through Iron Age Periods." In *Archaeology and History in Lydia from the Early Lydian Period to the Late Antiquity*, edited by E. Dündar, Ş. Aktaş, M. Koçak, and S. Erkoç. Koç University Press, pp. 15-32.

Rose, C. B. (2014). *The Archaeology of Greek and Roman Troy*. Cambridge University Press, pp. 46-78, 123-156.

Rutherford, I. (2008). "The Trojan War: The Afterlife of a Tradition in Lycia." In *Anatolian Interfaces: Hittites, Greeks and Their Neighbours*, edited by B. J. Collins, M. R. Bachvarova, and I. C. Rutherford. Oxbow Books, pp. 57-62.

Sagona, A., & Zimansky, P. (2009). *Ancient Turkey*. Routledge, pp. 245-278, 301-324.

Schachner, A. (2011). *Hattuscha: Auf der Suche nach dem sagenhaften Großreich der Hethiter*. C.H. Beck, pp. 102-134.

Sherratt, S. (2003). "The Mediterranean Economy: 'Globalization' at the End of the Second Millennium B.C.E." In *Symbiosis, Symbolism, and the Power of the Past: Canaan, Ancient Israel, and Their Neighbors from the Late Bronze Age through Roman Palaestina*, edited by W. G. Dever and S. Gitin. Eisenbrauns, pp. 37-62.

Singer, I. (1983). "Western Anatolia in the Thirteenth Century B.C. According to the Hittite Sources." *Anatolian Studies* 33, pp. 205-217.

Singer, I. (2006). "Ships Bound for Lukka: A New Interpretation of the Companion Letters RS 94.2530 and RS 94.2523." *Altorientalische Forschungen* 33(2), pp. 242-262.

Sommer, F. (1932). *Die Aḫḫijavā-Urkunden*. Verlag der Bayerischen Akademie der Wissenschaften, pp. 34-78, 112-156.

Souvatzi, S. G. (2020). "Kinship and Social Archaeology." *Cambridge Archaeological Journal* 30(1), pp. 123-139.

Taracha, P. (2009). *Religions of Second Millennium Anatolia*. Harrassowitz, pp. 87-123, 187-215.

Teffeteller, A. (2013). "Singers of Lazpa: Reconstructing Identities on Bronze Age Lesbos." In *Luwian Identities: Culture, Language and Religion Between Anatolia and the Aegean*, edited by A. Mouton, I. Rutherford, and I. Yakubovich. Brill, pp. 567-589.

Tomas, H. (2017). "Linear A in the Aegean: The Patterns of Distribution." In *Understanding Relations Between Scripts: The Aegean Writing Systems*, edited by P. M. Steele. Oxbow Books, pp. 9-24.

van den Hout, T. (2011). *The Elements of Hittite*. Cambridge University Press, pp. 1-18, 89-112.

Watkins, C. (1995). *How to Kill a Dragon: Aspects of Indo-European Poetics*. Oxford University Press, pp. 144-151, 421-428.

Weeden, M. (2013). "After the Hittites: The Kingdoms of Karkamish and Palistin in Northern Syria." *Bulletin of the Institute of Classical Studies* 56(2), pp. 1-20.

Woudhuizen, F. C. (2014). "Geography of Western Anatolia." In *Selected Luwian Hieroglyphic Texts: The Extended Version*. Innsbrucker Beiträge zur Kulturwissenschaft, pp. 364-377.

Yakubovich, I. (2010). *Sociolinguistics of the Luvian Language*. Brill, pp. 75-116, 189-235, 301-344.

Yakar, J. (2000). *Ethnoarchaeology of Anatolia: Rural Socio-Economy in the Bronze and Iron Ages*. Tel Aviv University, pp. 164-187, 225-243.

Yener, K. A. (2000). *The Domestication of Metals: The Rise of Complex Metal Industries in Anatolia*. Brill, pp. 71-94, 143-168.

Zangger, E. (2016). *The Luwian Civilization: The Missing Link in the Aegean Bronze Age*. Ege Yayınları, pp. 54-89, 167-198, 243-267.

Zangger, E., & Woudhuizen, F. (2018). "Rediscovered Luwian Hieroglyphic Inscriptions from Western Asia Minor." *Proceedings of the Dutch Archaeological and Historical Society* 49, pp. 239-251.

COMING SOON...

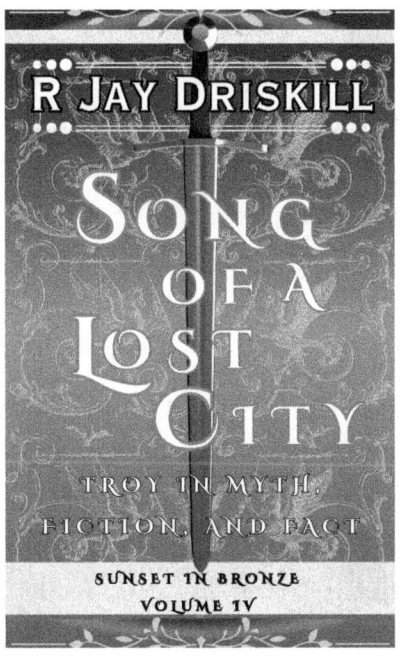

Sunset in Bronze Volume IV
Song of a Lost City: Troy in Myth, Fiction, and Fact
Discover the Truth Behind History's Greatest Legend

For three thousand years, Troy has captivated humanity's imagination. Now, leading archaeologist R Jay Driskill reveals the extraordinary story of how one of the world's most famous cities was lost to time—and found again through groundbreaking archaeological discoveries.

Journey from the windswept ruins of modern-day Turkey to the palaces of ancient kings as Driskill masterfully weaves together cutting-edge archaeology, forgotten diplomatic archives, and literary analysis to solve one of history's greatest mystery. Was Homer's Troy real? Did the Trojan War actually happen? The answers will surprise you.

What Recent Discoveries Reveal: • Troy was far larger than previously imagined—a Bronze Age superpower controlling crucial trade routes • Hittite diplomatic tablets document actual conflicts between Troy and Mycenaean Greeks • Archaeological evidence confirms violent destruction precisely when Greek tradition places the legendary war • The "Dark Age" transmission of oral tradition preserved authentic Bronze Age memories for centuries

A Detective Story 3,000 Years in the Making

This isn't just another archaeology book—it's a thrilling exploration of how historical events become cultural memory. Driskill demonstrates how Bronze Age catastrophe transformed into humanity's most enduring story, influencing everything from Roman imperial ideology to modern interpretations.

Perfect for Readers Who Love: • Eric Cline's accessible ancient history • Mary Beard's engaging classical scholarship • Popular archaeology and Bronze Age civilizations • The intersection of literature and historical evidence

The Ultimate Troy Experience

Experience the convergence of myth and reality at the crossroads of Europe and Asia, where the greatest story ever told began with fire, bronze, and human ambition.

ABOUT THE AUTHOR

R Jay Driskill is a professional archaeologist and bestselling author who transforms ancient mysteries into captivating narratives that educate and entertain. With academic credentials from the University of Florida and extensive fieldwork experience, Driskill brings authentic archaeological expertise to every page.

Specializing in historically accurate fiction and immersive non-fiction, Driskill's works have earned praise for their meticulous research, vivid storytelling, and ability to make complex historical concepts accessible to modern readers. Each book combines rigorous scholarship with page-turning adventure, offering readers both entertainment and genuine insight into humanity's fascinating past.

Whether you're a history enthusiast, archaeology buff, or simply love a well-crafted story, R Jay Driskill delivers meticulously researched narratives that will keep you engaged from first page to last.

Start your journey through time today – explore the complete collection and discover why readers call these books "unputdownable."

Visit rjaydriskill.com for exclusive content and upcoming releases.

If you enjoyed ***Ghosts of Arzawa***, please review at your vendor of choice.

www.ingramcontent.com/pod-product-compliance
Lightning Source LLC
Chambersburg PA
CBHW061611120626
46550CB00004B/1687